M000236388

Lexical Competence

Language, Speech, and Communication

Lexical Competence

Diego Marconi

A Bradford Book
The MIT Press
Cambridge, Massachusetts
London, England

© 1997 Massachusetts Institute of Technology

All rights reserved. No part of this book may be reproduced in any form by any electronic or mechanical means (including photocopying, recording, and information storage and retrieval) without permission in writing from the publisher.

This book was set in Bembo by Asco Trade Typesetting Ltd., Hong Kong, and was printed and bound in the United States of America.

First printing, 1997.

Library of Congress Cataloging-in-Publication Data

Marconi, Diego, 1947–
  Lexical competence / Diego Marconi.
        p.   cm. — (Language, speech, and communication)
  "A Bradford book."
  Includes bibliographical references and index.
  ISBN 0-262-13333-4 (hc : alk. paper)
  1. Semantics. 2. Competence and performance (Linguistics) I. Title. II. Series.
P325.5.L48M37   1997
401'.43—dc20   96-29014
                                                                    CIP

For Marilena

Once we give up the idea that individual competence has to be so strong as to actually determine extension, we can begin to study it in a fresh frame of mind.

H. Putnam, "The Meaning of 'Meaning' "

Contents

Acknowledgments

The bulk of the present work originated as a series of lectures at the Bolzano Summer School in Philosophy of Language in July 1992. I thank the organizers, Liliana Albertazzi and Roberto Poli, for giving me the opportunity to put some order into my scattered ideas on semantics and the lexicon. Among the participants, Roberto Casati and Achille Varzi were particularly active in the discussions. My lecture notes from the summer school were circulated rather widely and benefited from the comments of many friends and former students: Aldo Antonelli, Alessandra Damiani, Vittorio Di Tomaso, Giancarlo Mezzanatto, Alfredo Paternoster, Anna Maria Goy, and Dario Voltolini. The text of the 1992 lectures went through many changes before reaching the present form. One significant episode in their development was my participation in the San Marino School on Language and Understanding (June 1995), where I presented a new version of some of the ideas I had put forth in Bolzano and had the opportunity of discussing them with the participants and with Ray Jackendoff, who was coteaching the school with me. I am grateful to Patrizia Violi, tireless organizer of that school and of many San Marino events, which have been such an important part of the scientific life for all Italian philosophers of language. Otherwise, the sources of the materials in the book are the following.

The first part of chapter 1 was given as a lecture at the University of Palermo, one of a cycle directed by Nunzio La Fauci. It was later published in N. La Fauci (ed.), *Il telo di Pangloss* (Palermo, Italy: L'Epos, 1994).

Chapter 2 originated from several papers on holism read at the University of Rome, the University of Bologna, and the Rome International Workshop on Holism (December 1994). Among the people who heard them, I wish to thank Umberto Eco, Marcello Frixione, and

Marco Santambrogio. A previous version of a small part of the chapter was published in the *Bulletin of the Italian Association for Artificial Intelligence* (AI*IA) in 1994.

Chapter 3 contains materials from a paper given at the Dubrovnik Summer School on Meaning and Natural Kinds (1986), where it was discussed by David Charles, Nathan Salmon, and Tim Williamson. The paper was then published in *Lingua e Stile* ("Two Aspects of Lexical Competence," 1987). Later versions of that paper were read and commented upon by many people, including Pier Marco Bertinetto and Jim Higginbotham. In its present form, the chapter is based on a paper given to the Aristotelian Society in February 1995. Jonathan Dancy and Barry Smith are particularly to be thanked for their comments on that occasion. This paper was published in the *Proceedings* of the same year. The neuropsychological materials were presented at a seminar of the Center for Cognitive Science of the University of Turin and discussed with Bruno Bara, Leonardo Lesmo, Marina Zettin, and other members of the center. Advice from Remo Job and Giuliano Geminiani was also precious in this connection.

Most of chapter 4 is new. However, some materials come from two previous papers: one given at the Karlóvy-Váry Conference on Meaning (September 1993) and later published in the *Karlóvy-Váry Studies in Meaning and Reference* (Prague, 1995), the other presented at the conference Which Semantics? (Bolzano, Italy; December 1995). The section on truth conditions benefited from a discussion with Richard Rorty.

Chapter 5 is based on a paper read at the Catholic University of Milan in January 1995 and then again at the conference on 'Thought and Ontology' in Genoa (November 1995), where Mike Martin, Scott Sturgeon, and Alberto Voltolini took part in the discussion. A much earlier version had been presented at a conference on reference in Padua in 1991 and discussed with Joseph Almog, Keith Donnellan, Paolo Leonardi, and Ernesto Napoli.

An early version of what is now chapter 6 was given as a lecture to the John Von Neumann Society in Budapest in 1990 and later published in the French journal *Sémiotiques* (1991). An Italian translation appeared in *Epistemologia* (1993). A later version was delivered at a meeting of the Fellows of the Pittsburgh Center for Philosophy of Science in Athens in May 1992. Jonathan Berg was a most effective commentator. Among other people who commented on some version of the paper, I would like to mention Andrea Bonomi, Michele Di Francesco, Marcello Frixione, Carlo Penco, Philip Pettit, Nicholas Rescher, Marco Santambrogio, and Patrizia Violi.

Pieranna Garavaso's comments on the first three chapters of the book were especially helpful.

Two colleagues and friends, Paolo Casalegno and Carlo Penco, supported me in different ways through the whole enterprise. It is fair to say that the book would not have been written without Carlo's encouragement and it would have been much worse than it is without Paolo's criticism. I am deeply grateful to both of them.

Lexical Competence

Introduction

This book is about a single philosophical problem, namely, what is the difference between a system, natural or artificial, that can be said to understand a natural language and one that cannot. Originally, the question came to me in connection with the artificial natural-language-processing systems I had been studying in the early 1980s. What was wrong with them, essentially? Why did it seem so clear to so many people that such systems did not *really* understand language? What, if anything, could be done to endow them with genuine semantic competence? It was natural to think that to answer such questions, it would be at least useful to investigate our own semantic competence, that is, to wonder what kind of knowledge and abilities *we* possess that make it possible for us to understand language.

From the beginning, I concentrated on the understanding of *words*: not words such as 'all', 'and', and 'necessarily' but rather words such as 'yellow', 'book', and 'kick'. The reason was twofold. On the one hand, the research programs generated within the tradition of philosophical semantics stemming from Frege, which, in general, I found far superior to the alternatives in their approach to the study of meaning in natural languages, did not appear to adequately account for word meaning (the nature and some of the roots of such inadequacy are explored in chapter 1). Lexical semantics was perceived by many people as a problem area for model-theoretic semantics and other research programs centering on the notion of truth conditions. Moreover, it appeared that such inadequacy at the lexical level was at least partly responsible for the difficulty of deriving from the Fregean tradition really satisfactory answers to questions concerning competence. The tradition tended to identify knowledge of meaning (that is, semantic competence) with knowledge of the truth conditions of sentences. But then, truth conditions were spelled out in such a way that knowledge of them could hardly be identified with full semantic competence, and one reason seemed to be that the semantic values of most lexical units were left unspecified. True, there were meaning postulates and other devices that were supposed to account for lexical meaning (some of the issues that arise in connection with them are discussed in chapter 2); however, their insufficiency in explicating the full content of lexical competence had already been pointed out, particularly by Barbara Partee (1981).

On the other hand, setting the problem in terms of understanding and competence immediately brought words to the foreground. It seemed clear, for example, that an artificial system that could deal with natural-language sentences in several ways but ignored the meanings of their constituent words, no matter how such meanings were to be identified, could not be regarded as competent. Such a system could not know the difference between 'The cat is on the mat' and 'The book is on the table', or anyway, not in the same sense in which a competent human speaker could be said to know it. Clearly, *lexical* competence, the ability to use words, is an essential ingredient of semantic competence. So the question became, What does our ability to use words consist of? What kind of knowledge, and which abilities, underlie it?

It seemed to me that to be able to use a word is, on the one hand, to have access to a network of connections between that word and other words and linguistic expressions: it is to know that cats are animals, that in order to arrive somewhere one has to move, that an illness is something one may be cured of, and so forth. On the other hand, to be able to use a word is to know how to map lexical items onto the real world, that is, to be capable of both *naming* (selecting the right word in response to a given object or circumstance) and *application* (selecting the right object or circumstance in response to a given word). The two abilities are, to a large extent, independent of each other. They are described in some detail in chapter 3.[1] The former ability can be called *inferential*, for it underlies our inferential performances (such as, for example, interpreting a general regulation concerning animals as applying to cats); the latter may be called *referential*. Natural-language "understanding" systems of the standard kind could then be described as *inferentially confined*: they are incapable of referential performances, for their only access to the world is by way of linguistic description. Such systems could make steps in the direction of genuine understanding only by being connected to the world in a way that would be closer to how *we* are connected to the world, that is, in perception and action (some suggestions to this effect can be found in chapter 6).

I later discovered, thanks to Glyn Humphreys and other neuropsychologists, that empirical research on brain-injured persons confirmed, to some extent, the intuitive picture of lexical competence I had been sketching. Inferential and referential abilities appeared to be separate. Many cases had been reported of intact inferential competence going together with badly impaired referential ability. Recently the converse case has also been described: it is the case of a woman who is totally unable to verbally characterize common objects that she can, however, name. To her, a telephone is just that, a thing named 'telephone'. Nothing else. Such cases, and the emerging picture of lexical competence, are discussed in the second half of chapter 3.

It is sometimes argued that philosophy should not concern itself with the day-by-day returns of scientific research: they are notoriously unstable, their interpretation is far from straightforward, and they often force one into the Procustean bed of each researcher's theoretical prejudice. Philosophy, it is claimed, should not be made to depend on such dubious materials. However, even granting that the results of scientific research are, indeed, precarious (though some of them less than others), I disagree on the general principle: I don't think that philosophical research should be seen as less tentative and more secure than scientific research. I regard the idea that philosophy ought to be somehow preserved from the vicissitudes of empirical knowledge as stemming from Platonistic bias: it is assumed that philosophical inquiry is concerned with a separate realm of objects, that it is blessed with some form of direct access to its objects (whatever they are), or both. Neither is the case. Philosophy is science's faithful though staunchly critical companion, in good or bad weather.

In the late 1970s and the 1980s many people put forward "dual" pictures of meaning (though not of competence). Yet what is properly called 'dual-aspect semantics', the theory defended by McGinn, Block, Loar, Fodor (at some point), and others, cannot be the basis for a dual picture of competence such as the one I am proposing, for in dual-aspect semantics the referential component is conceived *externalistically*. Indeed, part of the motivation for having a dual-component theory was that

Putnam and others were believed to have shown that at least an aspect of meaning was not "in the head": it was determined by external circumstances, natural and social. By contrast, referential competence is a cognitive ability of the human mind: in this sense, it is entirely "in the head." Reference as conceived in the dual-aspect picture is an objective property of words: there is no guarantee that *anybody's* referential competence with a word is, or ever will be, adequate to that word's reference. Therefore, referential competence in my sense cannot be equated with knowledge of reference in the dualists' (or, more generally, the externalists') sense. Indeed, a particularly aggressive externalist would say that as I use it, 'referential competence' is a misnomer.

There is an easy way out of such a contrast: it consists in neatly separating the theory of competence from the theory of meaning. One could concede meaning to the externalists or the dualists, that is, one could grant that lexical semantic competence, understood as a complex of (individual) knowledge and abilities, falls short of knowledge of meaning, where meaning, or part of meaning, is conceived externalistically. This would not keep competence, and even referential competence, from being an object worthy of inquiry. However, I am not sure that such an easy solution would be satisfactory, for it seems to me that there is a terrain of intersection, and therefore of possible disagreement, between the theory of competence and the externalistic views on meaning, and this is the phenomena of the use of language. How is language use to be described? For example, should we say that Putnam is really using 'elm' to refer to elms, even though· he systematically confuses elms with beeches (so that he may date a friend "under the big elm" and show up, at the right time, under a beech)? Or again, should we say that Burge's Bert, who believes arthritis to be an affliction of both the muscles and the joints, really shares the expert's concept of arthritis in spite of such incorrect beliefs? Or, paradigmatically, did the inhabitants of Twin Earth refer to XYZ (never to H_2O) by their use of the word 'water' even before 1750, when nobody could tell the two substances apart and any Twin Earthian would have called H_2O 'water'? In all such cases, it seems to me, the theory of competence and externalism (and dualism) tend to part company. In chapters 4 and 5, I try to show that the use of language can be accounted for in terms of competence by taking into account the normative environment within which individual competences are located. Such a normative environment, in turn, can be described in quasi-naturalistic terms, without assuming the existence of absolute norms and standards. Of course, such an account, even if satisfactory, would not amount to a refutation of externalism. Its intended effect would rather be that of making the externalists' meaning into an idle wheel, playing no useful role in the description of language use. In this respect, as mine is an attempt at bringing semantics down from heaven to earth, I anticipate that many will be dissatisfied, for heaven is, of course, a much better place.

The Bothersome Issue of Lexical Meaning

The Fregean Tradition and the Lexicon

There isn't much on lexical meaning in the tradition of philosophical semantics: the tradition has focused on other aspects of meaning, those that have been called, and I will persist in calling, *structural* or *compositional*. This is surprising, in view of the fact that, as Hilary Putnam put it in 1970, "it is ... the phenomenon of writing (and needing) dictionaries ... that gives rise to the whole idea of 'semantic theory'" (Putnam 1975b, 150).[1] When the word 'meaning' occurs in ordinary parlance, it is most often connected with individual words: we may wonder what's the meaning of 'cremate', or what does 'crimson' mean exactly, or whether 'profligate' and 'licentious' have the same meaning. Nonphilosophers seldom, if at all, wonder about the meaning of 'if ... then ...', or about how the past tense or the imperfect aspect affect the meaning of a sentence, or about the way in which the meaning of 'John runs' results from, or is composed out of, the meanings of 'John' and 'run'—typical issues in compositional semantics. Such intuitions and linguistic habits may, of course, need correction; nevertheless, it is surprising that they be utterly disregarded.

It is all the more surprising, as the tradition did not begin like that. Many, if not most, of the semantic issues that Frege raised in his seminal papers of the year 1892 (1980a) were concerned with individual words—words such as 'Aristotle', 'man', 'Venus', 'horse', and 'Vienna'.[2] True, the emphasis on the compositional side of semantics must also be traced back to the influence of Frege. By his insistence on truth as the basic notion of logic, on the connection of thoughts and truth as the basic issue in semantics, on sentences as 'the proper means of expression for a thought',[3] and on a constituent's contribution to the truth conditions of the sentences in which it occurs as its essential semantic value, Frege paved the way for compositional semantics. However, Frege never entirely lost his interest in what he called the *Gedankenbausteine*,[4] the building blocks of thoughts: he kept asking questions about the content of the individual words' contribution to sentential meaning, that is, about the semantic values of individual words, or in short, about lexical meaning. In spite of Russell's and other people's criticism, he never gave up the notion of *sense* for individual expressions, that is, the idea that the semantic contribution of a constituent does not reduce to its denotation.

The Eclipse of Lexical Meaning

By the late 1920s this was all but forgotten. Why? One reason was that logic, "the theory of forms and of inference," as Wittgenstein called it in the *Tractatus* (1922, 6.1224), had come to be regarded as the key to semantics. And logic, of course, was only concerned with structural issues.

Another reason that structural issues prevailed was that there were thought to be *no* lexical semantic issues. Take the *Tractatus*, the most influential book on semantics before Tarski. In the *Tractatus,* lexical units are compressed into names, whose entire semantic function consists in their naming whatever objects they do in fact name. Whether or not such "names" are thought to coincide with the words of a natural language, or with a subset of them, there is simply nothing a semantic theory could say about their semantic function over and beyond the simple fact that each of them names whatever it names.[5] Genuine objects have internal properties, and so do their names,[6] but such properties are regarded as purely combinatorial. In this respect, the semantics of names is rather like syntax. The internal properties of a name (whatever they are) are not conceived of as making up its "semantic content": the semantic content (the *Bedeutung*) is just the object named, and as for sense, they have none. Everything else in language is composition.

Or take another very influential work of the old school, Carnap's *Logical Syntax of Language* (1937). Here semantic interpretation reduces to translation: "In the present work, by the interpretation of a language we shall always mean ... the method of explicit statements.... The interpretation of the expressions of a language S_1 is ... given by means of a translation into a language S_2" (1937, 228). Typically, the interpretation of a lexical unit of S_1 consists in having a lexical unit of S_2 correspond to it. In one of Carnap's examples, the k descriptive unary predicates 'P_1', ..., 'P_k' are "interpreted" by being stipulated to be "equivalent in meaning" (Carnap's own words, 1937, 230) to the English words 'red', ..., 'blue', and other color words. Clearly, within such a framework the problem of lexical meaning does not arise. The meaning of a word is simply given by another, supposedly interpreted word. There is neither any attempt at explicating the meaning of individual words nor any awareness that such an explication would be needed as part of the business of semantics.

Tarski and the Semantic Taxonomy of the Lexicon

Then there was Tarski and the short-lived identification of semantics with the theory of reference. It is important to remark that Tarskian "semantics" by itself is not especially oblivious of the lexicon. Indeed, in the analysis of lexical meaning, Tarski went beyond most of his predecessors in the Fregean tradition. In a Tarskian interpretation of a first-order language, individual constants are assigned objects in the domain of interpretation, unary predicates are assigned sets of objects, binary predicates (relations) are assigned sets of ordered pairs, and so on; and function symbols are assigned the appropriate functions over the domain. Thus Tarski classified the descriptive constants of a language, its lexical units, as to the logical type of their reference, that is, he classified them into words that designate individuals, words that designate sets of individuals, etc. Working with syntactically well-behaved artificial languages, he could unproblematically stick to the assumption of a one-one correspondence between grammatical categories and "semantic" categories: if a word is a unary predicate syntactically, then it designates a set of individuals, and conversely; and similarly for all other categories. The assumption was inherited by everybody working within the framework of model-theoretic semantics, and it was applied even to *natural* languages, most notably by Richard Montague and his disciples.[7] As we will see, there are difficulties with this assumption in the case of natural languages, and such difficulties have been a stumbling block for lexical semantics.[8]

However, Tarski did not go beyond a taxonomy of lexical units based on type of reference. He provided no explicit representation of the

semantic difference between two words of the same type (unary predicates such as 'dog' and 'run', or binary predicates such as 'beat' and 'left
of'). His was a skeletal lexical semantics. He did not *need* to go any further, for that was enough to make his point, namely, the availability of a
method for the construction of a definition of truth for a language that
met his own formal and material constraints.

It is occasionally pointed out that in the case of *some* lexical units,
Tarski went further.[9] In the case of *logical* words (such as 'and', 'not', 'all',
etc.), Tarski's account is fully satisfactory as an explication of the words'
meanings. To the extent that such a contention can be upheld,[10] it is
doubtful that the successful account of such words' semantic values is to
be credited to Tarski rather than (say) Frege or Wittgenstein. Anyway,
suppose it is true that in the case of the so-called "logical constants" we
are perfectly happy with one or the other of the extant accounts: either
Frege's, or Tarski's, or maybe the proof-theoretical account provided by
a natural-deduction system. We do indeed feel there is a difference in
informativeness between a Tarskian semantic account of the connectives
and an analogous account of, say, unary predicates. Is this, then, the
problem of lexical meaning? Would we like to have for *all* words what
Tarski (or Frege or Gentzen) gave us for a mere handful of words (the
"logical words")? Do we "expect to find [something] like a truth function answering to 'walk'"?[11]

Yes and no. What we feel would be needed in the case of such
words as 'walk' or 'painting', 'sepia' or 'inducement' is close to a truth
function in being an *explicit instruction* for the use of the word.[12] This is
what Tarskian semantics (or Montague semantics, for that matter) does
not provide us with, for such instructions would be different for non-
synonymous words, whereas whatever lexical information we get from
Tarskian semantics is the same for 'table', 'book', and 'walk' (but more
on this later).[13] On the other hand, what we· need is not *exactly* like a
truth function, for, obviously, no rule for the manipulation of truth values is going to do the job. There is probably more to the meaning of
'and' than is captured by the truth-table for conjunction.[14] Still, in the
case of 'and'—as in the case of 'not', 'or', and even 'if ... then ...'—we
do feel that many of our semantic intuitions are accounted for by the
appropriate truth functions. The truth functions do represent at least
rough instructions for the use of the logical words. On the other hand, to

know that 'walk' refers to a set of individuals is too skeletal a piece of information to serve as an instruction.

Quine Rehabilitates the Distinction of Sense and Reference

In 1943 (1952) Quine's *Notes on Existence and Necessity* made the analytic community aware that there was more to meaning than simple reference (or "designation," as Quine called it): Tarskian semantics can *not* be interpreted as a theory of meaning. Quine himself was essentially interested in ontic commitments and the behavior of modal and generally intensional contexts with respect to quantification. However, he thought that his problems could be best presented as stemming from a confusion of meaning and designation (Quine 1952, 77). He thus proceeded to point out their difference. For example, nondesignating words such as 'Pegasus' are not therefore meaningless. Indeed, it is precisely the meaning of 'Pegasus' that allows us to establish that the word does not designate, that is, has no reference (Quine 1952, 83). Moreover, if meaning were just reference, we ought to be able to say that all truths of the form $a = b$, even thoroughly factual truths such as 'the Morning Star = the Evening Star', state a relation of synonymy between a and b, one that could be grasped by anybody who knew the language, whereas, of course, it is only by researching reality that we can establish such truths (Quine 1952, 83).[15] In general, Quine saw the relation of meaning and designation as follows: There are uses of words such that only their designations matter for what we now call the truth conditions of the sentences in which they occur, and there are other uses, such as uses within modal and generally intensional contexts, where more than designation is at issue. In such uses, substitutivity of coreferential expressions fails. In such cases, says Quine talking about the special case of proper names, "the statement depends not only upon the [designated] object but on the form of the [designating] name" (1952, 78). If we assumed that all there is to the semantic value of a word were its reference, this would be inexplicable.

Not much later, Quine was led to the persuasion that the notion of meaning is hopelessly obscure and therefore unusable for any scientific purpose, so that we ought to simply dispense, within science at any rate, with the nonextensional part of language (that is, the part of language where reference does not suffice to determine truth conditions).

Ironically, however, Quine's remarks of 1943 (1952), together with Church's Fregean revival of the early 1950s,[16] contributed to the renaissance of meaning as distinct from reference. The outstanding document of the renaissance is Carnap's book of 1947 (1956b), *Meaning and Necessity*. A few years thereafter came the article "Meaning Postulates" (1952 [1956c]), which was later reprinted as an appendix to *Meaning and Necessity*. This article contains, or so I claim, the most important addition to lexical semantics after the Tarskian taxonomy of logical types.

Intensions

The key notion of Carnap's book is the notion of an intension. *Intensions*, in a modern formulation, are functions from indices, for example, possible worlds, to the appropriate extensions.[17] For instance, the intension of a 1-place predicate such as 'dog' ('____ is a dog') is a function assigning to each possible world a set of individuals, intuitively, the dogs of that possible world. As with Tarski's referents, so with Carnap's intensions, an intension's logical type is determined by the grammatical category of the expression with which the intension is associated: the intension of every proper name is a function from possible worlds to individuals, the intension of every 1-place predicate is a function from possible worlds to sets of individuals, and so on. Essentially, Carnap's scheme repeats Tarski's, adding one parameter.

What are intensions *for*? They serve to distinguish between expressions that have intuitively different meanings, though their reference is the same. The difference is interpreted as a difference in intension: such expressions denote the same entity (set, truth value, etc.) in the real world, but not in every possible world. There is at least one possible world in which their extensions differ. Thus there is (at least) one possible world where Venus is not the Morning Star, or where some animals that have a heart have no kidneys. We are no longer forced to regard as semantically identical all expressions that happen to have the same reference. As we know, besides saving the intuitions in the general case, this is very helpful in the analysis of modal constructions and *somewhat* helpful in the analysis of propositional attitudes (though not helpful enough, unfortunately, but this is another story).

Carnap's system does not make the intensions of the descriptive constants *explicit*: in this sense, even Carnap, like Tarski, does not make any distinction between 'cat' and 'table', that is, between expressions that belong to the same grammatical category and therefore are assigned intensions of the same logical type (in this case, functions from possible worlds to sets of individuals). One *presumes* that the intensions are different, but one cannot see exactly how. This has several consequences: First of all, if meanings are intensions (the notion of intension "explicates" the intuitive notion of meaning), then the meanings of the descriptive constants are not really given in Carnap's system. Second, and consequently, if sentential meaning is identified with a sentence's truth conditions, then the meaning of a sentence is itself only "virtually" given.[18]

One consequence, to which Carnap himself was sensitive, is the following. The system in itself does not make any difference between 'Egyptian cats were an object of worship' and 'Cats are animals'. Both sentences are (presumably) true in the actual world, and either true or false in each possible world. Yet it can be argued that while there are possible worlds in which the Egyptians did not worship cats, there are no possible worlds in which cats are not animals,[19] or in which bachelors are married, or in which circles are square. This problem, the impossibility of singling out, in the context of Carnap's "pure" system, the analytically true or analytically false sentences whose truth or falsity depends on meaning, not on logic, arises as a corollary of the way intensions have been conceived: obviously, if intensions are constrained *only* as to their logical type, relations among intensions will themselves only be constrained by type restrictions, which is not enough to single out the meaning-analytic sentences, be they true or false.

Meaning Postulates

Carnap's solution to this problem was the theory of meaning postulates. Essentially, a *meaning postulate* is a stipulation on the relation between lexical items; more precisely, a stipulation on the relation between their referents or (in Carnap's terminology) extensions. By setting down a meaning postulate such as

(MP) $(\forall x)(\text{bachelor}(x) \supset \sim\text{married}(x))$,

we stipulate that whatever individual is in the extension of 'bachelor' is not in the extension of 'married': the two extensions are disjoint.[20]

Carnap insists (1956c, 225) that a meaning postulate may or may not reflect linguistic usage or the semanticist's intuitions about it: more than anything, it expresses the semanticist's "intentions with respect to the meanings, that is, the ways of use of the descriptive constants" (1956c, 225). Thus a meaning postulate is a genuine stipulation rather than an explication, and the semanticist should not too much worry about the actual features of linguistic usage (which are often fuzzy anyway).

I introduced meaning postulates as constraints on the relations among extensions of words. However, given Carnap's theoretical context, the question immediately arises whether they should not rather be conceived of as stipulations about the *intensions* of words. The issue can be put as follows: do we want to say that 'If John is a bachelor, then he is not married' is true in all possible worlds *in which MP holds*, or do we prefer to say that it is true in all *admissible* possible worlds?[21] In other words, are we prepared to countenance possible worlds where John, though a bachelor, might be married, or do we want to rule them out from the start, that is, just by laying down (MP)? Intuitions are that the first option would amount to a relativization of language to possible worlds: in those possible worlds in which John could be both a bachelor and married, the two words would have a different *meaning*. Characteristically, Carnap saw the matter differently. He looked at the two options as more or less equivalent. Remember that he saw meaning postulates not as mirroring linguistic usage but rather as expressing the semanticist's decisions. Anyway, later theoreticians mostly chose the second option: to assert a meaning postulate like (MP) is to stipulate that it be true in all possible worlds. Thus meaning postulates are constraints on possible worlds.[22]

Carnap's main theoretical intent in introducing meaning postulates was to explicate the notion of analiticity. As we saw, in the "pure" system of *Meaning and Necessity* (1956b), a sentence such as (1) does not come out true in all possible worlds (that is, is not L-true, in Carnap's terminology), for, to put it briefly, all descriptive constants in the language are independent of one another both extensionally and intensionally: in any possible world, John may belong to the extension of 'bachelor', to the extension of 'married', to both, or to neither.

(1)   If John is a bachelor, then he is not married.

Consequently, L-truth does not coincide with the intuitive notion of analyticity: among the intuitively analytic sentences, only the truths of logic (such as 'John is a bachelor or John is not a bachelor') come out L-true, whereas sentences like (1) do not. Once meaning postulates have been introduced, we can define analyticity to cover both kinds of sentences, either by saying that S is analytic if and only if it is entailed by the meaning postulates (first option) or by saying that S is analytic if and only if it holds in all admissible possible worlds (second option), where the admissible possible worlds are just those in which the meaning postulates hold.[23]

The function of meaning postulates is often described, equivalently, as having to do with *inference* rather than analyticity, more particularly, with so-called *semantically based* inference.[24]

The following inferences are intuitively valid:

(2) John is a bachelor.

　　 John is not married.

(3) These are roses.

　　 These are flowers.

(4) John ran.

　　 John moved.

(5) John saw Bill run.

　　 Bill ran

Moreover, they seem to be recognized as such by any competent speaker, or contrapositively, we tend to deny competence to a speaker who does not immediately recognize the validity of (2) through (5).[25] We are willing to say that such a speaker wouldn't know what 'rose' means, what 'run' means, etc. On the other hand, such inferences do not come out valid in virtue of first-order logic alone, and this fact sets them apart from other inferences such as the following:

(6) John ran.

　　 Either John ran, or John stayed at home.

(7) Greta is a cow.

　　 There are cows.

However, if we add to first-order logic the appropriate meaning postulates, we can indeed validate (2) through (5). Thus, meaning postulates may be thought to capture the aspect of lexical meaning whose knowledge is brought to bear in the ability to recognize the validity of (2) to

(5). I will call this aspect the *inferential* aspect, while postponing the issue of whether it coincides with the whole of lexical meaning (or the even more interesting question of whether the relevant ability coincides with the whole of lexical semantic competence).[26]

What Is Semantic Interpretation?

Aside from solving the particular problem Carnap wanted to solve (singling out meaning-analytic truths and falsities), do meaning postulates represent an adequate account of lexical meaning? To answer this, let us ask a much broader question, namely, what is bona fide semantic interpretation?

Take a sentence such as (8):

(8)   There is a book on the table.

Suppose that we have an algorithm that can translate the language to which (8) belongs (let it be English) into a formal language L whose vocabulary and grammar are fully specified.[27] Suppose that the translation of (8) is (9):

(9) $(\exists x_1)(B^1 x_1 \;\&\; O^2(x_1, (\iota x_2 \,.\, T^1 x_2)))$

One can easily see that (9) by itself does not constitute a semantic interpretation (let alone *the* semantic interpretation) of (8), the obvious reason being that L, the language to which (9) belongs, is itself an uninterpreted language. Its expressions are fully determined syntactically, but totally devoid of meaning in any plausible sense of the word. Strictly, one should not even say that (9) is a *translation* of (8) into L (as we customarily say): translations are into meaningful languages. Frege (1980b, 61) characterized cognitive meaning as the part of meaning that is preserved under translation, but in order to preserve (cognitive) meaning, translation must be into a language whose expressions *have* meaning.

Now suppose that we provide an interpretation of L, and consequently of (9), *in the usual sense of 'interpretation'*, that is, by systematically specifying the truth conditions of the formulas of L. This is a topic that we will have to deal with in greater detail in one of the next chapters. If such a specification is standard, we obtain something very much like the following.

Translation (9) is true (in an interpretation I) if and only if there exists an object $o_1 \in \mathrm{Dmn}_I$ (the domain of I) and an object $o_2 \in \mathrm{Dmn}_I$ such that

- $o_1 \in I(B^1)$,
- $o_2 \in I(T^1)$,
- for every $o \in \mathrm{Dmn}_I$, $o \notin I(T^1)$ or $o = o_2$,
- $\langle o_1, o_2 \rangle \in I(O_2)$.

Is this a semantic interpretation of (8)? To avoid problems with the distinction between (8) and (9), let us suppose that the identification of (8) and (9) is forced: for instance, (9) is just (8), as in Montague grammar. Now, then, have we reached an interpretation of (8)? The answer is, No, for the interpretation of the descriptive constants is not explicitly specified. Remember, we are assuming that the interpretation is standard; in a standard interpretation, we specify only the logical types of $I(B)$, $I(T)$, etc. (by stating, for example, that $I(B) \subseteq \mathrm{Dmn}_I$, that is, it is a set of individuals, etc.).[28] We do not actually specify the denotations or the intensions of the descriptive constants. In this sense, standard semantic interpretation does not choose among infinitely many distinct possible models of a language. Montague was quite aware of this.[29] However, if by 'semantic interpretation' we mean an explicit representation of what a competent speaker understands when she understands (8),[30] then intuitively, we have not yet reached the level of genuine semantic interpretation. By understanding (8), you come to know more than you have been told so far. That is because you know what 'table', 'book', and 'on' *mean*, and to know this, whatever it is, is to know more than their logical types.

Let us stop briefly at this point to take care of an immediate objection. It could be pointed out that, whatever the interest of spelling out the content of semantic competence in full, that is not the proper task of a theory of meaning.[31] Requiring a theory of meaning to show that 'Grenada is a U.S. state' does not mean that snow is purple would be like requiring the theory of truth to prove that snow is white. This would be improper, it is argued, for a theory of truth is an account of the *concept* of truth, which does not require that the *extension* of the concept be specified (it is an intensional account). Now, it is surely conceivable that a theory may give an account of the notion of meaning without specifying meanings for sentences or other expressions of this or that language. If the Wittgensteinian slogan "Meaning is use" can be taken as a theory, such a theory certainly does not specify meanings. Another example might be Grice's theory relating meaning to intentions (with a '*t*'). On the other hand, however, this is not what model-theoretic semantics and other theories in the same family are about. They are not proposed as intensional accounts of the notion of meaning; they do not aim at clarifying the notion of meaning by defining it in terms of supposedly clearer or more familiar notions. Such theories purport to be talking about individual sentences and other expressions of a given language (such as English), not just about the notion of meaning. And they purport to provide information, *semantic* information, concerning such linguistic objects. The point I am urging here is simply that the information they provide, whatever its merit, does not amount to (what it would be natural to regard as) *complete* information about the sentences' meaning.

Meaning Postulates Do Not suffice

So, suppose we add a set of meaning postulates. Indeed, suppose we throw in a complete set of meaning postulates for the language of (8)—an idealized notion, but not a meaningless one. What we are adding is the set of postulates needed to validate *all* inferences accessible to a competent speaker of English, inferences such as the following:

There is a book on the table.
_____
There is a physical object on the table.

There is a book on the table.
_____
There is a piece of furniture.

Now we can no longer claim that the interpretation isn't genuine for we are not told what the individual words mean, though we have been told a lot of what a competent speaker knows about 'table', 'book', etc. Is this the whole story concerning word meaning, and therefore the whole story concerning semantic interpretation? Again, no. As Partee has remarked, "No amount of such intralinguistic connections [or meaning postulates] can serve to tie down the intensions with respect to their extralinguistic content. For that there must be some language-to-world *grounding*" (1981, 71; italics added).[32]

This has at least three possible interpretations. On the *mathematical* interpretation (which may be the one Partee had in mind) the point is that no set of meaning postulates can characterize the intended interpretation from among all logically possible interpretations.[33] Meaning postulates do rule out lots of interpretations, such as those in which, say, 'table' is interpreted as synonymous with 'cup' or tables do not turn out to be a subset of pieces of furniture. However, they do not single out one interpretation, the one on which 'table' refers to tables in the real world, 'book' refers to books, and so on. This is simply because of the Löwenheim–Skolem theorem: any consistent first-order theory has an infinity of nonisomorphic models.[34]

On the *semantic* interpretation, the point is that a meaningless (that is, uninterpreted) linguistic symbol cannot be made meaningful by being connected, in any way whatsoever, to more uninterpreted symbols. If you don't know Chinese, a Chinese definition for a Chinese word will not make you understand the word.[35] This is so no matter how many such connections you line up, no matter how many meaning postulates you write, no matter how big your Chinese dictionary is: there is no magic feat called 'holism' that can do the trick.[36]

Finally, on the *cognitive* interpretation, the one that will mostly engage us in this book, the point is that we, as competent speakers of English, know something about words such as 'book', 'table', and 'on' that is not captured by the meaning postulates for these words (or for all other English words, for that matter). Consequently, the informational content of (8) is not exhausted by its semantic interpretation-*cum*-meaning postulates, along the lines we have been following so far. That is, when we understand (8), we get more information than is made explicit by its translation into a well-regimented, interpreted first-order (or for that matter, second-order) language plus the relevant meaning postulates. What we know is, very briefly, how to apply such words in the real world. We know how to react to the order 'Keep off the table!' we can answer the question 'Is there a table in this room?' etc.—we will come back to this ability. No amount of meaning postulates is going to explicate this ability: to know that books are physical objects, made of cardboard and paper, of size typically ranging from 3×4 inches to 9×12 inches is not going to allow us to recognize a book on a table, not unless we know how to apply 'cardboard', 'paper', and many other words. But again, such know-how is not the job of meaning postulates. So, meaning postulates do not tell the whole story about lexical meaning; the inferential aspect is not the whole of lexical meaning.

With these remarks in mind, let us go back to Carnap. After stating the meaning postulate relating (the formal counterparts of) 'bachelor' and 'married', Carnap remarked the following: "Even now we do not give rules of designation for 'B[achelor]' and 'M[arried]'. They are not needed for the explication of analiticity but only for that of factual (synthetic) truth" (1956c, 224). Carnap was quite right that "rules of designation," that is, referential connections, were not needed for the explication of analiticity. In fact, analiticity, if one wants to have such a notion, can be seen as derivability from meaning postulates (it follows that meaning postulates are themselves trivially analytic, as they should be). He was likewise absolutely right that rules of designation *are* needed for factual truth: we cannot determine whether 'John is a bachelor' is true on the basis of a meaning postulate (unless, of course, we already know that he is a married male). However, he was mistaken in thinking that referential connections are needed *only* for factual truth. They are also needed for semantic competence.

Is There More Than Meaning Postulates on the Market?

Of course, after Carnap proposed meaning postulates in 1952 (1956c), other theories of the representation of lexical meaning were put forward: to name just a few, Katz's decompositional semantics (Katz and Fodor 1963; Katz 1972, 1987); semantic networks (Quillian 1968; see Lehmann 1992), which have been widely influential within artificial intelligence; and Pustejovsky's generative lexicon (Pustejovsky 1991). Whether such theories are equivalent to meaning-postulate theory is a matter of controversy: a lot hinges on what one means by 'equivalent' and by 'meaning-postulate theory'. For example, Israel (1983) has claimed that at least some systems of representation based on semantic networks (for example, Shapiro 1971) are not equivalent to first-order theories having meaning postulates as axioms. More precisely, what was shown is that such systems *can* be given semantic accounts that "range fairly far and wide beyond the confines of standard first-order logic" (Israel 1983, 2), and that such non-first-order accounts are mandatory if one wants to take seriously the intuitions underlying semantic networks. However, meaning postulates are not necessarily first-order; consequently, I do not see why going beyond the boundaries of first-order languages would rule out meaning postulates as a form of representation.

Katz too claimed (1987, 192–194) that his semantic method was far superior to the method of meaning postulates (and therefore different from it), at least in accounting for semantic inferences. In Katz's theory, senses of words are structured entities, whose representations are called

(a)

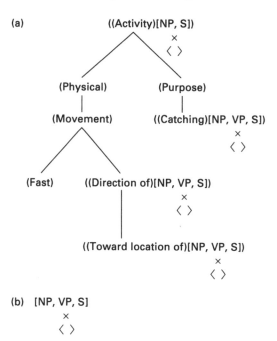

(b) [NP, VP, S]
     ×
    ⟨ ⟩

Figure 1.1
Tree (a) gives the sense of 'chase' (from Katz 1987). Sublabels that one finds at some nodes, such as (b), must be understood as variables: they indicate "positions in a semantic marker at which other semantic markers can be embedded" (Katz 1987, 187); at the same time, they identify the category of the semantic representation that can fill the variable position. For instance, [NP, VP, S] singles out the grammatical function of a direct object. The angle brackets '⟨ ⟩' are a placeholder for possible selectional restrictions, that is, restrictions on the semantic content of the representations that can occupy the variable position. This kind of information is used to compute representations of whole sentences from the representations of their constituent words. I will not elaborate on this.

semantic markers (by analogy with syntactic phrase markers). A semantic marker is a tree with labeled nodes; the tree's structure mirrors the structure of the represented sense, and the labels identify the sense's *conceptual components*. The tree in figure 1.1 represents the sense of 'chase'.

Within this framework, the justification of semantic inferences, such as the inference below, is, according to Katz, simply a matter of inspection: one just has to check that the semantic marker representing the relevant sense of 'follow' is a subtree of the semantic marker of 'chase'.

The police chased the demonstrators.
_____

The police followed the demonstrators.

Once the premise (or rather, its semantic representation) is written down, the conclusion is written down as well. By contrast, the method of meaning postulates requires one to appeal to "principles of deduction" in order to derive an entailment: in the above case, the conclusion can indeed by drawn from the premise together with a meaning postulate such as '$(\forall x)(\forall y)(\text{chase}(x, y) \supset \text{follow}(x, y))$', *given a few inference rules* (see Katz 1987, 193). Thus the method of meaning postulates does not distinguish between semantic inference and first-order inference in general, thereby ignoring a striking difference: in the case of semantic inference (but not in the general case) "the truth conditions of the conclusion *are* an explicit part of the truth conditions of the premiss" (Katz 1987, 193).

It appears, however, that in contrasting his method with the method of meaning postulates, Katz is relying too heavily on the immediacy of inspection. Deciding whether a given tree is a subtree of another can be a painstaking task if the "big" tree is big enough. Granted, it is an *easy* task: a computer can carry it out (in polynomial time) given a few *rules* for the exploration of the (putative) supertree. However, it is a task that needs carrying out according to rules. That in the simplest cases the solution is "practically immediate" does not make the problem inherently different from the problem of deriving a conclusion from one or more premises and meaning postulates: even here, simple cases are just that—simple.[37]

Anyway, I do not wish to claim that no forms of representation of lexical meaning have ever been proposed that differ from meaning postulates in *any* significant respect. What I *do* wish to claim is that none of them differ from meaning postulates as far as the issue of reference is concerned. Semantic networks, semantic markers, and Pustejovsky's representations are not more grounded, in any of the three senses that have been distinguished, than sets of meaning postulates.[38]

Prototypes and Reference

Beginning in 1973, Eleanor Rosch put forth a new theory of the mental representation of concepts. Concepts such as *furniture* or *bird*, she claimed, are not represented just as "[sets of] criterial features with clear-cut boundaries," so that any item can be conceived as either falling or not falling under the concept, according to whether or not it met the relevant criteria; rather, "items within categories may be considered differentially representative of the meaning of the category-term" (Rosch 1975a, 193–194). Several experiments seemed to show that the application of concepts was no simple yes-or-no business: some items (the "good examples") were more easily identified as falling under a concept than others (the "poor examples"). Thus an automobile was (perceived as) a better example of *vehicle* than a rowboat, and much better than an elevator; a carrot was more readily identified as falling under the concept *vegetable* than a pumpkin. If concepts were represented merely by criteria, such differences would be inexplicable when occurring between items that met the criteria equally well. It is thus plausible to assume that the mental representations of category words are somehow closer to good examples than to bad examples of the category: the mental representation of the concept *bird* is "closer" to a robin than to an ostrich.[39] A robin was perceived as a more "birdish" bird than an ostrich or, as people would say, closer to the *prototype* of a bird (or to the *prototypical* bird).[40]

Nothing in Rosch's experiments licensed the conclusion that there are individual mental entities corresponding to the prototypes or that the mental representation of a category word such as 'bird' has a mental entity at its center somehow resembling a robin, nor did she ever literally advance any such claim. What her experiments did support was the thesis that any theory of the mental representation of certain natural categories had to account for *prototype effects*, that is, for the relevance of the "goodness of the example" metric to the application of concepts in perception, naming, etc. However, as Rosch herself admitted later on,[41] there were ambiguities in the early formulations of the theory that led to the reification of prototypes, or rather, as Lakoff has shown,[42] to several distinct reifications. Prototypes were identified with feature bundles in the mind and with imagelike exemplars of a category.[43] As a consequence, prototypes were often thrown into one basket with Putnam's *stereotypes*.[44]

Stereotypes were introduced by Putnam in 1970 (1975b) partly to account for the content of lexical semantic competence in the case of natural-kind words such as 'tiger' and 'gold'. A competent speaker associates with such words an oversimplified theory that is not necessarily true of all tigers or of all gold: the theory is a description of normal, or typical, tigers (gold). Thus, although there are albino tigers, the theory associated with 'tiger' describes tigers as striped; although native gold is rather white, the theory associated with 'gold' decribes gold as yellow.

What is described by such oversimplified theories are *stereotypes* of the natural kinds. From later writings (particularly Putnam 1975c) we learn that stereotypes are, in Putnam's theory as in ordinary parlance, "conventional ideas" containing several "features" (such as, for tigers, being fierce, living in the jungle, being yellow with black stripes, being a meat-eater, etc.). Stereotypes are not necessarily true of all, or even of most, members of the extensions of the words they are associated with; however, knowledge of the stereotype is necessary for one to be judged a competent speaker by one's linguistic community.

Putnam was not very precise about the nature of stereotypes (Are they abstract ideas or mental entities? Are they essentially linguistic, or are they closer to pictures? Should we use the word 'stereotype' to refer to a certain amount of *information*, or should we reserve it for whatever such information is *about*, for example, the normal tiger?), nor did he need to be for the purpose of his theory. In fact, as is well known, Putnam had framed a theory of natural-kind words that had as a consequence that most speakers of English do not *really* know the meaning of 'tiger', 'gold', and other such relatively common words. Thus the questions immediately arose, What *do* they know in connection with such words? How can we mark the difference between competent and incompetent speakers if we are no longer allowed to draw it in terms of "knowing the meaning" of words? Stereotypes were the answer to these questions: the word 'stereotype' hinted at the kind and amount of information a competent speaker possesses in association with 'lemon', 'water', or 'tiger'.

Information of this kind, and the nature of its association with at least some category words, is best represented, according to many, by means of a data structure called a *frame*, which had been proposed by Minsky as a way of representing "stereotyped situations" (1975, 212). Minsky himself suggested that frames could be used to represent word senses (1975, 236, 245). A standard account of how this could be done is the following. Take the word 'tiger'. We want to represent both the features necessarily associated with the word and the features *typically* associated with it (the features of the typical tiger, so to speak).[45] Therefore, we make a distinction between the *range of possible values* a property may have, and its *default value*. A property's default value is the value that the property receives in the lack of more specific information. Thus if I am told a story concerning a tiger without being told about where it

Table 1.1
The frame for *tiger*

Property	Possible values	Default value
Is a	felin	
Weight	< 180 kg	120 kg
Height	< 106 cm	80 cm
Length	< 250 cm	180 cm
Color	yellow with black stripes white black yellow	yellow with black stripes
Habitat	jungle wetlands borders of rivers	jungle
Eats	antelope cattle deer warthog monkey man	antelope
Etc.		

Note: Usually there is more than this in a frame. For example, frames often include procedures, called 'demons', that are automatically activated in certain circumstances, as when a slot has been given a certain value (if-added demons) or when the value of a given slot can be determined indirectly, for example, by carrying out a computation (if-needed demons). Intuitively, the demons correspond to inferences one might (but need not) carry out from whatever knowledge is packed into the frame itself, or to inferences based on both frame knowledge and outside information. Frames, like semantic networks, depend, for their representational power, on the algorithms for their management.

lives, it is reasonable for me to take it for granted that the animal in question lives in the jungle. If I am not explicitly told the tiger's color, I more or less automatically assume that it is a normal tiger, that is, yellow with black stripes. And so on. Of course, tigers *need not* live in the jungle, and this is something we also want to represent, that is, we want the word to be associated with a list of possible habitats, the range of possible values for the property *habitat*. Similarly for other properties. A fragment of a plausible frame for 'tiger' might look somewhat like what is given in table 1.1.

The set of the default values in a frame was often identified with a stereotype in Putnam's sense: default values of properties are stereotypical features. However, such an identification does not literally correspond to Putnam's theory. In the frame for *tiger, feline* is taken to be a necessary characteristic of tigers, not a default value, but according to Putnam (1975c, 252) it is part of the tiger stereotype in that it would be part of the answer to the question "What is the meaning of 'tiger'?" (meant as a question about standard semantic competence). More generally, the distinction between necessary features (represented by ranges of possible values) and typical features (represented by default values) does not coincide with any distinction in Putnam's theory.[46] Nevertheless, sets of default values and stereotypes do share important properties: first, they both try to cash out the notion of typicality; second, they both involve *defeasible* information.[47] The former common feature was the basis for regarding frames as the best representation of stereotypes, or even as identical with stereotypes. The following text by Johnson-Laird can stand for many others:

If you ask what is meant by a characteristic component, then perhaps the best answer is based on Marvin Minsky's notion of a "frame." A frame system is intended to be a structured piece of knowledge about some typical entity or state of affairs. It contains variables into which go the specific values of a given instance.... The values of many variables can be specified by default.... If there is no information about the number of legs that a particular tiger possesses, then the default value is *four*. A prototype, or theory about a class, is simply a system that specifies all the default values. (1986, 107)

You may have noticed that Johnson-Laird appears to be talking about *prototypes* rather than stereotypes. As a matter of fact, previous references to Putnam make it clear that what he wants are stereotypes, not prototypes. However, his confusion is symptomatic: prototypes, once they had been reified, were easily conflated with both frames and stereotypes. If the prototype of, say, bird was an exemplar in the mind, it could be identified with the stereotype associated with 'bird' (stereotypes, after all, were somehow 'in the mind', according to Putnam), and it could be described by the default values in the *bird* frame. In common parlance, a prototype became something like the psychologist's stereotype,[48] whereas stereotypes were the philosopher's prototypes, and frames were the computer scientist's way of representing either.

All of this would be utterly irrelevant to our present concerns were it not for the fact that the conflation of stereotypes, prototypes, and frames led to the misguided idea that semantic competence could be *fully* accounted for by a theory that made room for prototypes (stereotypes, etc.) alongside meaning postulates and compositional rules. Prototypes were perceived as the missing ingredient whose addition would somehow "bridge the gap" between language and the world.

Actually, such a bold claim was never put forth by anybody I know of, or anyway, not in so many words. However, one does find bits and pieces of the following picture, which I shall label "Nobody's semantic theory of many common nouns":

• Many words (such as natural-kind words but not only those) are not used on the basis of necessary and jointly sufficient conditions for their application: most speakers don't know such conditions.[49]
• What ordinary speakers do know in connection with such words are stereotypes, that is, something like frames (i.e., schematic descriptions of normal members of the relevant classes).
• Cognitive psychology shows that such stereotypes (the psychologists call them 'prototypes') are psychologically real: that's how the meaning of many words is mentally represented.
• Prototypes, being mentally real entities, are not linguistic (which would be in need of semantic interpretation); they are mental, and therefore connected with perception, perhaps even *made* of "perceptual primitives." Prototypes are inherently grounded.
• The connection of language to the world is by way of association with mental entities, the prototypes, which are themselves "in touch" with perception.

It helps if one is able to imagine prototypes as tiny pictures in the mind, for it is very hard to think of an *uninterpreted* picture (it can be done, of course): if prototypes are pictures, they are *ipso facto* connected with the world.[50]

In Nobody's theory, certain structures—data structures such as frames, naive theories such as the stereotypes—are regarded as grounded by being identified with *mental* structures, the prototypes, which are considered as inherently grounded. That is, 'stereotype' is considered as *just another name* for prototypes. However, this is not what stereotypes or frames are. Putnam's stereotypes and frames in themselves are *inferential* structures: there is nothing referential about them. Indeed, they support *default inference*. The ability to carry out default inference is part of *inferential* competence and does not "reach out" to the world or to perception. Consider the following inference:

Tweety is a bird.
Tweety flies.

That this inference is sound ceteris paribus or in normal cases or in normal worlds or whatever does not help to determine the reference of 'bird' (or 'flies'). It does not reduce the number of admissible models more than a meaning postulate would. It does not capture a speaker's ability to name birds or to draw a certain picture rather than another when prompted with the word 'bird'. And it does not "take us out of language." Default inference is an object worthy of study and is irreducible to standard inference; it is nevertheless inference and not reference.[51] This is not to say that stereotypes or frames cannot be grounded: they are as capable of being grounded as, say, meaning postulates. However, they cannot be seen as inherently grounded.

Couldn't it be objected that stereotypes, though themselves ungrounded, could be grounded by being *associated* with prototypes? Unfortunately, this suggestion turns out to be rather empty. First of all, it is to be doubted that *there are* prototypes, that is, that prototype effects must be accounted for by postulating individual mental structures, associated with individual words, that would be the mental equivalents of sets of default values in frames. Surely the experimental evidence does not force such a hypothesis upon us. Besides, as several critics have remarked, the hypothesis would have to face no end of difficulties.[52] Prototype effects are indeed well established.[53] Thus it is fair to say that any theory of lexical semantic competence should account for them. However, this appears to entail very little as to the overall architecture of such a theory.

Second, even if there were (reified) prototypes, the claim that they are inherently grounded is unsubsantiated until their role in perception, naming, etc., is made more precise. For example, what exactly does it mean to *compare* a prototype, either as an exemplar or as a set of mental features, with the output of visual perception? Such questions are not answered simply by saying that prototypes, being mental structures, are intrinsically intentional or inherently interpreted: one wishes to know how it *works*. Until this is explained, the insufficiency of meaning postulates in spelling out lexical competence is not remedied by stereotypes, frames, or other structures supporting default inference.

The Delimitation of Inferential Meaning

How Do We Choose the Meaning Postulates?

We saw that meaning postulates (or other equivalent forms of repre-sentation) cannot adequately express lexical semantic competence: they cannot really account for its whole content. There is, however, another crucial issue: how do we *choose* the meaning postulates? *Which* sentences actually represent the part or aspect of lexical competence expressed by meaning postulates? For example, is (1) a candidate meaning postulate for the word 'table'?

(1) My aunt's coffee table is 7 years old.

Probably not. Why not?[1] One answer could be, Because the information expressed by (1), even if true, is not *constitutive* of the meaning of 'table'. One might be ignorant of (1) and yet be competent in the use of 'table'. Of a speaker who didn't know or believe that my aunt's coffee table is 7 years old, we wouldn't say that she doesn't know what 'table' means, whereas if she didn't know that tables have a top and (typically) four legs, we would probably regard her as linguistically incompetent.

Analytic/Synthetic and Quine's Criticism

The criterion we just applied used to be brought back to the analytic/ synthetic distinction. All true sentences of a language in which a given word occurs divide into two disjoint sets.[2] Some sentences are true by virtue of what the occurring words mean. For instance, the truth of (2) is manifest to any competent speaker of English, whereas the truth of (1) is not.

(2)   Tables have tops.

The former sentences are called 'analytic', the latter 'synthetic'. Analytic sentences collectively express the information required and sufficient for competent use of words. Consequently, a sentences is a meaning postulate for a word w just in case it is one of the analytic sentences in which w occurs; a sentence S in which w occurs is analytic just in case a speaker ought to believe S in order to be competent in his use of w.[3] The reader will remember that Carnap introduced the notion of a meaning postulate to explicate the notion of analyticity. Like all logical positivists, he regarded the analytic/synthetic distinction as well founded.

As everybody knows, the analytic/synthetic dichotomy came under scrutiny in the early 1950s. In his famous article "Two Dogmas of Empiricism" (1953) Quine challenged the scientific viability of the concept "analytic" by showing that it could not be noncircularly defined. Analyticity presupposes synonymy, which in its turn presupposes analyticity. I personally believe that Quine only showed that there cannot be a definition of analyticity that does not rely upon our intuitions of synonymy (hyponymy, antonymy, etc.). I don't see anything wrong in taking such intuitions as basic and building the definition of analyticity upon them, perhaps once we have reached reflective equilibrium between our intuitions and the needs of the theory, just as we define justice on the basis of our intuitions of fairness. However, I too will propose that we give up the analytic/synthetic dichotomy, although for reasons different from Quine's. One reason is that the old notion of the analytic, the notion that the logical positivists thought they needed, was required to do too many jobs, some of them incompatible. Analytic sentences were thought to be identical with (a) necessary truths, (b) a priori truths, (c) unrevisable pieces of knowledge, and (d) sentences constitutive of (lexical) semantic competence. However, these concepts are extensionally distinct: there is no set of sentences that exactly instantiates all four properties. Kripke (1970) is believed to have shown that (a) and (b) do not extensionally coincide: there are necessary truths that are not a priori, and there are a priori truths that are not necessary. Whether or not his arguments to this effect are sound, it can be argued that (c) and (d) do not coincide extensionally. For instance, 'Cats are animals' is probably constitutive of competence but it is not unrevisable, as Putnam has shown, whereas 'The number 37 is the thirteenth prime number' is highly unrevisable but hardly constitutive of our competence concerning any of the occurring words.[4] The point seems to be that low revisability depends on factors that have nothing to do with competence, such as belonging to a tightly knit body of knowledge, belonging to a pervasive body of knowledge, occupying an inferentially crucial position within a body of knowledge, and so forth. Moreover, competence is connected with commonsense knowledge (though not identical with it), whereas unrevisability is often attributed to items of "objective," that is, entrenched scientific knowledge.[5]

Perhaps even Quine's own point was not so much to deny that sentences such as 'A round shape is circular' or 'Bachelors are unmarried' are somewhat peculiar. He wanted to challenge an all-purpose philosophical notion that was intended to play a crucial role in positivistic epistemology. As Hilary Putnam saw as early as 1962 (1975a), Quine was trying to discredit a whole philosophical framework of which the distinction was an essential ingredient. For Putnam, such a framework included the ideas of "deep" synonymy (such as the synonymy of, say, 'chair' with an allegedly equivalent expression in "the language of sense data") and "deep" grammar (involving the supposedly Wittgensteinian idea that all necessity could be traced back to "the rules of language") (Putnam 1975a, 37–38). Analyticity was a weapon in the hands of both the reductionists and the "deep grammarians." Therefore, Quine was right in attacking the analytic/synthetic distinction if this means rejecting the kind of philosophical machinery that the distinction was meant to grease.[6] But he was wrong, according to Putnam, in denying that there was *any* such distinction, for there is indeed an analytic/synthetic distinction, albeit a "trivial" one and one that "cuts no philosophical ice." It encompasses such classic cases as 'All bachelors are unmarried' but simply does not apply to the sort of statements that most philosophers of the 1930s and 1940s had in mind in connection with the notion of analyticity. For example, it is just inappropriate to ask whether the principles of logic are analytic.[7]

Putnam was surely right in pointing out that Quine had been after bigger game than just synonymy in natural languages; however, he was more interested in explaining why *he* thought that the analytic/synthetic distinction was philosophically dangerous than in identifying Quine's own target of 1951 (1953). Recently another picture of Quine's polemic has been offered by Paul Horwich. According to Horwich, Quine intended to show that "our everyday semantic notions are not as precise as they would need to be for the philosophical purpose to which Carnap and the other logical empiricists would have liked to put them" (Horwich 1992, 107). The logical empiricists wanted the truths of logic, mathematics, and a good deal of natural science to be "determined by the rules of language," so that skeptical assault against them would be reduced to the vague and obscure proposal to adopt a different language.[8] In other words, the empiricists wanted the truths of logic (and mathematics, etc.) to be integral to semantic competence relative to the respective languages, and *therefore* unrevisable *within* such languages. What Quine did was to undermine the very notion of the "rules of language" by showing that "they cannot be specified on the basis of the behavioural facts" (Horwich 1992, 99).[9] Therefore, the rules of language could not be appealed to in order to secure as much as the positivists wanted them to secure.

This differs to some extent from Quine's own reassessment of the argument of "Two Dogmas" in 1986 and then again in 1991. According to Horwich, Quine meant to challenge the positivists' account of the *truth* of logic (and mathematics, etc.), whereas for Quine himself, the issue was their *meaningfulness*. The logical positivists needed analyticity, according to Quine, in order to make the mathematical and logical truths *meaningful*, for, obviously, their meaning could not be made to coincide with their empirical content (as they have none). Once one gives up the "second dogma," the need for analyticity "as a key notion of epistemology" disappears.[10] For if we "see logic and mathematics rather as meshing with physics and other sciences for the joint implication of observable consequences, the question of limiting empirical content to some sentences at the expense of others no longer arises" (Quine 1986, 207; compare Quine 1991, 269).

This is not quite convincing as it stands, for if one has, as Quine believed he had, powerful independent arguments against the dogma of reductionism, why should one bother to criticize a distinction (the analytic/synthetic distinction) needed only if the dogma is adhered to? Not that such criticism would have been entirely superfluous: it would have provided an additional argument against the second dogma ("Look, if you stick to reductionism you are going to need a notion of analyticity in order to make logic and mathematics meaningful; but the analytic/ synthetic distinction is untenable"). Still, one feels some lack of proportion between the weaponry displayed by Quine against the distinction and the rather modest polemic value he attributed to it in 1986.

It looks more plausible to regard Quine's attack against the distinction as having broader scope than either Quine himself or Horwich are willing to grant. In "Two Dogmas" (1953 [1951]) Quine wanted to dismantle the positivistic picture of human knowledge as consisting of two sharply separated domains: the domain of empirical knowledge, which was circumscribed in terms of possible verification, and the domain of the pure sciences (logic, mathematics, part of physics), which inherited the features that previous centuries had attributed to the "truths of reason." Quine wanted to replace such a picture with a unitary account in which logic and mathematics would be seen "rather as meshing with physics and other sciences for the joint implication of observable consequences." To attain his overall theoretical aim, he thought he had to show that there are *no* truths that are both immune from revision based on experience and directly accessible to the linguistically informed mind, that is, that there are no analytic sentences. He did so indirectly by showing that the analytic/synthetic distinction is ungrounded, so that we have no clear *notion* of an analytic sentence. In so doing, he went overboard twice: he didn't need to show that the *very notion* of analyticity was empty, for it was enough for him to show that it is by no means clear that the *logical and mathematical truths* are analytic, and he didn't need to prove anything general concerning logic and mathematics, for it would have been enough for him to show that *some* of the truths of interest to the positivists are either revisable or not constitutive of semantic competence (what he actually thought and said was, of course, that they were revisable [Quine 1953, 43; compare Quine 1986, 620]). But he had a logician's taste for proving the strongest result one can prove (or believes one can prove), rather than the one required by the nature of the argument.

This was fortunate, in a way, because it helped to expose the inherent weakness of the very idea of analyticity (which, in fact, never fully recovered from Quine's aggression). On the other hand, it left many people, including Quine himself (1991, 270), rather uneasy about 'Bachelors are unmarried'. For even if we grant that not all sentences constitutive of semantic competence are unrevisable and, conversely, that not all unrevisable (or hardly revisable) truths are constitutive of semantic competence, there may well be sentences that are both. These are the "trivial" cases for which Putnam (1975a) thought one could safely use the label 'analytic'. Quine himself made some room for a "humbler" notion of analyticity, devoid of epistemological potentialities and restricted to the domain of "empirical semantics" (Quine 1986, 208).[11] He noticed that there are sentences "that we learn to recognize as true in the very process of learning one or another of the component words." 'No bachelor is married' is, of course, a paradigm case. The logical words, 'if', 'not', 'or', 'and' are another case: to have learned such words without having learned that 'if p then p', 'not both p and not p', 'p or not p' are all true "is simply not to have learned them" (Quine 1986, 94–95). "Some truths are learned by learning words": this is for Quine the "worthwhile insight" that makes up the only content of the notion of analyticity as "an intelligible and reasonable notion" freed of all epistemological hooks. By this Quine appears to mean that no one will ever be tempted to regard mathematical theorems, or even complex tautologies, as analytic in *this* sense, that is, as the kind of truths one learns by learning words. We are not taught the word 'prime' by being taught to appreciate the truth of Euclid's theorem, nor do we learn the idiom 'if ... then ... ' by learning Peirce's law.

Actually, the case of the logical truths is the one that Quine is most uneasy about, as is shown by his oscillations on the matter. In *The Roots of Reference* (1973), the first version of the "humble theory" of analiticity, he makes a distinction between logical truths that are "bound up with the very learning" of the logical words and logical laws that, though no less true by our lights, are not so bound up: the law of the excluded middle is an example of the latter.[12] "Perhaps then," he there concludes, "the law of excluded middle ... should be seen as synthetic" (1973, 80). In 1986, as we saw, this view appears to be reasserted, except that here Quine gives no examples of nonanalytic logical truths, *and the excluded middle is one of his examples of truths that* ARE *learned by learning the occurring words!* Finally, in 1991 Quine forfeits the distinction and includes all truths of logic "in [his] narrow sense," that is, up to first-order logic with identity, among the (humble) analytic truths.[13] The reason he gives for the inclusion is deductive closure: "Truths deducible from analytic ones by analytic steps would count as analytic in turn." It is hard to see what has been left of logic's "meshing with physics and other sciences for the joint implication of observable consequences" as the ground of its meaningfulness: it now seems that the truths of logic are simply what we learn in learning the logical words, or consequences thereof.[14]

Which, then, is Quine's final view of "humble" analyticity? Does he hold (3) or (4)?

(3)   There are a few sentences constitutive of competence, which are indeed unrevisable (whereas many among the *allegedly* analytic truths are revisable).

(4)   There are a few sentences constitutive of competence, and even they are revisable.

The example of the logical truths (such as the law of the excluded middle, etc.) would induce us to conclude that (4) is Quine's considered opinion, for he has said over and over that he regards even the logical principles as revisable in principle. On the other hand, given what Quine has to say concerning the connection between learning words and learning truths (learning the word 'bachelor' and learning that bachelors are males, adult, and unmarried), it would seem that to forfeit the truth of, for example, 'Bachelors are unmarried' just *is* to give up the word 'bachelor' as one has learned it; in this sense, "humble" analytic truths are unrevisable and Quine's considered view is expressed by (3). One could reconcile (3) and (4) (in the spirit of Quine's own slogan "Change of logic, change of subject" [1970, 81]) by concluding that humble analytic truths are indeed revisable, *and* revising them *amounts to* giving up certain words (or, equivalently, changing their meaning). This view is explicitly endorsed by Quine himself, at least as far as the logical truths are concerned: "In elementary logic a change of theory *is* a change of meaning. Repudiation of the law of excluded middle would be a change of meaning, and no less a change of theory for that" (Quine 1991, 270).

Quine's view, then, is just that there are a number of true sentences that are constitutive of competence relative to certain words occurring in them, and these are the reasonably analytic sentences. We will see in a while that there are reasons to doubt that such an identification (roughly, of analyticity with the content of inferential semantic competence) does complete justice to our intuitions.

Attempts at Reviving the Distinction

Bierwisch and Kiefer

Quine's criticism of the full-fledged notion of analyticity was immensely successful: after Quine, very few people tried to reinstate the analytic/

synthetic dichotomy or to give criteria for the delimitation of lexical meaning.[15] One such attempt, which has received some attention in the literature, is due to Bierwisch and Kiefer (1970). But, as we will see, the attempt is a total failure.

According to Bierwisch and Kiefer, for semantic purposes a lexical entry should be divided into two parts. The core of the entry includes all (and only) "those semantic specifications that determine ... its place within the system of dictionary entries, that is, delimit it from other (non-synonymous) entries" (1970, 69–70). The periphery, on the other hand, consists of those semantic specifications that "contribute to the meaning of a lexical entry without distinguishing it from other dictionary entries" (1970, 69–70). For instance, 'artifact' would belong to the core of 'spoon', whereas 'having such and such an average size' or 'not used in Asiatic cultures' would belong to its periphery. Obviously, the distinction of core and periphery is relative to a dictionary (that is, a set of entries), and therefore to a language. Since Bierwisch and Kiefer maintain that "the distinction [of core and periphery] correponds essentially to that between linguistic and encyclopedic knowledge," it follows that "there is no language-independent borderline between linguistic and encyclopedic knowledge in general" (1970, 72).

One wonders what kind of delimitation is this. Is lexical meaning *stricto sensu* supposed to coincide with the core? Then it is odd that the periphery is also said to "contribute to [the entry's] meaning." Should we then say that lexical meaning is really core plus periphery? In this case, the identification of the core/periphery distinction with the distinction between dictionaries and encyclopedias is less than plausible, for the whole point of the dictionary/encyclopedia distinction as a theoretical distinction (as opposed to a practical distinction between cultural objects) is to sort out information into semantically relevant and semantically irrelevant, that is, into specifications that do contribute to a word's meaning and specifications that do not. Moreover, if we take the identification of the two dichotomies seriously, we have to face at least two disturbing consequences. On the one hand, all encyclopedic information turns out to contribute to word meaning: for instance, chemical information concerning photosynthesis and historical information concerning the origins of agriculture turn out to "contribute to the meaning" of 'plant'. This is not so bad in itself, but it certainly does not go well with the intention of delimiting lexical meaning. On the other hand, if all information is either dictionary or encyclopedia information and lexical meaning is core plus periphery, then there is simply no piece of information that does not at least contribute to word meaning. We are left with the utter trivialization of the proposed delimitation, unless there is information that is neither dictionary nor encyclopedia information (perhaps 'My aunt's coffee table is 7 years old' would be a candidate). But then we haven't even begun to solve what turns out to be the real delimitation problem, that is, the problem of distinguishing between meaning-relevant information (be it dictionary or encyclopedia, core or periphery) and meaning-irrelevant information.

Suppose that, in spite of all this, we grant Bierwisch and Kiefer the following restatement of their theory: all information is relevant to the meaning of a word ("contributes" to its meaning), but part of it, the core, is more relevant, in that it semantically characterizes the word with respect to all other words in a given vocabulary, such as the vocabulary of Italian or of English. Still, Bierwisch and Kiefer's theory won't do if lexical meaning is conceived as the content of semantic competence, that is, if a word's core, in the sense of Bierwisch and Kiefer, must include all and only those specifications necessary for competent use of the word, for there may be information that, though not required to delimit the word with respect to other words of the language, is nonetheless crucial for competent use of the word. To see this, consider the phenomenon of so-called lexical gaps. Take a language *L* that has an individual word meaning a device for crushing olives but no individual word meaning a device for crushing nuts. Italian is such a language: the word which means a device for crushing olives is 'frantoio'. In Italian, there would be no need to include in the core of 'frantoio' the specification that the relevant crushing is to affect olives (rather than other small fruits), for there is no word such that the specification 'olives' would delimit 'frantoio' with respect to that word. Nevertheless, if a speaker did not know that 'frantoio' is to be used in connection with the crushing of olives but not in connection with the crushing of other small fruits, we would not regard her as competent (with respect to that particular word). Thus the core cannot be the meaning, not even the essential, or minimal, meaning.[16]

There appears to be a tacit consensus, among both linguists and philosophers of language, to the effect that the delimitation of lexical meaning with respect to factual or encyclopedic or world knowledge has become a moot issue after Quine. Even Bierwisch and Kiefer's proposal is instructive in this respect: it seems that with their distinction between specifications that characterize the meaning of a word and specifications that (merely) contribute to it, they are trying to eat their cake and have it too, as if they wished to delimit lexical meaning somehow without ruling out any specification as utterly irrelevant to it.

Artificial intelligence

On the other hand, the need for a delimitation of (inferential) lexical meaning seems to be very much alive in artificial intelligence. Even today, the belief seems to be widespread among AI researchers that "there is a boundary somewhere" (White 1991, 140).[17] If we knew exactly where it lay, our natural-language-understanding systems might perform better (White 1991, 149). As things stand, "the actual decision as to which component certain knowledge should go into [that is, whether in the lexical or in the world-knowledge component of a given system] depends more on software engineering, human factors, and efficiency issues than on capturing the natural linguistic/knowledge boundary" (White 1991, 142).

Such an "unprincipled" position may be the present consensus among the AI researchers who are at all interested in the matter. The prevailing view may be stated as follows: There is a natural distinction of lexical knowledge and world knowledge. Where exactly it should be drawn, we do not know. However, we do need to draw it *somewhere* for the purposes of building effective AI systems. Therefore, we are free to draw it more or less *anywhere* (within limits), depending on such external criteria as computational economy and so forth.

In the recent past, sharper views were expressed within the AI community, particularly by people working on issues of knowledge representation. "The conceptual separation of definitions and assertions has played a part in every KL-ONE-like system, including KL-ONE itself" (Woods and Schmolze 1992, 155), and the KL-ONE family itself has played a crucial role in the history of knowledge representation. However, in all cases I know of, the distinction appears to have been presupposed rather than justified. Researchers have been busy explaining how the two kinds of knowledge (lexical and factual) should be represented, how the data structures representing either kind should be dealt with, how and to what extent they ought to communicate with each other, and so forth, much more than they have been concerned with explaining *on what grounds* the relevant information is to be divided into lexical and factual. In other words, it seems to be assumed that information already comes divided into two sorts, so that one can focus on how either sort is to be represented, not just for the system's own sake but also to preserve the distinction—which is regarded as a worthy end in itself.

Let us consider the example of KRYPTON, a prestigious member of the KL-ONE family (Brachman, Fikes, and Levesque 1983). KRYPTON "clearly distinguishes between definitional and factual information" (1983, 413). This is absolutely true, in a sense: the two kinds of information are not simply expressed in different formalisms; they even have physically separate realizations. Brachman, Fikes, and Levesque (1983, 418) stress that each data structure must be uniquely interpretable *either* as expressing a factual assertion *or* as expressing (part of) the meaning of a word. The separation is brought about by having information stored in two separate "boxes," the assertional box (A box) and the Terminological box (T box). These are different and physically distinct formalisms. The T box represents taxonomies of structured terms: it "allows us to ... answer questions about analytical relationships among these terms" (1983, 418). The A box represents descriptive *theories* of the relevant domain. The T box contains (the formal equivalents of) *noun phrases* in subsumption or disjunction relations: thus, for example, the formal counterpart of 'person with at least 1 child' subsumes the formal counterpart of 'person with at least 3 children'. The A box contains the formal equivalents of *sentences*, such as 'Every person with at least 3 children owns a car'. Whatever information is in the A box is assertional and therefore not terminological: even the formal counterpart of a universally quantified biconditional ('For every x, x is Q if and only if x is P_1 & x is P_2 & ... & x is P_n') is regarded as having "no definitional import" (1983, 419).

If one already knows whether a given piece of information is definitional rather than factual, one thereby knows how to deal with it within the KRYPTON framework: one knows how to represent it and how it will be processed by the system (the two boxes are managed by different algorithms). However, how are we to know whether a given piece of information ought to be considered as definitional rather than factual (one is tempted to say, whether it *is* definitional or factual)? As the A box is supposed to contain the counterparts of sentences, one might think of adopting a straightforward linguistic criterion: every information intuitively expressed by a sentence goes into the A box, and nothing else does. This, however, won't do, for even the contents of the T box could likewise be regarded as the formal counterparts of English sentences: that [DOG] is subsumed by [MAMMAL] could be stated by asserting, 'The concept "dog" is subsumed by the concept "mammal" ' (or ' "dog" is a hyponym of "mammal" ', and so forth). What's wrong with such sentences? Why should the information they convey not go into the A box?

Suppose that we could rule out such sentences (for example, as being "metalinguistic," either explicitly or disguisedly). The problem is actually deeper. Take the information that dogs are mammals, as expressed by the sentence 'Dogs are mammals', a regular object-language sentence. Should we regard it as definitional or rather as factual (after all, it *is* a fact that dogs are mammals)? Should it be represented in the T box as establishing that [MAMMAL] subsumes [DOG], or should it go into the A box as a straightforward universal assertion? Surely Brachman, Fikes, and Levesque do not want to have it both ways. Indeed, they are even opposed to the possibility of having an assertional "copy" of the terminological fact that [MAMMAL] subsumes [DOG] (1983, 425). The issue arises because one would reasonably want the inferential device working on the contents of the A box to be able to exploit the definitional contents of the T box: one would want the system to be able to derive 'Greta is a mammal' from the assertion (in the A box) that Greta is a cow plus the terminological fact that [MAMMAL] subsumes [COW], as established from the T box. However, simply having the terminological fact induce the assertion $(\forall x)(\text{cow}(x) \supset \text{mammal}(x))$ would not do, according to the authors of KRYPTON, for it would obfuscate the distinction between definitional and assertional information. This is, in their opinion, exactly what happens in systems based on first-order logic, where definitions are commonly rendered as universally quantified biconditionals—"a treatment which simply fails to distinguish them from the more arbitrary facts that happen to have the same logical form" (1983, 425 n. 8). To summarize,

• There is a distinction of principle between definitions and assertions.
• Such a distinction must be preserved in formal representation. Therefore, definitions cannot be captured by universally quantified biconditionals, for there are assertions of facts that have exactly that form.

• Even having definitions *entail* universally quantified biconditionals or conditionals is dangerous and confusing (aside from being a redundancy in the system).[18]

All of this does not tell us whether 'Dogs are mammals' is definitional or assertional. KRYPTON's insistence on how important the distinction is does not appear to engender a criterion for drawing it.

Three Reasons for Not Jumping to the Conclusion That Everything Matters

Intuitions

No matter what one thinks of Quine's critique of the analytic/synthetic distinction, a tenable version of the dichotomy seems very hard to come by. Thus it is probably wiser to give up the attempt at delimiting lexical meaning (more precisely, the inferential side of lexical meaning, for this is what we have been talking about in this chapter). However, we should not hasten to conclude that all truths, or all beliefs are meaning-relevant, and this for three reasons. The first has to do with intuitions. There are lots of pieces of information that it would be extremely unnatural to regard as meaning-relevant or constitutive of competence or part of the dictionary. We already encountered some of them. We should not do violence to our intuitions just for the sake of theoretical simplicity. True, we do not have a *rationale* for such intuitions: we have no theory to sort out bits of information (or sentences) into those that are meaning-relevant and those that are not. However, this in itself is no reason simply to dispose of our intuitions, to the extent that we have any.[19]

Moreover, perhaps we can rationalize our intuitions of meaning-relevance to some extent by showing how they work, that is, by showing what sorts of considerations are brought to bear in our judgments of meaning-relevance. For it seems that our assessment of a piece of information as more dictionarylike or more encyclopedic is not altogether haphazard: there are regularities, which can be brought back to more basic intuitions. Certain features of a piece of information (or of its linguistic expression) tend to be regarded as encyclopedic, whereas the complementary features tend to be perceived as semantic, or dictionarylike. Thus (a) being contingent, (b) being about an individual, or having existential form, (c) not being constitutive of normal linguistic competence are encyclopedic features, while their opposites—being necessary, being universal, being constitutive of competence—are semantic.[20] A piece of information that has all of (a) through (c) will be regarded as closer to the encyclopedia (and farther from the dictionary), and the opposite will be true of information lacking all three of (a) through (c). Thus few will take the information that George's train came in at 4:10 as semantic, and few will consider the knowledge that wholes have parts as encyclopedic. But, of course, most information falls in between. The hypothesis we are exploring makes two predictions: (1) Ceteris paribus, a piece of information perceived as a necessary truth will be regarded as "more semantic" than a contingent truth; information considered to be strictly required for a competent use of language will be perceived as more semantic than another not so regarded; and information of a universal form will be seen as more semantic than information about individuals. (2) Two bits of information judged to possess the same number of encyclopedic features will be perceived as more or less on a par, that is, as equally distant, more or less, from the dictionary and from the encyclopedia.

The 'ceteris paribus' clause in (1) above should be taken seriously: it means that, for example, if two bits of information are both perceived as constitutive of normal competence and they are both expressed by sentences of a universal form but one is perceived as a necessary truth whereas the other is not, then the necessary truth will be seen as more semantic. Thus 'Bachelors are unmarried' is more semantic than 'Ovens are used to bake cakes'. Similarly for two pieces of information that are both nonconstitutive of competence: 'Water is H_2O' (universal, *necessary*, nonconstitutive) is more semantic than 'Manx cats have no tails' (universal, *contingent*, nonconstitutive). And so forth. On the other hand, prediction (2), the following items should be perceived as more or less at the same distance from the dictionary and from the encyclopedia: 'Mont Blanc is a mountain' (*individual*, necessary, constitutive), 'Wool is taken from sheep' (universal, *contingent*, constitutive), 'Gold has atomic number 79' (universal, necessary, *nonconstitutive*). In other words, the three parameters (a), (b), and (c) define a sort of elementary *metric*, the dictionary/encyclopedia metric, on the set of truths (table 2.1). Of course, much is demanded for one to begin to agree with this suggestion. First of all, it must be granted that we do have intuitions of the required kinds: modal intuitions and intuitions about linguistic competence (that we can recognize a sentence's logical form is perhaps not so con-

Table 2.1
The position of various sentences on the dictionary/encyclopedia metric

---

Dictionarylike

Bachelors are unmarried.
(universal, necessary, constitutive)

Mont Blanc is a mountain.
(*particular*, necessary, constitutive)

Wool is taken from sheep.
(universal,[a] *contingent*, constitutive)

Gold has atomic no. 79.
(universal, necessary, *nonconstitutive*)

Thirty-seven is the 13th prime no.
(*particular*, necessary, *nonconstitutive*)

Manx cats have no tails.
(universal, *contingent*, *nonconstitutive*)

France is a republic.
(*particular*, *contingent*, constitutive)

Napoleon died in May 1821.
(*particular*, *contingent*, *nonconstitutive*)

Encyclopedic

Boldface type indicates the metric poles. ▼ is a metric divider. Sentences are in roman type. Characteristics of the sentences are in parentheses. Dictionarylike characteristics are in roman type. Encylopedic characteristics are italicized.
a. This is a generic, rather than genuinely universal, sentence. However, the distinction does not seem to make any difference for the present purpose.

troversial). Second, it must be accepted that such intuitions are not, in themselves, intuitions about semantic import (which would trivialize the suggestion). This may be doubted, particularly in the case of the constitutive/nonconstitutive distinction, for after all, isn't belonging in the dictionary *just* being constitutive of normal competence? My answer is that, in spite of appearances, it is not. Notice, in fact, that if it were, then all pieces of information perceived as constitutive of normal competence ought to be on a par as to their distance from the dictionary and from the encyclopedia *independently of the other two parameters*: thus 'Bachelors are unmarried' should be on a par with 'Wool is taken from sheep' and with 'France is a republic'. I take it that it is obviously not so.[21]

On the other hand, to appreciate the present proposal it is not required that you agree with my intuitions in each single case. Disagreement on individual pieces of information do not affect my main claim, namely, that our (intuitive) judgments of semantic relevance are based on the interplay of our intuitions concerning the three pairs of features that I have singled out. This in turn may, of course, be challenged: the list may not be exhaustive; other features may turn out to be relevant. However, I predict that any other feature put forward as affecting our intuitions of semantic relevance will be shown to interact with the three features I just proposed.

I should point out that the rationalization of our intuitions that I have just proposed is *not* a new version of the analytic/synthetic distinction, not even a "fuzzy" version or a "multidimensional" one. The analytic/synthetic distinction is a "deep" distinction: it is based on certain real properties that true sentences are alleged to have (or lack). More precisely, it is a distinction between two kinds of grounds for the truth of a true sentence: a true sentence may be true by virtue of its meaning (if it is analytic) or it may be true by virtue of how the world happens to be (if it is synthetic). Whether or not a sentence is or is not analytic has nothing to do, in itself, with the fact that it is *recognized* to be such by this or that speaker, or even by a majority of speakers.[22] The dictionary/encyclopedia metric, on the other hand, is a "shallow," or phenomenological, taxonomy: it is based not on a sentence's objective properties but simply on our intuitive judgment of the sentence relative to the three parameters (a) to (c). Therefore, the taxonomy would be falsified by massive disagreement, for it does not appeal to any deep facts about language or information over and beyond the speakers' intuitions.[23]

There is no encyclopedic competence

The second reason for not regarding all information as relevant to competence is that it would be hard to answer the question, *Whose* competence? In other words, it would be hard to think of any real-life speaker who would even approximate such encyclopedic competence. This is one important difference between lexical semantic competence, on the one hand, and structural semantic competence and syntactic competence, on the other. Like syntactic competence, structural semantic competence can be identified with, or anyway represented as, implicit knowledge of a limited number of rules, such as the rule that computes the meaning of 'John runs' out of the meanings of 'John' and 'runs', or the rule that computes the meaning of 'the king' from the meaning of 'king'.[24] It is not too great an idealization to assume that such knowledge is actually shared by all competent speakers of a natural language.

David Dowty (1980, 390–391) expressed doubts that "compositional model-theoretic semantics" can be viewed as "somehow an acceptable model of the process of comprehending a sentence" beyond what he labeled "the thesis of the parallel structure of reference and understanding," according to which if a compositional procedure is shown to be necessary in a theory of truth and reference, then the same compositional analysis is necessary in a theory of language understanding (1980, 383). Such doubts may seem to apply to the contention just put forth, for the compositional rules of model-theoretic semantics are the obvious model for structural semantic rules. Dowty's reason for his doubts is that "the formal definition of entailment" for a language includes much more than is actually computed in the act of comprehending a sentence; in other words, only a very small subset of the huge number of entailments that model theory ascribes to a sentence are actually computed as the sentence is understood by a speaker. Here Dowty is (correctly, I believe) identifying the model-theoretic meaning of a sentence with the set of its entailments.[25] And he is certainly right in pointing out that whatever is computed in an individual act of comprehension does not coincide with a sentence's meaning in *this* sense. However, much less is required to substantiate the claim that an ordinary speaker may be endowed with (structural) semantic rules of the *kind* of the compositional rules of model-theoretic semantics. What is meant is simply that to grasp the meaning of a compound expression, an ordinary speaker must be able to put together bits of semantic information by way of rules whose prima facie application depends on the structural properties of the expressions singled out as constituents. What is required is for syntactic structure to induce semantic processing: it is required that the understanding of 'The cat is on the mat' be not an *altogether* different story from the understanding of 'The book is on the table'. It is certainly not required that the rule we use to compute the meaning of 'John runs' be exactly the rule that is provided by Montague's "Proper Treatment of Quantification in Ordinary English" (1974b). Nor is it necessary that the semantic object that gets computed, the sentence's meaning, be identified with an element of a system whose relations with the other elements are all given *by fiat* once the object itself is given (as with "propositions" in model-theoretic semantics), not, at any rate, if by 'given' one means brought to consciousness. Actually, what is required is even less than what is expressed by Dowty's thesis of parallel structure, for it is not to be taken for granted that compositional understanding, as carried out by finite minds, can satisfy the exacting demands of a theory of truth and reference in the model-theoretic tradition.

With lexical semantic competence, that is, the ability to understand and use words, things are different. In the case of words, genuine competence cannot be idealized to include encyclopedic knowledge (not even into encyclopedic knowledge in the narrow sense, including beliefs about Julius Caesar but not including beliefs about my aunt). The gap is just too wide. We do not work that way: if people like you and me are competent users of whatever natural language we speak, then it cannot be the case that lexical competence coincides with encyclopedic knowledge, not even "idealized" competence.

Holism

The third reason that not all truths are meaning-relevant is connected with the issue of holism. Anybody who doubts the possibility of delimiting lexical meaning, drawing the analytic/synthetic distinction, etc., is bound to face the charge of semantic holism. And if we say that all information in whose expression a word *w* occurs is constitutive of the meaning of *w*, this is one brand of holism.

Semantic holism in general is the doctrine according to which the semantic value of an element of a linguistic system, whatever it may be, *depends on* the whole system. 'Depends on' may be read in more than one way. For example, it may be read *epistemologically*: one cannot *account for* an element's semantic value without bringing in the whole system ('bringing in' is ambiguous here: which features of the system are relevant?). Or it may be read *ontologically*: an element's semantic value is *determined by* the system, or by certain properties of the system or of all its elements. In what follows, we will mostly be concerned with ontological holism.

There are bland versions of semantic holism that are quite defensible in themselves and do not raise particular problems for a theory of semantic competence. One such is *structural* holism, as I shall call it. It is best introduced by an example. According to a standard account, the meaning of the word 'not' as a sentential connective consists in reversing the truth value of the sentence it is applied to: if 'Elias is just' is true then 'Elias is not just' is false, whereas if the former sentence is false, then the latter is true. Whether or not this is the whole story about the meaning of (sentential) 'not', few doubt that it is a substantial part of the story. To know the meaning of 'not' is to know (implicitly perhaps) at least this much. Now in a sense, such knowledge may be said to involve the whole language to which 'not' belongs, for the semantic role of 'not' is defined with respect to *any sentence* of the language. Therefore, it could be claimed, to be fully competent in the use of 'not', one must know what counts as a sentence of the language, but such knowledge is (in a sense) knowledge of the whole language.

It is indeed, but only in a sense: it is knowledge of a *structural* property of the (whole) language. In this sense, all words of a language like English are such that competence in their use includes knowledge of some structural property of the language. Thus, to be competent in the use of 'gold', one has to know that it is a mass noun, and to be competent in the use of 'discover', one must know that it is a factive verb.[26] Therefore, it could be said that a holistic factor is included in our knowledge of the meaning of any word. This, however, is not to say that to use *any* word competently, one must be aware of *all* the semantic properties of *all* expressions of the language. Surely, in order to be competent in the use of 'not', one does not have to know what 'sesquipedalian' means or what the difference is between 'voluntarily' and 'deliberately'. Any view entailing such consequences deserves the name of 'serious semantic holism'. Structural holism has not got much to do with serious semantic holism. For *structural* holism, competence with a word *w* belonging to the lexicon of a language *L* involves command of some structural property *P* of *L*. For *serious* holism, competence with a word *w* involves command of *all* properties *P* of *L* and competence with *all* expressions *e* (including *all* words) of *L*. Structural holism would be close to (though still not identical with) serious holism only if competence with a word reduced to command of structural properties of *L*. But, evidently, such cannot be the case: competence with individual words does not reduce to command of structural properties (this is just what being an individual word is about). To be competent with, say, 'remember', one must know the semantic difference between 'remember' and 'recall', and no degree of command of the structural properties of English is going to yield such knowledge.

If structural holism may be regarded as plausible, serious holism, on the other hand, is totally implausible as an account of the semantic phenomena. Aside from the well-worn and seemingly harmless metaphors according to which "the meaning of a sign is its place in the linguistic system" or "its use in the language game" or "its position in the network," serious semantic holism is the view on which the meaning of a linguistic expression e belonging to a language L is determined by all expressions of L together with the rules for their use. In terms of competence, holism can be read as the claim that to understand e, one must know the meanings of all the expressions of L. Serious semantic holism looks convincing only as long as it is couched in the rhetoric of networks with a center and a periphery. As soon as we realize what the phrase 'the whole language' means, holism begins to look slightly crazy. It is all the more surprising that there seem to be so many arguments in its favor, and so strong.[27] As we will see, there even seems to be a very simple argument leading straight to semantic holism from the almost commonsensical assumption that the meaning of word w is "given" by a few sentences $S_1, \ldots, S_n$ of the language to which w belongs.

Recently a number of devastating consequences of holism were again pointed out by J. Fodor and E. Lepore (1992). It appears that holism, taken seriously, entails incommensurability of theories, the impossibility of linguistic diacrony, and the impossibility of any generalization concerning the intentional states of people (thus the impossibility of psychology, economics, and so forth). According to Fodor and Lepore, these are all consequences of holism in their sense. In their sense, "holistic properties are properties such that, if anything has them, then *lots* of other things must have them too" (1992, 2). Thus for example, the property of being a natural number is holistic (if there is a natural number, there are lots of them). 'Holistic' in this sense is more specific than, and should be contrasted with, 'nonatomic' or, in Fodor and Lepore's unfortunate coinage, 'anatomic': a property is *anatomic* just in case if x has it, there is at least one y (y other than x) that also has it. For instance, the property of being a member of a cooperative is anatomic.[28] A nonanatomic property is atomistic. An *atomistic* property is one that might be instantiated by only one individual: being a citizen of Boston exactly 1.83 m tall is atomistic in this sense.

Garden-variety semantic holism can be "reduced" to Fodor and Lepore ($=$FL) holism in the following way: take the property of contributing to determining the meaning of expression E of L as a property of expressions of L; if this property is FL-holistic and if all analogous properties involving the other expressions of L are likewise FL-holistic, what we get is traditional (ontological) semantic holism, or at any rate one version of it (the version in which 'the whole of L' is interpreted as 'all expressions of L').[29] Thus traditional holism can be defined in terms of FL-holism.[30] Anyway, it appears that the dreadful consequences that Fodor and Lepore draw from FL-holism could equally well be derived from holism in the traditional sense.

However, the consequence I find hardest to swallow, and hardest to avoid, is one they don't seem to be considering. Suppose that sentence understanding is a *compositional* process, in which the meaning of a sentence, whatever it may be, is constructed from the constituents' semantic values, the construction process being somehow governed by the sentence's syntactic structure.[31] Such an assumption is both widespread and strongly motivated. Now suppose that holism holds, so that a constituent's semantic value (like the semantic value of every expression of any language) is a function of the linguistic system as a whole, in any prima facie plausible sense:[32] for example, a function of the system's structural properties *and* the semantic values of the system's other units. It follows that understanding any sentence involves the understander's entire semantic competence, for it requires that information be used relative to the whole linguistic system, structure and elements. Understanding would thus be impossibile for a mind like the human mind in memory and computational resources. Only God would understand the sentence 'All men are mortal'. Perhaps this isn't so bad in itself: some philosophers would have approved of it. What is *really* bad is that we would be left without any notion of what *human* understanding is like. We would only know that the computations of which our understanding consists are radically inadequate, but we would not know how to characterize them. What are the data the computations are based on? How are the data chosen? How are computed semantic values connected with the constituents' *real* (that is, holistic) semantic values?

From the standpoint of a theory of semantic competence, one cannot but look for an alternative to holism. One such alternative is surely *atomism*, the view according to which the meaning of an expression depends only "on some punctuate symbol/world relation" (Fodor and Lepore 1992, 32). In an *ideational* version of atomism, the meaning of an expression might be an individual mental entity, such as a symbol in Fodor's language of thought.[33] However, the atomistic alternative is ruled out if one favors *eliminative* over *hypostatic* theories of meaning, that is, if one wants to countenance (and be able to answer) questions such as 'Does *x* mean the same as *y*?' without thereby accepting statements of the form 'The meaning of *x* is *z*', where *z* is an individual entity of whatever ontological species.[34] For atomism is tendentially, if not necessarily, hypostatic.

Molecularism

One is then led to explore the alternative of molecularism. In the *molecularist* picture (as applied to comprehension) each act of understanding only uses a finite and reasonably small amount of information.[35] Understanding a sentence does not involve the understander's entire semantic competence (or a great big chunk of it, as in Fodor and Lepore's version of holism[36]), but neither does it involve only "punctuate relations" between each symbol and the world.

However, molecularism also came under attack by Fodor and Lepore: they thought themselves to have shown that molecularism is incompatible with the rejection of the analytic/synthetic distinction. If they were right, molecularism would not be a live option for us.

Fodor and Lepore's argument is aimed at molecularism as applied to belief, that is, at the claim that if we share the belief that *p*, there are other beliefs we must also share, but we do not have to share *all* our other beliefs. Their argument is condensed in the following sentence: "But distinguishing between those [beliefs] that do [have to be shared] and those that don't depends on invoking the analytic/synthetic distinction, for believing *p* requires accepting the *analytic* inferences in which *p* figures" (1992, 31). More clearly, if other beliefs must be shared besides *p*, they cannot but be those beliefs that follow analytically from the belief that *p*. Fodor and Lepore's contention seems to be that whenever we make a selection among beliefs where the selection is of the beliefs that have to be shared if *p* is shared, there has to be a *criterion* of the selection, but any such criterion embodies some form of the analytic/

synthetic distinction. However, is there really a selection going on? What does the molecularist really hold?

According to Fodor and Lepore, the molecularist's position is captured by the following:

(5) $(\forall p)(\exists q)(q \neq p \;\&\; \Box(p$ is shared $\supset q$ is shared$))$

That is, there are beliefs that must be shared whenever p is shared. This, of course, is not the same as (6):

(6) $(\forall p)\Box(p$ is shared $\supset (\exists q)(q \neq p \;\&\; q$ is shared$))$

That is, necessarily, whenever p is shared, there are other beliefs that are also shared.[37] Is the molecularist committed to (5), as Fodor and Lepore believe he is, or is the weaker (6) a better formulation of his intuitions? Moreover, does (5) really imply or presuppose the analytic/synthetic distinction, as in Fodor and Lepore's account?

Let us start with the second question. The answer should be weakly affirmative, I believe, for if certain given beliefs must be shared (whenever p is shared), there appears to be something like a "privileged neighborhood" of the belief that p. Suppose that p is the belief that gold is a metal. It is natural to include in the set of qs that must be shared the belief that metals are minerals and the belief that many precious objects are made of gold, but not the belief that cats are feline or the belief that some philosophers play volleyball. Such beliefs might, of course, be also shared, but why *must* they? It is thus natural to conclude that the privileged neighborhood in question is but a way of representing the set of beliefs that are *analytically* connected with p ('Gold is a metal'). There is some plausibility (though less than logical validity) in such an argument. If one has to choose a set of beliefs necessarily associated with p by whoever believes that p, it is natural to pick such beliefs as are naturally conceived of as analytically connected with p (Jacob 1993, 21).

In this respect, (5) is different from (6): (6) doesn't say that certain other beliefs must be shared; it says that there must be other shared beliefs if p is shared. From the standpoint of (6), there is no reason why such beliefs should be analytically connected with p: they might concern altogether different matters.

Where does the molecularist stand? He could be represented as reasoning along the following lines: suppose that A and B both believe that gold is a metal. In addition, each of them has lots of other beliefs concerning gold, metals, and countless other things. *Some* such beliefs must be common to them if we are to say that they both believe *that gold is a metal*, not different though homonymical propositions. However, the molecularist says, they need not share *all* beliefs on gold or metals; they need not even share the beliefs that each of them regards as most important, crucial, or "constitutive of the meaning" of 'gold' or 'metal'. *A* may strongly associate with the word 'gold' the property of being yellow, whereas *B*, who was trained as a metallurgist, may rather associate the property of being white with the same word. *A*'s firm belief that gold is yellow may thus not be shared by *B*. Are we prepared to claim that consequently, *A* and *B* do not *really* share even the belief that gold is a metal? Or would we then insist that therefore, 'Gold is yellow' is not analytic, or that it is not analytic in *B*'s idiolect? It seems to me that the notion of analytic is totally irrelevant in the present context. There is *no* general criterion to decide which beliefs about gold must be shared, although some beliefs have to be shared.[38]

The point I am trying to emphasize is that two (or more) speakers may be said to share a common language, in the ordinary sense of that phrase, even though they only share some beliefs. We already saw (p. 44) that there is an asymmetry between lexical semantic competence and structural semantic competence: at the lexical level, individual competence, even idealized individual competence, does not coincide with encyclopedic knowledge, that is, with the totality of true beliefs that can be ascribed to the linguistic community as a collective entity. We also saw that it is extremely hard to isolate a plausible subset of encyclopedic knowledge as being constitutive of (lexical) semantic competence, that is, a set of propositions we all ought to know or believe in order to be regarded as lexically competent. As a matter of fact, each of us knows or believes partly different things (partly different subsets of the collective encyclopedia), yet we are all competent in the use of our language. Could lexical competence be defined as the *intersection* of such different individual competences? In principle, no, for we have no guarantee that the intersection of all competences is rich enough to be considered adequate as a competence (it is quite possible that the set of beliefs we all share about, say, gold is very small, too small to constitute an adequate competence with 'gold'). It remains that we regard the notion of absolute competence as empty at the lexical level: on this level, we only have *competences*, in the plural. We ought to speak not of a unique lexical competence, only of individual competences. In this sense, there is no language, only idiolects.[39]

If such an account is plausible, then (5) does not capture the molecularist's view, for there is no individual belief (no q) that must be shared if p is. Each belief, no matter how "analytic," could fail to be shared. On the other hand, (6) is not entirely satisfactory either. For if A and B, beside believing that gold is a metal, also share the beliefs that Napoleon was French and that lemurs live in Madagascar (and no other beliefs), then (6) is satisfied, but the molecularist's intuitions are not.[40] The molecularist wants other beliefs *about gold and metals* to be shared. Therefore, (6) should be modified, perhaps as follows:

(7) $\Box(p[\alpha_1 \ldots \alpha_n]$ is shared

$\supset (\forall i_{1 \leq i \leq n})(\exists q[\alpha_i])(q[\alpha_i] \neq p \ \& \ q[\alpha_i]$ is shared$))$

Here $\alpha_1, \ldots, \alpha_n$ are predicates occurring in p. What (7) says is that if, for example, A and B share a belief about gold and metals, then they share other beliefs about gold and other beliefs about metals (though there are no beliefs about either topic that they are bound to share).[41]

Now all this concerned molecularism as applied to beliefs. What is the connection with the kind of molecularism we felt the need of when discussing the compositionality of comprehension? That kind of molecularism was a claim about competence: it was the claim that an understander's competence is so organized that only a finite (and reasonably small) amount of competence is mobilized in each act of understanding, and not his entire competence. The connection with the preceding discussion is the following: if Fodor and Lepore's argument against molecularism of belief were sound, an analogous argument would hold against molecularism of comprehension. Such an argument would show that molecularism of comprehension presupposes the analytic/synthetic distinction, for this kind of molecularism holds that understanding p requires the mobilization of only certain contents of competence (not the entire content: that would be holism). But *which* contents must be mobilized, Fodor and Lepore would ask? Surely such as are analytically connected with the words occurring in the expression that is understood: it's the *meanings of the words* that are mobilized. Or again, *if* there are contents that *must* be mobilized, the principle by which they are singled out is a form of the analytic/synthetic distinction.

However, as we saw in the case of belief molecularism, there are no contents that must be mobilized: *some* contents must be, and those that are so mobilized may be different for each understander, and even for an individual understander on different occasions of understanding (for distinct occurrences of one and the same word in different sentences, and even for different occasions of understanding the same sentence).[42] It is, of course, *possible* that (part of) the contents mobilized in understanding sentences in which the word 'cat' occurs be consistently the same for a given speaker, but such an eventuality is by no means forced by molecularism (or by anything else). If it were, we would have an analytic/synthetic distinction (or something like it) idiosyncratic to a given speaker and relative to a given lexical unit. Here the existence of an analytic/synthetic distinction is transformed into an *empirical* issue.[43]

The Truth in Holism

Let us now go back to the argument I hinted at on p. 48, leading from the harmless assumption that the meaning of each word of a language L is given by a few sentences of L, to semantic holism. The argument is the following. Assume $S_1, \ldots, S_n$ to be the (true) sentences of L on which the meaning of word w is said to depend, or by which it is said to be "given." Assume further that $v_1, \ldots, v_m$ are the words occurring in the S_i other than w. For each j, the meaning of v_j depends in turn on some true sentences of L in which v_j occurs, some of which are other than each of the S_is: say these are $S_{n+1}, \ldots, S_k$. Thus the meaning of w depends on these too. By iterating this reasoning, we are likely to reach "the whole of L," or all true sentences of L. Of course, the argument is even stronger if one assumes that the meaning of w is "encyclopedically" determined by *all* true sentences of L in which w occurs.

The argument, however, is unconvincing. Let us try to apply it to semantic competence. Suppose we say that a system H is **inferentially competent relative** to w if (and only if) its database includes all S_i of w. Again, let $v_1, \ldots, v_m$ be the constituents of the S_i other than w. Clearly, the argument goes, it makes sense to say that $S_i(w, v_j)$ belongs to the content of H's competence only if H is inferentially competent relative to v_j. Therefore, H is (inferentially) competent relative to w only if it is competent relative to $v_1, \ldots, v_m$, and so on. The argument's apparent plausibility rests on examples like this: suppose that 'Roses are flowers' is part of the content of the system's competence relative to 'rose'. If the system doesn't know what 'flower' means, how can that sentence give any flesh to its competence relative to 'rose'? However, this is exactly where the fallacy hides. For if the content of (inferential) competence has been reduced to knowledge of certain relations among words, it is incorrect to require or presuppose that such relations involve not the words themselves but their meanings. *There are no meanings*, only relations among words, expressed by sentences such as 'Roses are flowers', 'If one walks, one moves', etc. This is clearly seen in the case of an artificial system: for the system, the "meaning" of 'rose', as far as its inferential aspect is concerned, is but the inclusion of certain sentences and/or inferential sequences in the database.[44]

Clearly, we are as a matter of fact competent with many words of the language we know (though to a different extent). Thus it is quite natural to feel that knowledge that roses are flowers is part of our competence with 'rose' because we know what 'flower' means; if we didn't, such knowledge would be no knowledge at all, and thus no contribution to our competence with 'rose'. Now we do in fact know a lot about flowers, and this fact indirectly extends and strengthens our competence with 'rose' (this is the truth in holism). By contrast, we (or at least I) know very little about angiosperms. Consequently, knowing (as I do) that roses are angiosperms does not *extend* or *strengthen* my competence with 'rose'. However, *it is part of my competence*: it is not as if the information were empty because it doesn't lead me anywhere *else*.

As I anticipated, the moral is the following: we feel that our knowledge of how to use a word is inextricably intertwined with our knowledge of how to use many other words. This is true up to a point: it does not entail that to be able to use one word, we must know how to use all other words, nor that we must know how to use the other words to the same extent as we know how to use the original word.

Conclusion on Meaning Postulates

How, in conclusion, do we choose the meaning postulates? Does it make sense to select any? The answer I would suggest is based on three premises, which have been argued for in this chapter. First of all, there is no absolute criterion to tell meaning-relevant from meaning-irrelevant information (in this sense, there is no analytic/synthetic distinction).

Second, we should not therefore conclude that the only reasonable choice of meaning postulates makes them coincide with the encyclopedia, that is, with the set of propositions that are collectively believed by the linguistic community at a given stage in history (for example, the present stage). Such a radical option would be forced on us by certain forms of semantic holism, but we found no reason to adhere to *any* form of semantic holism except structural holism. Moreover, such an option would be inconsistent with the idea that meaning postulates represent one side or aspect of lexical semantic *competence*, for there is no encyclopedic competence, nor does individual competence idealize to encyclopedic competence.

Third, given the variety of individual competences on the inferential level, we cannot expect any choice of meaning postulates to represent any more than (the inferential side of) one particular competence. We should give up any attempt at capturing "communitarian" inferential competence, or the common core of all individual competences: neither the union nor the intersection of individual competences are reasonable candidates, for the intersection is bound to be too small and insignificant, while the union is most likely inconsistent.

Still, there may be reasons (within an AI project, for example) to try to write down a set of sentences (or pieces of information, in any format) that would reasonably represent the inferential side of *some* competence. In this case, the *dictionary* ought to be our guide. Dictionaries are excellent repositories of information that several generations of expert speakers have perceived as meaning-relevant, and the knowledge of dictionary contents has been regarded as contributing to competence.[45] As we will see better in chapter 5, dictionaries are not absolute standards, nor should they be seen as embodying any more than the information considered by lexicographers as useful for a socially adequate use of the language (in which opinion, naturally, they may be mistaken). Of course, any but the most elementary dictionary far exceeds the lexical competence of most individual speakers; nevertheless, dictionaries are helpful in that they (mostly) include *the right kind* of information, while not presenting such information in philosophically misleading form (as being "analytic," for example). A reasonable selection from a good dictionary can be a basis for a set of meaning postulates intended to represent (one side of) the lexical competence of a very competent speaker.

3

On the Structure of Lexical Competence

Two Aspects of Lexical Competence

I have repeatedly emphasized that meaning postulates do not exhaust the content of lexical semantic competence. A competent speaker knows more than is expressed by meaning postulates.[1] What more? What do we typically know and what can we typically do whenever we are regarded as competent in the use of a word? Consider the word 'spoon'. We all know a lot about spoons: we can describe a spoon, explain its use, tell how spoons are normally acquired and where they are usually kept; we know what materials spoons are (mostly) made of, how long they may last, what kind of deterioration they are subject to. Moreover, most of us can draw a reasonable picture of a spoon, one that would be recognized as such by most observers; we can in turn also recognize drawings of spoons, photographs of spoons, and, of course, real spoons. Consequently, we usually have no trouble answering questions such as 'Are there any spoons in the drawer?' or obeying orders such as 'Fetch me a spoon!' provided there are spoons in the vicinity. To know the word 'spoon', to be competent in its use, is or includes the possession of all these simple abilities.

Many words are like 'spoon' in this respect: most speakers are fully competent in their use, that is, they can easily carry out the performances just mentioned. But many more words, perhaps the majority of words in a standard English vocabulary, are *not* at all like 'spoon'. Competence in their use varies widely from speaker to speaker. A zoologist knows a lot in connection with the word 'macaque', he knows many true sentences where the word occurs, whereas I only know that macaques are monkeys. A zoologist can recognize a macaque and tell one from a Barbary ape, I cannot (although I could easily tell a macaque from a gorilla). A chemist knows more than most of us about asbestos, and he can identify asbestos in many ways, including by way of certain tests that we don't know how to apply. Such differences in richness, articulation, and subtlety among the competences of several speakers were described long ago by Putnam (1975c) as one effect of the 'division of linguistic labor'. Putnam took the division of linguistic labor to rest on the division of *non*linguistic labor (1975c, 228), which seems to imply that each subclass of "semantic experts" coincides with a professional class (the botanists, the chemists, etc.). This is not necessarily so: if a person spent her life among manatees, she may have become extremely good at recognizing manatees, better than any trained zoologist. She would never confuse a manatee with a dugong, not even on first sight (a zoologist might), because of those particular ways and looks that manatees have, with which she is better acquainted than anybody else.

Of course, that same person might be utterly ignorant of manatees' anatomy and physiology, of their evolutionary history, and of their place in the zoological taxonomy. The trained zoologist knows much that she might not know. Thus it seems that Putnam was right after all: the scientist's expertise is far superior to the layperson's. On the other hand, scientists may be very bookish persons. We can imagine a scientist who knows everything one can learn from books about the butterfly *Aulularia Clemensi* but has never seen one (his books had no pictures). If he ever gets to the Amazonian forest and an *A. Clemensi* flies by, he may fail to recognize it.[2] He is indeed equipped with the cognitive resources needed to identify it, for he knows the butterfly's shape, size, colors, length of feelers, etc. (so if a native were to catch the butterfly for him, he would eventually recognize it, given enough time). However, his ability to apply the butterfly's name to the real animal is much inferior to the native's, who has been playing with *A. Clemensi* all his life.

The difference we have been hinting at, between the competence of the native (or the friend of manatees) and that of the scientist is not simply one of quantity. It is a difference between two kinds or aspects of (lexical) semantic competence, one consisting in the knowledge of true sentences in which a certain word is used, the other relevant to the application of the word in the real world. The genuine expert (not the bookish one) is endowed with both: he can spot a macaque half a mile off, and he is familiar with scores of scientific articles about macaques.

We, on the other hand, are not like him (and the scientist himself is not like that, with respect to most words): very often the two aspects of competence do not match. I, for instance, am pretty familiar with primroses: I could pick a primrose for you without risk of picking a ranunculus instead. However, I know close to nothing about primroses: not their classification, not their anatomy, nothing that could be used to effectively distinguish primroses from other, macroscopically similar flowers. I couldn't even put into words whatever criteria I use to single out primroses. Similarly with many other words, whether for natural or for artificial kinds: I know very little about cathode-ray tubes or microwave ovens or antennas, though I can use the words appropriately most of the time to refer to the corresponding artifacts. Surely my scanty knowledge is insufficient to sustain my (more or less) adequate referential performance.

Notice the difference between the distinction I am drawing and the one implicit in the notion of the division of linguistic labor. Putnam (1975c) made a distinction between speakers who were very competent (as competent as one can be) in the use of certain words and less competent speakers, whose use of such words is somehow parasitic upon the experts' competence.[3] By contrast, the distinction I am pointing out primarily concerns individual competence: a speaker may be quite competent referentially, that is, in the application of certain words, while being deeply ignorant of their referents' nature and properties. Derivatively, individual speakers may differ from each other like the bookish zoologist and the native: one may possess excellent referential competence and poor knowledge (like the native); another may possess excellent knowledge but poor referential competence (like the bookish zoologist).

The nonreferential side of competence has been characterized in terms of *knowledge*: the bookish zoologist knows a lot about *A. Clemensi*; I know very little about microwave ovens or macaques. However, the ability I am trying to circumscribe is more general and dynamic: it is the ability to manage a network of connections among words, underlying such performances as semantic inference, paraphrase, definition, retrieval of a word from its definition, finding a synonym, and so forth. In Marconi 1991 (see also 1987) I called this the *inferential* aspect of lexical semantic competence, having in mind the fact that artificial systems that try to model human lexical competence actually succeed in modeling (only) this side of competence and that such systems are essentially inferential devices. Yet the ability to draw semantic inferences is also crucial to lexical competence. We expect anybody who knows what 'cat' means to be aware that provisions concerning animals are relevant to cats; of one who did not know that to eat one ordinarily has to open one's mouth, we would say he does not know what 'eat' means; and so on. By contrast, referential competence, or the referential side of competence, is the ability to map lexical items onto the world. An ordinary speaker can tell cats from cows, can point to a numeral on paper, can describe a person as running rather than walking. Of one who were incapable of such performances in ordinary circumstances, we would say that he or she does not know what the relevant words mean.

In recent years several people, working from different points of view, have pointed out the distinction and partial independence of the two aspects of lexical competence. Moravcsik (1981, 15) neatly distinguished knowledge of meaning from the capacity to identify extensions ("identificational skill," as he called it), noting that one may possess the former but not the latter, but he wanted to exclude referential ability from linguistic competence (though he admitted that in some cases it might be part of linguistic competence, as with the words 'up' and 'down'). We will examine this objection later on in this chapter (pp. 64–66). Johnson-Laird insisted that knowledge of semantic relations is not the whole of semantic competence: thus theories of meaning that rely on meaning postulates, or other equivalent formalisms, in order to represent meaning are bound to be inadequate, for "unless a theory relates language to the world ..., it is not a complete theory of meaning" (1983, 230). Indeed, more than anybody else I know of, Johnson-Laird stressed that semantic relations do not determine truth conditions, and that a complete account of semantic competence needs a theory of the mapping of lexical items onto the world as a cognitive process, not just the assumption that some such mapping exists, as we have in model-theoretic semantics. In Johnson-Laird's own theory, such a mapping is mediated by mental constructions, mental models, that may or may not be embeddable in the actual world. Language understanding consists in the construction of mental models of the sentences (or more complex texts) being understood.

Johnson-Laird (1983) did not recognize, however, the independence of the two aspects, inferential and referential, for he apparently believed that the referential determines the inferential: if we could map language onto mental models in the appropriate way, we could "read off" semantic relations among words directly from the model. Discounting the connection between mental models and perception,[4] this amounts to the claim that *perfect* referential ability would yield full inferential competence. If one had a perfect referential algorithm for 'rose' (such as would pick out all and only the roses among all objects in the world) and an equally perfect algorithm for 'flower', the truth of 'Roses are flowers' would follow from such algorithms, in the sense that all the objects picked out by the algorithm for 'rose' would also be picked out by the algorithm for 'flower'.

Even if this is conceded in principle, it scarcely needs arguing that average speakers do not possess such perfect referential ability. Moreover, in real life we do not seem to *derive* the knowledge that, say, dolphins are mammals from our ability to recognize dolphins plus our ability to recognize mammals. Even those of us who do have such referential abilities know independently that dolphins are mammals. Similarly, semantic inferences do not generally depend on the exercise of referential abilities: to infer from 'This is a couch' to 'This is a piece of furniture' we do not think of how we identify couches, then of how we recognize pieces of furniture. The dependence of inferential competence on referential competence is no more plausible than the converse dependence.

The independence of meaning and reference was stressed in so-called "dual aspect" theories, which wanted to have both mental states (inferential roles, conceptual roles, narrow contents, etc.), to solipsistically determine behavior, and objective causal relations with the world, to fix reference and take care of Twin Earth problems.[5] Dual theorists have occasionally emphasized some of the phenomena highlighted here to point out the independence of the two aspects of meaning. However, their views should not be conflated with the picture I am presenting. First of all, dual-aspect theories are theories of *meaning*, whereas I am offering an account of *competence*. Everything I am talking about takes place "in the head" (of course, "the head" is in touch with the world, thanks to perception and motion). Consequently, the referential aspect of lexical semantic competence is a cognitive ability of the human mind (or rather, as we will see, a family of such abilities) and should not be conceived of as the introflection of a purely objective, causal relation between a speaker and his or her environment.[6] Thus in the present context I will have little to say concerning "real" reference, the internalism/externalism controversy, or truth versus verification. Some of these problems will be taken up in chapter 4 in connection with a radical objection to my view, namely, the (externalistic) charge of irrelevance to the concerns of semantics.

Interaction of the Two Aspects

So far I have been stressing the independence of the two aspects. This must be qualified. We saw that the bookish zoologist could have recognized *A. Clemensi*, thanks to a detailed description of that rare butterfly. He would have been using his referential competence relative to color words, geometric predicates, expressions of measure, etc., as a substitute for direct referential competence relative to the word '*Aulularia Clemensi*'. But, of course, access to the butterfly description is possible thanks to the scientist's *inferential* competence. Often, particularly with less common words, we use our inferential competence to carry out referential tasks when we lack direct referential competence. "Someone who has learned from books what a guanaco looks like may never have been caused to accede to 'That's a guanaco' by seeing a guanaco, and yet be prepared ... to accede when he does see one" (Davidson 1991, 195). If one has mastered dictionary definitions of words such as, say, 'opal', 'caulking', or 'Sienna', one may be in a position to apply them. This is one thing that is right about the idea of semantic primitives: our ability to apply words may be based on the ability to apply other, more common words, such as color words, except that there needn't be anything particularly primitive about them.[7] For example, color words or shape words such as 'square' and 'round' are definable. Some of them may be "cognitively basic": for example, some color words are among the first words learned, their application is usually fast (the task of deciding whether something is red is usually a cognitively easy task), and a single mental image can stand for the whole range of application. However, they share such features with words for "basic-level concepts" (such as 'cat' or 'chair'), which few would regard as primitive.[8] Moreover, color words and shape words are by no means the only mediators of referential competence: *any* word of which we have specially good referential competence can play such a role. Again, words for basic-level concepts, many of which are common and with which we are often particularly competent, are entirely on a par with color words in this respect ("A peregrine is a kind of *hawk*," "Cumuli are *clouds*," "A chiffonier is a high narrow *chest of drawers*," etc.).[9]

Not that such feature-based procedures are *necessary* to the application of words like 'caulking' or 'guanaco': it is conceivable that a speaker may simply and directly know how to apply them because, so to speak, she simply knows what things or actions of these kinds *look like*. Besides, referential performances based on feature-by-feature procedures are inherently harder and more tentative than direct performances: a referential competence that were indirect for most words would be seriously impaired. Riddoch and Humphreys describe the case of H. J. A., a neurological patient whose referential competence relied entirely on feature-by-feature procedures: "He reported that when told the name of a picture he was able to retrieve a list of characteristic features of the object which he matched against the pictures" (1987b, 53).[10] H. J. A.'s performance in naming objects or objects in photographs from vision was poor: 65 percent correct with objects, 37.5 percent with photographs. Interestingly, he was much better at pointing to pictures corresponding to given words (up to 95 percent correct). In fact, if one has to rely on feature-by-feature procedures, then it can be plausibly predicted that recognition and naming are going to be inherently harder than application. For in recognition, one has to single out salient features that can play the role of cues and match groups of such features against a presumably vast catalog of "feature bundles" in order to identify an object, whereas in application (the word to object direction), each word may be associated with a finite list of features to be checked against the objects or their photographs. Even in application, however, H. J. A.'s performance was substandard.[11] If all our referential procedures were feature-based, we would be like H. J. A., that is, much less efficient than we are, though this does not prevent *some* referential performances from being assisted by inferential competence.

Conversely, we may enrich our inferential competence by reflecting on our application of a word. A child, for example, may be led to conjecture a connection between 'man' and 'male' by reflecting on how the words are applied by himself and the people around him. It may dawn on us that 'panda' is not the name of a single species by noticing how different the animals are that are so labeled in the Paris zoo. Thus referential competence may also buttress the inferential side.

Another qualification: the distinction between the two aspects of semantic competence, inferential and referential, is not relevant to all words in the lexicon of a natural language (see Jackendoff 1992, 56–57). To be competent in the use of words such as 'unlikely', 'derive', or 'nevertheless' is *just* to be able to use such words in inferences. Such words are not applied to the real world, though they may occur in sentences that are used to describe facts of the world. In the same vein, Harman remarked that "it is possible that there are certain sorts of theoretical terms, like 'quark', that play no role in perception at all, so that the content of the concepts they express is determined entirely by inferential role" (1987, 61). Notice that this is not to say that words like 'quark' or 'derive' or the numerals have no *reference*.[12] In the context of a theory of reference, there may be reasons to have such expressions refer to abstract entities precisely to account for their inferential role in a (relatively) simple way. The present account, however, is not a theory of reference.

Referential Competence and Recognition

Referential competence has been characterized as the ability to apply words to the real world: it underlies such performances as naming, answering questions concerning the obtaining situation, obeying orders such as 'Close the door!', following directions, etc. These performances are partly based on the ability to *recognize* objects and actions. This, in turn, is not a purely linguistic ability; under a certain description it can even be regarded as *non*linguistic. As we will see, certain performances can naturally be described as cases of recognition without naming: a subject may recognize an object without being able to retrieve its name. This may have led some philosophers to deny that referential competence is part of semantic competence. For example, Moravcsik (1981, 15) claimed that the layperson's inability to identify instances of a disease is no lack of *linguistic* competence (but, one would suppose, of medical science). Similarly, a speaker may know very well what 'koala bear' *means* and yet be unable to identify one until he visits Australia (or a zoo) and learns what koalas look like; when this happens, we don't say that the speaker in question is rounding out his linguistic competence. Or again, Wilks (1982) remarked that he knew enough of the meaning of 'uranium' to use the word effectively even though he could not recog-

nize uranium and knew no one who could. Thus, it is claimed, referential ability is not necessary for semantic competence (Wilks); indeed, it
would be an abuse of language to regard it as at all relevant to linguistic
competence (Moravcsik). We say that we know the meaning of 'x' (for
example, 'uranium' or 'koala') even when we are unable to identify
instances of x. Thus, 'knowing the meaning' is not used so as to include
referential competence. Besides, the ability to identify instances of uranium is obviously not part of semantic competence, for it is part of
something else, namely chemical knowledge.

I do not share the belief in the rigid separation of linguistic and
scientific knowledge that is presupposed by the objection above. As
Alonzo Church once wrote, "That 'the number of planets' denotes the
number nine is a fact as much of astronomy as it is of the semantics of the
English language" (1951b, 105). So I have nothing against counting an
ability as part of both medical competence, say, and semantic competence.
As to Wilks's contention that recognitional ability is not necessary for
semantic competence, it can be construed in two different ways, weak
and strong. In the weak interpretation, it is claimed that one can have
some competence relative to a word although one lacks full referential
competence relative to that same word. In this sense, the thesis is true: if
I know a lot about uranium without being able to recognize uranium in
the real world, it will not be denied that I am competent with the word
'uranium'. Notice, however, that such an inability does not necessarily
amount to a complete lack of referential competence. I cannot recognize
uranium, but if I am presented, on a tabletop, say, with a fruit I don't
know, an animal I never saw before, and a bit of uranium and I am asked
to pick the uranium, I will easily do it. As far as uranium is concerned, I
no doubt lack full recognitional ability, but I do possess some ability to
discriminate. It makes sense to regard such ability as part of referential
competence.

Wilks's thesis in the weak version does not entail that recognitional
ability is irrelevant to semantic competence. In the strong version, however, the thesis holds that it is possible to have full semantic competence
with a word although one has no referential competence with it—not
even any ability to discriminate, as in the case of uranium. In this form,
the thesis is (first of all) very hard to test: if a speaker has even limited
competence relative to a word, she usually has some ability to discriminate in its application. If one knows anything at all concerning opals,

one knows that they are precious stones, so one can tell opals from cats or books. If the word 'pangolin' is not totally unknown to you, you know that pangolins are animals (not celestial bodies or Indian military men). On the other hand, in ordinary cases the strong thesis seems false: if I cannot tell cats from tigers, violins from cellos, my competence will be considered as defective, whatever my zoological or musical learning. Notice, however, that our judgment of the relative importance of referential competence for lexical competence as such is highly sensitive to social norms and the distribution of competences and skills throughout the linguistic community. If I cannot recognize uranium but I know that it is an element with heavy atomic weight, radioactive under certain circumstances, and so forth, few would say that I don't know what 'uranium' means. If I know that dolphins are sea mammals frequently spotted even in the Mediterranean, etc., but I do not have the faintest idea of what a dolphin looks like, there may be doubts concerning my competence. And finally, if I cannot recognize a dog, people in the community will tend to say that I do not know what 'dog' means, whatever my zoological competence about dogs. Thus for common words, referential competence is more easily regarded as an integral part of semantic competence.[13]

Aren't referential and inferential competence just two sides of the same coin? In particular, can't referential competence be turned into inferential competence simply by being put into words, so to speak, that is, by being converted into linguistic description? Isn't the distinction of the two aspects of lexical competence merely a matter of *format*? After all, it might be observed, if a speaker can recognize dandelions, why can't he *say how* he goes about recognizing them? Why can't he *spell out* his criteria? It is important to note that things don't work this way, except perhaps in a few cases ('square' might be one such case). First of all, in general, we are not aware of which features of a kind of object (of cats or children or slowly moving objects) actually play a role in our recognition of them. As Gareth Evans remarked about the recognition of people, "Perhaps . . . information about the object's appearance is stored in the nervous system, but this is not information which the *subject* has, or in any sense *uses* to effect an identification" (1982, 288).[14] Well, maybe in *some* sense the subject does use such information; surely not, however, in the sense of consciously accessing it and consciously putting it to use. Second, some features playing a role in recognition are likely to be, say, ratios of distances between specified parts of an object (Evans 1982, 290). Such features *could* be put into words, at least in principle, but if they were, they would hardly be acknowledged by the speaker as the criteria he uses ("how he goes about recognizing dandelions") or as part of his inferential competence relevant to the case. The point is not that the content of referential competence eludes linguistic expression, but that such an expression, even if possible, would not be plausibly regarded as part of a speaker's competence in any sense. This provides one reason for disagreement with Howard Wettstein's account of semantics in "Has Semantics Rested on a Mistake?" (1986). For the fact that, as he says, "perfectly competent speakers are often in no position ... to specify the rules that determine the references of expressions" (1986, 203) does not by itself make such rules noncognitive. Similarly, the fact that no speakers are aware of the procedures by which they judge a sequence of words to be grammatical or ungrammatical does not make such procedures noncognitive.[15]

The Mental Reality of the Distinction between the Inferential and the Referential

So far I have tried to show that an important part of our dealings with words can be described *as if* they depended on two separate (though often cooperating) systems, one taking care of word-word relations, the other managing the application of the lexicon to the world as accessed in perceptual and motor interactions. In itself, this shows nothing at all about the mind (or the brain). Separation of the two systems might be just a feature of a convenient representation of our lexical performance. However, neuropsychological evidence appears to indicate that the separation of the two systems is mentally real, in the sense that one ability can be lost or severely impaired as a consequence of brain damage while the other is more or less fully preserved. With normal speakers, one component may be more developed or more efficient than the other; however, both components *work*. On the other hand, with some brain-damaged people, one of the two doesn't work at all or doesn't work properly.

For instance, F. R. A., a patient described by McCarthy and Warrington (1986), performed normally on language tests not involving visual input and displayed normal visual abilities as long as the tasks did

not involve language,[16] but he made 47 percent errors in naming pictures. Errors reduced to 1 percent when he was asked to name the same
items from a verbal description—from our point of view, a purely
inferential performance.[17] Another patient, A. B., had a verbal IQ of 122
and was able to define *supplication* as 'making a serious request for help'
but made 53 percent errors in a task involving naming, or identifying by
description, photographs of common objects (Warrington 1975). J. B., a
patient reported by Riddoch and Humphreys (1987a), was bad at naming
visually presented objects (45.5 percent correct), but he was 100 percent
correct on matching words to definitions. In a task in which he had to
separate two associated objects from a distractor (for example, a cup and
a saucer from a colander), J. B. scored 54.2 percent correct when real
objects were presented to him, and 100 percent correct with spoken
names of objects (1987a, 155). Still another patient, E. S. T., was 100
percent correct in pairing synonyms,[18] but only 27 percent correct in
naming pictures (Kay and Ellis 1987). It thus seems that inferential
competence, as I called it, can be preserved even when referential competence is severely impaired.

Until recently, the converse occurrence had not been reported:
there were no clear cases of people whose referential competence was
preserved while their inferential competence was lost or severely
impaired. However, Brennen and his associates (1996) have now described an Alzheimer patient, a 74-year-old French woman, Mme.
D. T., whose performance appears to exhibit just these features. When
presented with line drawings of objects, she could correctly name 33 out
of 37 of them (or 89 percent), while she could verbally characterize or
"define" only 13 (or 35 percent). She also proved unable to answer
simple questions concerning the objects she had just named, such as 'Is a
plane larger than a car?' "When presented with a picture of a telephone
she named it and, when asked what it was, she said 'It's a telephone,
that's all,' but was unable to give any supplementary information"
(Brennen et al. 1996, 104). Mme. D. T. was also much better at naming
(pictures of) objects than at associating them with related objects from
among groups of three objects, two of which were distractors (for
example, associating a kennel with a dog rather than a cat or a brush).[19]
Thus, it appears that referential competence can be preserved even when
inferential abilities are gone, although such cases are far from frequent.

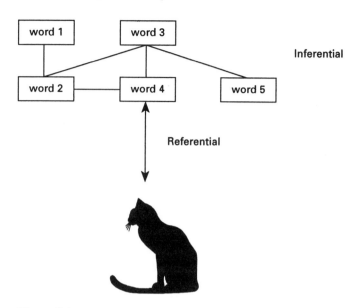

Figure 3.1
The structure of lexical semantic competence: a primitive picture.

Therefore, the neuropsychological data seem to support the intuitive picture sketched in figure 3.1.

However, this picture is belied by other data. First of all, referential competence, management of word-world connections, involves separate abilities. There is evidence that *application* proper is dissociated from *naming*. By 'application' I mean the ability involved in such performances as drawing a picture of an object from its name or picking out the picture (photograph, drawing) or the real object appropriate to a given word, for example, choosing the picture of a lemon rather than that of an orange in response to the word 'lemon'. Application is management of the word-to-picture direction. Naming involves the opposite direction, that is, picture to word. It turns out that application can be preserved even when naming is lost or impaired: many cases have been reported of patients who could easily pick out the picture appropriate to a given word, even in the presence of close distractors, whereas they were unable to name objects or pictures (even the very same pictures they had chosen in response to words). Thus, for example, E. S. T., who could name but few pictures, was 97 percent correct on word-to-picture connections (limited to concrete words) (Kay and Ellis 1987, 616).[20] Similarly, K. R.

was 100 percent correct on picture-word matching in spite of a profound naming deficit (limited to animals) (Hart and Gordon 1992). S. F., whose naming performance was very poor (between 20.8 percent and 23.3 percent correct), could draw objects from their names and selectively match pictures to words (Miceli, Giustolisi, and Caramazza 1991).

Second, naming cannot really be considered as a one-stage process, as if words were directly connected with objects or pictures of objects. We regarded naming as the retrieval of the word associated with a given object: *how* the retrieval is effected did not concern us, except that it didn't seem to involve the same kind of information or the same procedures as are activated in inferential performances (such as defining a word). Neuropsychological research provides reasons for complicating the picture. There are people who appear to recognize an object—they know what it is or "is about"—and yet cannot name it. Such patients are often able to mime the objects they cannot name (Warrington 1985, 341–342; Riddoch and Humphreys 1987a, 132; Shallice 1988, 292 ff.) or anyway to provide evidence that they are aware of their properties and functions. For example, E. S. T. would respond to the picture of a snowman, which he could not name, by uttering the words "It's cold; it's a man ... cold ... frozen." S. F. "claimed that he 'knew' the item, but was unable to find its name." These patients are often described as unable to access the *output lexicons*, that is, the words themselves (in either their phonological or graphic format), as opposed to the concepts, or semantic representations. Such a description presupposes a distinction, which is not part of the primitive picture, between words (or the mental representations of words) and other entities ("concepts"?) accessible from both words and pictures and providing access to both words and pictures.

The distinction appears to be forced upon us by another case as well (the converse case, so to speak). T. O. .B., a patient described by McCarthy and Warrington (1988), was asked to say what he knew about several objects presented to him. He performed well with both spoken names and pictures of inanimate objects, still well with pictures of animals, but when the stimulus was the spoken name of an animal, his performance got worse. To the *picture* of a dolphin he responded with a rich and accurate description, whereas the *word* 'dolphin' only elicited the response "A fish or a bird." "When asked to define the word 'rhinoceros', he responded, "Animal, can't give you any functions." But when shown the picture of a rhinoceros, he responded, "Enormous, weighs over one ton, lives in Africa" (McCarthy and Warrington 1988, 429). If we disregard the category-specific nature of T. O. B.'s deficit, his pattern of performance is anyway inconsistent with the primitive picture (figure 3.1). For in the primitive picture, access to the inferential network from a picture is necessarily mediated by the name associated with the picture. Therefore, if knowledge about dolphins is at all accessible from the picture of a dolphin (as it obviously is in T. O. B.'s case), it should a fortiori be accessible from the word 'dolphin' (as it is not). In the case of successful recognition without naming, we were led to conjecture impaired access of the output lexicon *from* the semantic lexicon. T. O. B.'s deficit could be described in terms of impaired access *to* the semantic lexicon *from* the phonological output lexicon. In fact, the semantic lexicon itself appears to be in good shape, witness T. O. B.'s ability to engage in rich verbal descriptions from pictures. This also shows that the (phonological) output lexicon is accessible *from* the semantic lexicon.[21]

Once we have introduced the distinction between the semantic lexicon and the output lexicons, both naming and application are transformed into *two*-stage processes. For naming, it is one thing to *recognize* an object or a picture and another to find the word for it. Naming an object or a picture requires that both stages are carried through in sequence. A naming deficit can result if either stage is affected.[22] Similarly with application: it is one thing to "understand" a word in the sense of being able to exhibit a synonym or a definition (inferential competence), and quite another to be able to appropriately use the word as a label for a picture or an object.[23]

Notice that inferential competence can no longer be described (as in the primitive picture) as the ability to manage a network of relations among *words*. The distinction between word forms (output lexicons) and the semantic lexicon obliges us to redescribe the kind of performances in which inferential competence is typically displayed (such as paraphrasing, semantically based inference, etc.) as following word-word routes *through* the semantic lexicon. The overall picture resulting from these modifications is sketched in figure 3.2.

Other complications, though interesting in themselves, need not concern us here, for they do not directly contradict the more mature picture. Perhaps the most striking of such complications is connected with the issue of so called *category specificity*: it appears that impairments of semantic competence may be restricted along the lines of conceptual

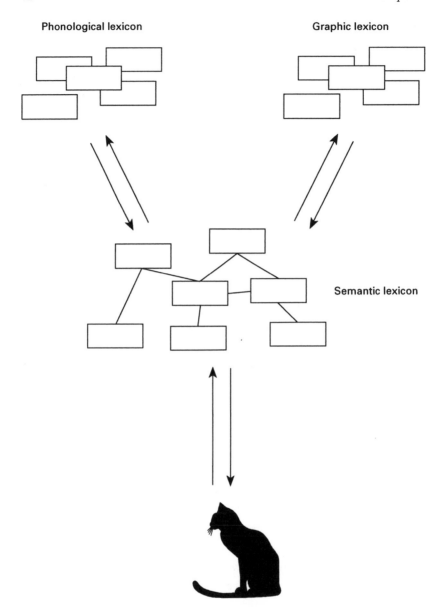

Figure 3.2
The structure of lexical semantic competence: a more mature picture.

dichotomies, such as animate versus inanimate and concrete versus abstract.[24] However, the conclusion that such dichotomies correspond to subsystems of the semantic lexicon is unwarranted. The organization of the lexicon may be based on oppositions that only happen to extensionally coincide with the dichotomies. For example, it may be that animate objects are (mainly) recognized on the basis of overall shape and color, whereas inanimate objects are recognized by individual cues as to function (Warrington and Shallice 1984, 849–850). If so, the "real" opposition structuring the lexicon would be the opposition between entries that are clusters of purely visual properties (including overall form) and entries that are pairs with the structure ⟨cueing visual feature, function⟩. The animate/inanimate opposition as such would play no role in the organization of the semantic lexicon.

Closer to our concerns is the hypothesis that inferential competence may include several conceptually distinct and mentally separate abilities. Thus the ability to define words (word to definition) may be dissociated from the ability to find the word corresponding to a given verbal definition or to a description of the word's referent (definition to word). S. F. made 31.2 percent errors in associating names of objects to oral descriptions, whereas his definition performance was good (Miceli, Giustolisi, and Caramazza 1991). S. F. was able to clearly define 'microphone', while he never succeeded in naming a microphone. This is further evidence of the separation of (one side of) referential competence from inferential abilities.

The Original Intuition

Let us go back to my initial intuition. There seemed to be two distinct abilities connected with the use of words, both of them constitutive of lexical semantic competence: one involved in inferential performances, the other concerned with word-world connections. They seemed to be separate, in that the same person could be very competent referentially with respect to a given word while not so competent inferentially (or, less commonly, vice versa). Moreover, the two sides of competence seemed to be relying on different *kinds* of informational resources. Are such intuitions borne out by the more mature picture? Is lexical semantic competence really organized into two separate systems, one taking care of intralinguistic connections, the other in charge of word-world connections?

There is indeed ample evidence that the referential functions (application and naming) are dissociated from inferential functions (such as defining and paraphrasing). Consequently, in the picture I have been drawing, the respective strengths of inferential and referential competence are allowed to vary independently; for example, the semantic lexicon may be rich, well structured, and well connected with both the input and output lexicons without this involving easy access from vision.

On the other hand, intralinguistic connections are mediated by a system (the semantic lexicon) that I assume is also involved in both application and naming, that is, in the exercise of referential competence. For example, in this model recognition is presented as involving access to the very same system of representations accessed in carrying out purely inferential tasks, such as definition and paraphrase. This in itself does nothing to reduce the relative independence of the two aspects of competence: inferential competence can be seen as the ability to manage the semantic network and connect it to the output lexicons both ways, whereas referential competence is the ability to find a name for an object (or a picture) that has been categorized in the semantic lexicon, and application is the ability to retrieve a semantic representation from a word and match it with an object or a picture. That referential competence has to "go through" the semantic system does not entail that it is based on inferential competence.

On the other hand, no difference between the *kind* of information involved in the exercise of inferential competence and that used in naming and application comes out of the picture. Intuitively, one would be tempted to postulate a privileged connection between the exercise of referential competence and knowledge of an object's visual properties. After all, both naming and application seem to require knowledge of what an object "looks like." From a neuropsychological viewpoint, such an intuition would be borne out if it could be shown that there is such a thing as a *visual subsystem* of the semantic system, playing a special role in referential performances such as naming from vision or word-picture matching. However, the evidence is far from clear-cut. Take the case of K. R., a woman who had a profound naming deficit restricted to names of animals (Hart and Gordon 1992). In addition, K. R. was unable to answer questions involving the *visual properties* of animals, questions such as 'What color are elephants?' and 'How many legs do elephants have?' as opposed to nonvisual questions such as 'Do elephants live on land, in the air, in the sea?' and 'Is an elephant edible?' which she had no trouble answering. It would be natural to conclude that K. R. had trouble accessing the visual semantic subsystem from language (she could not "visualize" elephants). But on the other hand, her application performance was perfect: she was 100 percent correct on picture-word matching, and she could point to parts of animals on request ('Show me the trunk'). But such performances also seem to require an ability to access "visual knowledge" from language.

Some neuropsychologists have found it relevant to distinguish between *structural* knowledge, that is, knowledge of an object's form (and possibly color), and "*semantic*" knowledge, as they call it, that is, knowledge of an object's functional properties and associations (Riddoch and Humphreys 1987a, 134; see also Shallice 1988, 291–297). Others have been thinking in terms of *modality-specific* subsystems, which would be accessible from one perceptual modality (for example, from vision or from touch) and not from others, or not so easily. Caramazza and his associates (1990) have argued against the thesis of modality-specific subsystems. They have claimed that distinct subsets of semantic information need not be represented in distinct, modality-specific formats (visual information needn't be in a "pictorial" format; it may be in a modality-neutral format). To think otherwise is just to conflate content with format. They have also argued that privileged access does not require that the semantic system be organized into subsystems directly accessible only from modality-congruent input representations. It is possible that the semantic representation accessed from the word 'fork' is the same as that accessed by a picture of a fork. That (representations of) visual properties are more easily accessed from vision can be explained by their being homogeneous with perceptually salient features: "Access to a semantic representation through an object will necessarily privilege those perceptual predicates that are perceptually salient in an object" (Caramazza et al. 1990). Such an alternative explanation of privileged access is unconvincing: visual features of an object, salient or not, are obviously not identical with "perceptual predicates" as elements of a semantic representation. To say that they "correspond" to such predicates or "resemble" them is notoriously uninformative. Therefore, Caramazza's alternative account amounts to a restatement that some parts of the semantic representations are more easily accessed from vision. However, it is perfectly right to maintain that this in itself does not entail that there are modality-specific subsystems if this in turn is taken to imply different representation formats for different kinds of semantic information or *exclusivity* of access from one or another perceptual modality.

Yet all this does not preclude that some segments of the semantic system may play different roles in different cognitive processes. Thus application (for example, picture-word matching) might normally rely on structural (rather than functional) information associated with words such as 'fork', and naming from vision might be based on the very same information, whereas inferential performances (such as definition) would make appeal to a much wider informational network. What matters for the subsystems hypothesis is neither difference of formats nor exclusivity of access, but privileged connection with distinct processes. Thus if it could be conclusively shown that certain referential performances can be impaired as a consequence of structural knowledge being selectively disrupted, this would be evidence for the existence of a structural subsystem of the semantic system. This in turn would buttress the intuition that the two sides of lexical competence, inferential and referential, rely mostly on different kinds of information.

Competence and "Objective" Reference

From my city bed in the dawn I see a raccoon
On my neighbour's roof.
He walks along in his wisdom in the gutter,
And passes from view
On his way to his striped spaceship to doff his disguise
And return to Mars
As a Martian
Raccoon.
Ernest Leverett, *SF*

In the last chapter I presented a picture of lexical competence based on
the idea of the relative independence of inferential and referential abilities. Lexical competence, considered as a whole, is here regarded as part
of overall linguistic competence; more particularly, it is regarded as part
of *semantic* competence, the knowledge and abilities that underly a
speaker's understanding of a language. We saw that another side of
semantic competence is *structural* semantic competence, or the ability to
understand a complex expression on the basis of an understanding of its
constituent parts.[1] The relations of semantic competence with syntactic
competence on one side and pragmatic competence on the other side,
though not a topic of this book, would surely require careful scrutiny.[2]

Just for illustration, let me present a couple of examples of how this
picture may help redescribing certain classic cases produced by semantic
externalists as counterexamples to the traditional, Fregean view of the
relations of meaning and reference. Take, first, the well-known case of
Putnam's incompetence concerning elms and beeches (Putnam 1975c,
226–227). Everybody will remember that Putnam admits to having
exactly the same mental representation or concept in connection with
both words (he can't tell the difference between an elm and a beech).

Nevertheless, the two words differ in reference, even as used by himself (for 'elm' refers to elms, not to the union of elms and beeches). Putnam claims that this shows that mental representations, or mental states, do not determine reference.

As an objection against traditional semantic theory, this is not very powerful. The traditional theorist supposedly believes that meaning determines reference and that meanings are mental entities, or at any rate, entities that can be grasped by our minds; he certainly does not claim that *any* mental entity that a speaker may happen to associate with a certain word determines the reference of that word, not even for that speaker. For the traditional theorist, what fixes the reference of 'elm' is the meaning of 'elm', which Putnam does not know, or not accurately enough. Putnam's remark that what is in his head does not determine the reference of 'elm' would be taken by the traditional theorist as a reminder of the publicness of language; he would reiterate that, indeed, what determines the reference of 'elm' for Putnam (as for everybody else) is *the meaning of 'elm'*, not any mental entity that *Putnam* associates with the word 'elm'.

On the other hand, the argument does not show that the reference of words such as 'elm' is to be conceived of as *objective*, rather than standard, that is, as determined by communitarian criteria.[3] To show this, one would have to prove that the reference of 'elm' is independent of what even the most expert speakers know about elms: Putnam's incompetence is irrelevant. In the elm/beech argument, Putnam is exploiting our willingness to concede that his (inadequate) representations do not match *standard* reference in order to persuade us to accept a notion of reference that *no* representations would be guaranteed of matching.

From my viewpoint, the elm/beech case can be simply described as follows. If a speaker's inferential competence concerning one or more words is socially inadequate, he may or may not be able to pick out the words' referents in a socially acceptable way, but he can hardly expect his inferential competence to be of much assistance in doing so. For example, if a speaker believes that any large house appliance is called 'refrigerator', this won't help him to apply the word correctly, that is, competently. That 'elm' refers to elms, not to beeches, may simply mean that a more competent speaker would apply the word to elms and not to beeches. If we wish, we may express this, though misleadingly, by saying that *in English* the word refers to elms, not to beeches, no matter who uses it.

Or take the simple case of whales: "Central to what most people used to associate with 'whale' was the description 'fish'. This description is false of whales. Yet all these people referred to whales by 'whale'. (Devitt and Sterelny 1987, 69). Of course they did: their referential competence picked out whales; that on the inferential level they regarded whales as a kind of fish had no influence. On the other hand, it is correct to say that they included whales in the reference of 'fish'. This case is different from the elm/beech case, for here we may suppose that the whale-namers' referential competence was good—they were very good at telling whales from (other) big fish—although some of their beliefs were wrong. In the elm/beech case, however, both Putnam's inferential competence and his referential competence are somewhat defective: he *both* knows too little about *Latifolia and* cannot tell elms from beeches.

Jackendoff on Lexical Meaning

My picture bears a strong similarity to Jackendoff's views about lexical meaning as he presented them in *Languages of the Mind* (1992).[4] According to Jackendoff, one factor of word meaning is "the connection of the concept expressed by the word to perception and action"; another factor is a word's "interaction with the inference rules," which Jackendoff wants to keep distinct from "its relationship to the rest of the lexicon," a third factor (in my view, inferential competence is conceived as taking care of both). That there is much agreement between our views, at least on the level of basic intuitions, is obvious. So, let me point out the differences:

First, Jackendoff has a fourth factor: he wants to pack into lexical meaning "the interaction of the word with the grammatical patterns of language" (1992, 57). Thus, in his view, it is part of the meaning of 'load' that 'X loaded a truck with furniture' entails that the truck was full of furniture at the end, whereas 'X loaded furniture onto the truck' carries no such entailment. I prefer to regard such inferences as depending on structural rather than lexical competence; I would hesitate to say, of one who could not carry out the appropriate inferences, that he or she does not know *what 'load' means*. However, this is perhaps a difference in theoretical architecture, with no great substantial import.

Second, Jackendoff insists that the connections between concepts and perception and action, though a "counterpart of what the philosophical tradition calls the *reference*" of a word, concern not real-world objects (or actions, etc.) but "the *mental representations* linked to the concept in the perceptual and motor modalities" (1992, 56).[5] In other words, he sees such quasi-referential connections as linking, say, the concept [*dog*] to the visual features of dogs as represented in the mind. He mentions Marr's 3-D models as embodying such features, or part of them (Jackendoff 1992, 44). In my view, referential competence is a family of abilities involving real-world entities *through* perception and action. We do not apply the word 'cat' to mental representations: we apply it to cats. When asked to fetch a book, we come back not with the mental representation of a book but with a real book. The performances in which referential competence is involved concern real-world entities, not representations. We should not let the fact that such performances *also* involve perception mislead us into thinking that referential competence is the ability to connect words, or the concepts they are associated with, to mental entities such as outputs of perceptual abilities (for example, vision). Take naming: we saw (chapter 3, p. 70) that naming is best conceived, on the basis of available evidence, as a two-stage process involving (a) recognition and (b) the retrieval of a name associated with a unit or a network in the semantic lexicon. Surely, referential competence cannot just be identified with the ability to carry out stage (b), for referential competence includes the ability to *name things and actions*, not just the ability to retrieve output words from the semantic lexicon (which ability is also part of the inferential side of competence). On the other hand, referential competence is not simply the ability to carry out stage (a), that is, recognition: we saw that there can be recognition without naming, whereas referential competence must involve language. Referential competence is the ability to carry out both stages in sequence.

Even recognition alone, however, involves more than just the connection between a word or a concept and one of Marr's 3-D models. First of all, it is far from established that all cases of visual recognition conform to Marr's pattern, that is, that they regularly involve a complex match between a mental catalog of 3-D models and shape information derived from the visual image (Marr 1982, 313 ff.).[6] Moreover, in Marr's theory, object recognition is the result of just such a complex match. Availability of a connection between a word or concept and a certain 3-D model is surely not enough for recognition: the ability to match the model with the output of vision is also necessary. Of course, 3-D models may be complex, informatively rich pictures, yet they do not include the *procedures* for their own application, that is, the procedures that make it possible to match a 3-D model with a given scene.[7] If "knowing the meaning" of a word only involved, on the referential side, command of its connection with a 3-D model, this would not suffice for its application. Finally, it should never be forgotten that though vision does play a central role in object recognition and though object recognition is in turn crucial for referential competence, on the other hand, referential competence, generally understood, involves a wide variety of perceptual and motor abilities, as Jackendoff himself points out (for example, 1992, 56). Therefore, it is clearly inappropriate to *identify* the referential aspect of lexical meaning with information that is only relevant to visual recognition.[8]

Third, Jackendoff's is a theory of lexical *meaning*, whereas I am presenting a picture of lexical *competence*. This may look like a purely nominal difference or, at most, a distinction of equally legitimate viewpoints, for after all, it might be observed, what is lexical semantic competence but knowledge of the meaning of words? A theory of competence along the present lines is just a theory of meaning in disguise.

Let me hasten to make it clear that I have no qualms with the *phrase* 'knowing the meaning of a word' if it is taken to be synonymous with 'being able to use a word'. In this sense, semantic competence is indeed knowledge of meaning. However, it is not knowledge of *meanings* as entities of any kind: in my picture, meanings are nowhere to be found. Inferential competence is command of a lexical network (probably, as we saw, command of a conceptual network plus input-output functions to graphic and phonetic word forms); referential competence is a family of abilities, all involving the interaction of language and perception. Thus the ability to use the word 'cat' (competence with 'cat') is indeed the outcome of a sum of knowing-thats and knowing-hows, but it cannot be reduced to knowledge *of* some entity, the meaning of 'cat'.

This is not simply a matter of not "hypostazising" meanings. There are, of course, plenty of good reasons for not wanting to include in one's ontology a domain of special, separate entities called 'meanings', but aside from this, given the intuitions that Jackendoff and I share, it is hard to see how individual meanings of words can be singled out with any definiteness. Take inferential competence. Inferential competence with a certain word (such as 'pellucid' or 'armadillo') is the ability to connect the word with other words, including the ability to answer questions, give definitions, retrieve the word from a reasonable definition, make inferences involving the word, etc. Each such performance may involve a somewhat different region of the vast network managed by a speaker's inferential competence. As I made clear in the last chapter, taking sides with molecularism against holism does not entail that every performance involving a certain word appeals to the same bits of information, to the same limited region in the lexical network. This being so, *what* could be identified as *the* inferential meaning of 'armadillo' for a given speaker— the sum total of all information that gets used in all inferential performances? New performances might require, and appeal to, inferential information not included that far. Even if we found a reasonable candidate for being *the* meaning of 'armadillo' in *X*'s idiolect, and I cannot see how we could, what would be gained by such an identification? On the other hand, it is easy to see what would be lost. As Wittgenstein told us long ago, we would lose the freedom to attend to each word's actual use and start looking for uniformities where there are none to be found.

Objections of One Kind

Two kinds of objections can be raised against the picture of competence that has been offered. It can be conceded that the phenomena of language understanding and use I have been discusssing so far are genuine, that they are indeed based on certain capacities we do possess, and that one might want to have a theory of all this. However, such a theory, which would be a *psychological* theory, if anything, would be *irrelevant* to the concerns of *genuine* semantics. There are at least three distinct viewpoints from which this kind of objection can be raised, corresponding to partly different ways of identifying the subject matter and concerns of semantics.

First, it can be said that semantics concerns *public* languages. Genuine semantics is a theory of meaning for, for example, English, not a description of this or that individual speaker's dealings with language. Theories of competence, no matter how general in scope, will never reach or even approximate the subject matter of semantics, for the features of a public language cannot be extracted from the content of individual competence, not even from the contents of all competences taken together, if this were at all conceivable.[9]

Second, it can be argued that no descriptive theory of semantic behavior as grounded in cognitive abilities (collectively labeled 'competence') can be relevant to semantics, for semantic values are *norms*: any attempt at making a descriptive theory of competence relevant to semantics would amount to a naturalization of semantics, which is just one version of the naturalistic fallacy.[10]

Third, one can hold that once semantic values are fixed (for example, by procedures such as baptisms), *reality* takes care of them. For example, once it has been established that certain animals are to be called 'lions', then 'lion' refers to all and only the objects that, as a matter of objective fact, have the same nature as those animals. Our use of 'lion', the procedures by which we identify lions, our beliefs about lions—all this is irrelevant to the reference of 'lion'. Our use may or may not conform to the established reference, we may be better or worse at identifying lions (zoologists are better), and so forth, but semantics has nothing to do with any of this, for semantics is concerned with semantic values, and these are not determined by use or cognitive procedures or beliefs.[11]

The three viewpoints, particularly (a) and (c), share a commitment to the notion of *truth conditions* as semantically pivotal: a sentence's meaning is identical with its truth conditions, and the meaning of a subsentential expression, such as a word, is its contribution to the truth conditions of the sentences in which it occurs. Naturally, the import of such claims entirely depends on how 'truth', 'truth conditions', and 'giving the truth conditions' are interpreted. There are interpretations under which I would have no quarrel with any of the above claims. However, it is often argued that such slogans must be taken in conjunction with (i) a robustly realistic notion of truth, which (ii) is explicated by Tarskian semantics or some of its successors, such as Montague-style model-theoretic semantics (see, for example, Field 1978, McGinn 1982, Block 1986). This cluster of theses tends to make the theory of competence irrelevant to semantics, for "objective" truth conditions are said to be determined by the real world, totally independently of our use of language. Thus semantics is about the truth conditions of, say, 'Lions are tawny'; these truth conditions in turn depend on facts of the world plus the fact that 'lion' refers to certain animals and 'tawny' refers to a certain color; such relations of reference are themselves objective (here (a) or (b) or (c) or some combination of them is invoked); individual competence never comes into the picture.

Objections of Another Kind

All these objections leave some room for a theory of semantic competence, although they deny that it has any relevance to semantics (and perhaps to the philosophy of language, as opposed to the *psychology* of language). Another set of objections are even more threatening, for they rely on considerations linked to (a), (b), and (c) to show that the kind of picture I have been offering cannot even be an acceptable account of the very phenomena it deals with; in other words, it is not even a good theory of competence. For example, Colin McGinn has argued that to account for linguistic communication, we need an *objective* notion of reference, for communication is intended to convey information about the world, and not simply "the solipsistic contents of the speaker's mind" (1982, 226). But if communication is about the world, then "the speaker must exploit signs standing in representational relations to things in the world." Such relations between words and the world must be "non-solipsistically articulated" (1982, 236), that is, they must be conceived of as objective. Consequently, any theory according to which "referential relations" between words and the world are essentially a matter of referential practices grounded in individual competence (as in my picture) is bound to fail as an account of communication.

Moreover, many people have argued that the use of language in general cannot be accounted for without assuming an objective notion of reference. For example, our use of natural-kind words presupposes that their reference is conceived by individual speakers as independent of, and irreducible to, their competence. This is allegedly shown, first of all, by speakers' dispositions to *defer* to more competent speakers. Thus if it had been possible to point out to Archimedes that some of the samples he was willing to call 'gold' (or rather, 'chrusós') were not *really* gold, he would not have replied "Ah, but that's according to *your* notion of gold; according to *my* criteria, they are indeed gold!" Instead, he would have been convinced by scientific arguments to accept the correction, which is based on superior knowledge of the substance gold (Putnam 1975c, 237–238). This shows that natural-kind and natural-substance words are used under the presupposition that their reference is eventually determined not by whatever criteria may be available at a given time to a given speaker (or even to a whole linguistic community) but rather by the nature of the species or stuff they are intended to name. Influenced by Putnam's ideas, Frank Keil carried out a series of experiments on children purportedly showing that "from an early age[12] we have a natural bias to go beyond characteristic features" in the application of natural-kind words and identification of their meanings: we tend to believe that "there is a deeper causal structure that is the essence of meaning." Thus, even if we do rely on characteristic features in our application of words (including natural kind words), "we usually do not consider those features to be the final criteria" by which the corresponding concepts are identified (Keil 1986, 138).[13] There is an underlying assumption that what really matters for the meaning of natural-kind words, as opposed to names of artifacts, is the "explanatory causal structure" of the relevant objects and phenomena. Such an assumption influences use, in that we are prepared to go beyond characteristic features whenever it is pointed out to us that they do not fit internal structure or causal history: if some animal looks like a raccoon, smells like a raccoon, and behaves like a raccoon but has the physiology and the genetic history of a skunk, then it is a skunk, not a raccoon, and if we have ever called it 'raccoon', we'll be ready to amend our ways and call it 'skunk' (perhaps 'very peculiar skunk').

My strategy in dealing with these objections will be the following. I will deal with the latter objections first, showing that they are not as damaging as they seem. I will then take up the charge of the irrelevance of my picture to semantics proper. I will try to show that much of its strength, though not all of it, derives from a certain conception of semantic normativity. The issue of normativity and how it ought to be conceived will be postponed until the next chapter. As to the residual strength of the charge of irrelevance, my point will be that to the extent that semantic theory is identified so as to exclude the theory of competence, semantics becomes irrelevant to use, that is, it cannot provide the basis for a reasonable account of language use (I will thus reverse charges, so to speak). Finally, I will discuss the proper place of formal semantics and the notion of truth conditions.

As I will frequently be talking about objective reference, let me first explain what I mean by the doctrine that reference is objective. By that phrase I will not be referring to the view according to which the reference of words is independent of an individual speaker's conscious *knowledge*.[14] Such a view can be reconciled with the picture I put forth. In fact, I emphasized (chapter 3, p. 66) that a speaker is usually unaware of the mechanisms by which she manages to apply even the most common words and that if such mechanisms were somehow spelled out, they would not be recognized as relevant to the speaker's use of words. Moreover, if by the opposition of individual knowledge and the "real" reference what is meant is simply that an individual speaker may not know a word's *socially standard* reference (believing, for example, that 'cat' refers to pandas or, less deviantly, being ignorant of the word's scientific definition), I obviously have no quarrel with such a doctrine. In the next chapter I will propose a redescription of the relevant phenomena. Nor I will be referring to the stronger view according to which reference is (also) independent of a speaker's *discriminating abilities* (Burge 1993, 325). This view too can be read normatively, that is, can be interpreted as pointing to possible discrepancies between individual competence and the social standards. Rather, I will understand by 'the doctrine that reference is objective' the view that words have the reference they have independently of whatever knowledge or ability is available to or within *the linguistic community as a whole*. Thus my paradigm of the doctrine will be Putnam's view of 1975c, according to which the word 'water' on Twin Earth referred to XYZ (*not* to H_2O) even before 1750, in spite of the fact that no speaker on either Earth or Twin Earth would have been able to discriminate in any way between the two substances, the fact that any speaker would have used 'water' to refer to both XYZ and H_2O (unless he or she was making a mistake), and the fact that nobody could have been in a position to *correct* an allegedly improper use of 'water' (that is, its use to designate a sample of H_2O). Thus, according to the doctrine of the objectivity of reference, the reference of a word is ultimately determined, granted some original intentional act of dubbing, by certain factual relations (often called 'causal connections') between speakers and the real world.[15] If it is assumed (as in the Twin Earth thought experiment) that such relations are essentialy the same for all speakers in a given linguistic community, then idiolectal reference coincides, for all speakers, with communitarian reference. Nothing else really matters: not knowledge (explicit or implicit), not discrimination abilities, not linguistic behavior (unless these are defined so as to include, or anyway depend on, objective relations with the environment) (see below, pp. 88–89).

Communication

Ever since Frege, it has seemed that communication and cultural inheritance require uniformity of meanings: if 'cat' did not mean the same for you and me, we could not talk to each other about the same animals; we would forever be equivocating. This familiar argument is not the one McGinn appeals to in order to prove the indispensability of objective reference for communication. As we saw, his view is rather that we need objective reference because communication is intended to be *about the real world*. It is hard not to agree with him on this point; however, it is equally hard to see how this can entail that in order for communication to be possible, we need *objective* reference, rather than some degree of *convergence* of the referential abilities and practices of the speakers.[16] Of course, the possibility of successful comunication is predicated on the assumption that, say, the word 'cat' is used by another speaker to refer to by and large the same objects to which I refer with that word. If we constantly disagreed in the application of words, communication would be impossible. But it is convegence of application that matters, not objective reference. Indeed, objective reference is *irrelevant* from the standpoint of communication. Let us go back to Twin Earth. 'Water' as a word of Twin Earthian English refers to XYZ, according to Putnam, even if the whole linguistic community of Twin Earth is unaware of the fact and even if all speakers are prepared to apply the word to H_2O as well. In such a situation, before 1750, to follow Putnam, Twin Earthian speakers would be successfully, consensually, and coherently communicating about what they take to be the real world. In this they would be mistaken, perhaps, but their mistake would not affect their intentions—they intend to communicate about the real world and real water, not just to convey "the solipsistic contents of their minds"—nor would it undermine the success of their acts of communication, for they would understand each other perfectly well.

Some would say that they wouldn't be communicating *about the real world* at all, for in the real world, XYZ is not H_2O. But in this sense, who of us is ever assured of talking about the real world (that is, of knowing exactly how things stand and using language accordingly)? Moreover, it would be quite surprising if such assurance could come *from a theory of reference*.[17] Obviously, we will never be sure of knowing exactly how things stand in the world, but if we were, this could hardly be attributed to our having come up with the right theory of reference. Perhaps two senses of 'talking about the real world' are conflated here: one having to do with the causal nature of perception and its systematicity, the other with the absolute correctness of our theories. In the first sense, most of us are talking about the real world most of the time, and so were the

Greeks, in spite of their false beliefs about whales and (possibly) gold, as well as the Twin Earthians before 1750. In this sense, 'talking about the real world' is to be contrasted with 'talking about a fanciful or hallucinatory world'. In the other sense, the Greeks were not talking about the real world. Nor were the Twin Earthians. Indeed, nor, probably, are we. In this sense, talking about the real world simply amounts to always being right about the world.

I just said that Twin Earthians "would understand each other" quite well. But would they? It could be objected that, on the contrary, they wouldn't understand each other at all. For a speaker, Sam, would take another speaker, Dudley, to be using the word 'water' to refer to XYZ or H_2O (for this is what he, Sam, "has in mind" in connection with 'water', though this is not how he would phrase it), whereas the word 'water' as used by Dudley, who is a speaker of standard Twin Earthian, only refers to XYZ, no matter what Dudley himself has in mind or thinks about water and in spite of his objective linguistic behavior (for Dudley would apply 'water' to both XYZ and H_2O, being unaware of the difference—this takes place before 1750). So Sam actually *mis*understands Dudley, for he takes him to be talking about either H_2O or XYZ, whereas Dudley is really talking about XYZ. Notice, however, that this is misunderstanding of a peculiar kind: it could not be pointed out by anybody in the linguistic community, no matter how learned in both linguistics and natural science. Dudley himself would not understand himself, or explain himself, any differently: he would insist that he is prepared to apply the word 'water' to either the Earthian or the Twin Earthian stuff. There is no single statement on whose truth value Sam and Dudley would be bound to disagree because of their misunderstanding (as usually is the case with misunderstandings). Thus it is hard to see how such a "misunderstanding," if that is what we want to call it, would impair communication between Sam and Dudley.

Some philosophers, including McGinn, have tried to pack the notion of objective reference into the notion of understanding:

On [my] view of semantic knowledge you understand an expression just if (a) you associate the right representation with it, and (b) the resulting states of your head are appropriately related, causally or contextually, to the referent of the expression. So people on Earth and Twin Earth understand 'water' differently after all. (1982, 238)[18]

This is confusing: does it follow that before 1750 *nobody* understood the word 'water' on either Earth or Twin Earth? For it is hard to see in what sense one could say that speakers on either planet were associating *the right* representation with the word, since whatever representations were available at that time did not discriminate between H_2O and XYZ. If, on the other hand, to have the right representation is just to have the common everyday notion of water (a liquid, transparent, boils at 100° C, etc.) then both Oscar$_1$ on Earth and his twin Oscar$_2$ on Twin Earth did understand the word 'water', though differently, as McGinn says. Yet such an "understanding," aside from being opaque to both Oscar$_1$ and Oscar$_2$,[19] would have been inconsistent with the linguistic behavior of both, for Oscar$_1$ would have been prepared to apply the word to XYZ as well, not just to H_2O, and Oscar$_2$ would have applied it to H_2O and not only to XYZ. A theory based on such a notion of understanding can hardly account for the use of language.[20]

A while ago I used the notion of convergence, and I will use it again in the sequel. As that notion is almost as unpopular as the notion of similarity of meaning among different speakers, an explanation is due. Two speakers are said to *converge* in their use of a given word *w* when they share a number of beliefs in whose expression they use the word *w*,[21] or when their referential practices, associated with word *w*, single out the same objects or phenomena, by and large. Thus if a cat comes by, they would both agree that it is indeed a cat (though in a few cases they may disagree). It may be suspected that *inferential* convergence is not really a viable notion, for it simply pushes the need for meaning identity one step back, so to speak: the argument being that two speakers may be said to converge on 'cat' by sharing (among other beliefs) the belief that cats are mammals only if they understand 'mammal' in the same way. The obvious answer is that they need only to converge on 'mammal' as well (inferentially, referentially, or both ways). Convergence, not identity of meanings or concepts, is all that is needed in order that several people may be said to have "beliefs and preferences with the same content" (Rey 1983, 249): they don't need to agree on each single cat or to share each and every belief about cats or to possess a mysterious entity, the concept cat, transcending both their inferential and discriminating abilities.

What if two speakers converge referentially but diverge inferentially on the same word? Say that they have radically different beliefs about cats (one of them thinks that cats are Martian robots) and yet they single out the very same objects as cats. Well, if they *really* diverge inferentially, they don't even share beliefs about the shape of cats, their habits, or their size, they are likely to diverge on much more than 'cat', and they are going to have great trouble communicating with each other. It might happen, but it does not appear to be a frequent case.

Deference and Reference

The phenomenon of *semantic deference* is real enough: we are all prepared to acknowledge that some speakers are more competent than we are on this or that word or family of words, and even that there may be speakers, for example, lexicographers, who are more competent than we are on many, perhaps most, words. Therefore, we are prepared to accept corrections to our semantic habits, both referential and inferential. The phenomenon concerns most words, certainly including natural-kind words. Does this show that our use of such words is predicated on the belief that their reference is regulated by the "deep" nature of the species and substances they refer to? Obviously not: it merely shows that we do not regard ourselves as semantic dictators, like Lewis Carroll's Humpty Dumpty. The phenomenon is by no means trivial: it will require careful discussion (see chapter 5, pp. 115–121). However, it does not particularly concern natural-kind or natural-substance words (we are not more prone to defer to the authority of experts in the case of 'lion' than in the case of 'trochaic' or 'thresher'); it is just an aspect of a more general and pervasive phenomenon, semantic normativity, and should be discussed under that heading.

It can be argued, however, that in the case of natural kinds and substances, such a description is not appropriate. Take my discussion of Archimedes concerning the reference of 'gold', or 'chrusós'. Archimedes defers not to our superior *linguistic* competence but to better knowledge of the substance gold. He is not recognizing that we know the dictionary meaning of 'chrusós' better than he (indeed, he knows it better than we, in a sense); rather, he is bowing to our greater scientific knowledge of the stuff itself. This shows that what matters is the substance's real constitution. Like us, Archimedes believes that 'chrusós' refers to whatever has the same "deep" nature as the standard samples of gold, and he has found reason to admit that we are more reliable on this matter than he is.

First of all, let me point out again that such an account presupposes an opposition of semantic knowledge and scientific knowledge, which I see no reason to accept (see chapter 3, p. 65). To neatly distinguish between dictionary knowledge and substantial knowledge, knowlege of words and knowledge of things, general lexical competence and domain expertise, is both impossible and useless. Almost always, our lexical semantic competence, both inferential and referential, includes information that would naturally be ranged as more dictionarylike alongside information that would naturally be regarded as more encyclopedic. Thus in the case of natural-substance words, such as 'gold', our referential competence may include the ability to use *tests* to determine whether the word applies. Referential competence need not be limited to the ability to apply macroscopic criteria based on prima facie perceptual properties such as shape, color, and the like. That most of our referential practices rely on such criteria most of the time does not entail that this is all there is to referential competence. Persons we call 'experts' are often especially good at the application of words relevant to a particular domain.[22] It is futile to regard them as experts of things rather than words. This would engender an intolerable opposition between knowing what gold is and knowing how the word 'gold' applies. But clearly, if you know the former, you also know the latter, and vice versa. This is not the opposition we want. The appropriate contrasts are between better and worse referential competence on the one hand and among competences of different kinds (serving different purposes in different circumstances) on the other hand.

It is also wrong to rigidly oppose discriminating abilities based on "natural," macroscopic criteria (supposedly characteristic of the layperson) to sophisticated abilities involving the use of elaborate tests, artificial instruments, and so forth, which would be the monopoly of experts. Think of physicians and their special "eye": an expert physician's ability to diagnose a particular illness by examining a patient does not necessarily involve either instruments or tests. It does require, however, a long and complex training, into which a lot of formal, verbalized knowledge goes. Similarly, our ability to apply such words as 'tool' or 'game', 'intelligent' or 'lazy', and hundreds of other words, is based on long training, involving the acquisition of much formal knowledge. And yet few would dream of opposing our competence on such words to our competence relative to 'chair' or 'scissors'.[23]

Thus, *pace* Georges Rey (1983, 249), the fact that we feel that "something might share all the usual perceptual features of a kind of plant or animal, but nevertheless fail quite definitely to *be* of that kind" is in itself no reason to oppose "the epistemological and the metaphysical roles of concepts." "The usual perceptual features" are naturally and usually contrasted not with essence or nature but with less superficial, more significant features, such as an expert would detect. So far metaphysics does not come into the picture; only the hierarchy of competences is involved. It is an entirely different matter if essence is contrasted not with superficial perceptual features but with all the features that communitarian science can identify.[24] Could some animal have all the features by which science identifies cats (including the appropriate DNA) and yet fail to be a cat? This is were metaphysics comes in.

Similarly, Keil's (1986) experiments show that children in fourth grade and older know that in our community, genealogy and physiology outweigh external appearance for purposes of identification of animal and plant species. The Putnamian belief that the application of natural-kind words is governed by the idea of a common nature, no matter how this is identified, does not surface in the experimental protocols. Indeed, both the experimenters and the subjects make constant reference to genetic and anatomic-physiological features of both animals and plants, that is, to features singled out as relevant to identification by scientific theories (or their naive counterparts) (Keil 1986, 139, 141, 142). It is with these that the superficial, external features are contrasted. The fact that many (adult) subjects confess to "not having any idea what internal factors would differentiate a skunk from a raccoon, but will nonetheless insist that there are such factors" (Keil 1987, 189) does not license the conclusion that they are Putnamian "essentialists,"[25] as long as they also insist that "members of the scientific community would know" the relevant factors (the subjects themselves mention internal organs, DNA etc.) (Keil 1987, 187, 189).[26] What all this shows is that members of our linguistic community are aware, from a relatively early age, that natural kinds are essentially identified not on the basis of external appearance but rather on the basis of scientific criteria of some kind or other. Again, metaphysics does not enter the picture. Adult use of natural-kind words seems to presuppose the idea that application of such words, aside from being nonarbitrary, as with all other words, is governed by special criteria best known to experts. This amounts to an assumption of semantic normativity, with a special role for scientific experts as far as natural kinds are concerned.

Publicness

We saw that communication requires convergence but does not presuppose the objectivity of reference (indeed, objective reference is irrelevant to communication), and we also saw that deference, in the case of
natural-kind and natural-substance words, does not of itself indicate that
the use of such words is based on essentialistic assumptions. The insufficiency of superficial criteria does not of itself imply that concepts have a
metaphysical identity (Rey) or that the superficial criteria are contrasted
with "nature" (Keil). So, at least *these* arguments, purporting to show that
one cannot even describe competence (and use, which is based on it)
without bringing in objective reference and the speakers' belief in it
(which surfaces in deference) are not compelling.

Let us now consider the charge of irrelevance to semantics, or
rather, the several arguments by which such a charge can be supported.
First, publicness. Semantics, it is argued, aims at describing public languages, not individual competences (Dummett 1986, 468–469; 1991,
87–88, 105–106). One will never reach the genuine subject matter of
semantics if one starts with the variable contents of competences.
Thinking that the study of competence might be relevant to semantics is
like believing that one could describe the rules of a certain game, chess,
say, by describing the players' attitudes to the game or their internalized
picture of what the rules are (Dummett 1991, 87). The perspective
should be reversed: one should conceive of individual competence as a
particular speaker's grasp of a certain public entity, a language. From this
perspective, the study of competence might prove to be of some interest
(though it is doubtful that it could be of interest for *semantics* proper).

What *is* publicness? The picture that first comes to mind when one
thinks of the publicness of language is the picture of *a set of physical realizations*: configurations of ink on paper, vibrations of an elastic medium,
etc. Such physical realizations are universally accessible in the sense in
which tables and lemons are accessible, and more so than either protons
or chromosomes; they are *public* in the sense of being accessible to any
observer endowed with normal perception. Perhaps it was publicness of
language in this sense that played an important role in language replacing
thought as the object of philosophical inquiry (the "linguistic turn"). Of
course, people were aware that, as a matter of fact, physical realizations
are all different from one another.[27] However, it looked possible in

principle (though, as we now know, extremely hard in point of fact) to
define equivalence relations among configurations of ink on paper (say)
so that one could define equivalence classes of such shapes, with which
linguistic expressions could eventually be identified. Thus the sentence
'New York is in France' could be identified with the equivalence class of
the token I just wrote—a public physical entity. Words and sentences are
abstract entities, but their tokens are concrete, public entities.[28]

However, even if words are open to view, it would seem that their
meanings are not. For, of course, a physical entity is one thing, and its role
as an element of a language is another thing.[29] Can one ascribe publicness to an *interpreted* language, that is, to the connections of linguistic
expressions with their semantic values? Mentalistic empiricism said that
one cannot; most of twentieth-century philosophical semantics tried to
show that one can.

As far as I know, semantic values, meanings, were conceived of as
public in either of two ways, both of them expressed by negative theses.
According to the first thesis, thesis A, meanings are not, and cannot be,
idiosyncratic. Meanings must be the same for all speakers. This is proved
by the facts of communication and cultural inheritance: if meanings were
idiosyncratic, we could not say 'Pythagoras' theorem'; we ought to say
'my theorem', 'his theorem', etc., for the words 'The sum of the squares,
etc., ' would have different meanings for different speakers. This thesis,
and the argument supporting it, are due to Frege.[30] Notice that the thesis
does not directly state the publicness of meanings, but only their *uniformity.* Frege, however, was an instinctive Platonist, and he went on to
infer a form of publicness. For, as he saw the matter, the only plausible
way to account for the uniformity of meanings was to regard them as
Platonic entities, the inhabitants of a Third Realm, equally accessible to
all minds.[31] They are accessible not, of course, in the same way as tables
and lemons, that is, through perception, but in some "analogous" way.
Frege did not see any other way of explaining the uniformity and stability of meanings, which we must grant, for communication is a fact.

According to the other thesis, thesis B, meanings are not something
that an individual speaker can *determine.* They are not *private,* in the sense
that they are not invented or modified at will by individual speakers. In
this sense, they are public. For Frege, meanings are public in the sense in
which tables and lemons are public: they are the tables and lemons of
another world. For Wittgenstein, to whom we owe thesis B, meanings

are public in the sense in which traffic regulations, or the directions for filling up a tax form, are.

Why should we admit that individual speakers are not "masters" of their meanings, as Lewis Carroll's Humpty Dumpty believed he was? Wittgenstein's answer is the private language argument: there simply are no private meanings; to assign a semantic value privately is to assign no semantic value at all.

Theses A and B are *independent* of each other: neither entails the other. They are two different ways of (negatively) conceiving of the publicness of meanings. Thesis B does not entail thesis A: meanings can be idiosyncratic, not uniform across speakers, not because each speaker has invented his own ad libitum but for other reasons. For example, in an empiricist framework, meanings might be different because the speakers' individual experiential histories are all different from one another.

On the other hand, thesis A does not entail thesis B. It is conceivable, though implausible, that meanings be uniform across speakers in spite of the fact that each speaker makes up his or her own. By preestablished harmony or sheer chance, speakers always manage to make up the same meanings. Some externalists come close to such a view when they imagine that all speakers form essentially the same concepts because they causally interact with one world with perceptual modalities that are essentially the same.[32] This is not identical with the miracle view of semantic uniformity, though, for on the externalist view, concepts are somehow induced by nature, not made by speakers.

As I just said, Frege's thesis does not really state that meanings are public. It is turned into a publicness thesis with the addition of the Platonist theory of the Third Realm. Meanings in themselves could be uniform *and* private.[33] With Wittgenstein, things are different. Here the publicness of language depends (according to a standard interpretation) on the communitarian nature of the processes by which meanings are regulated. The meanings of words are acquired by each speaker through her participation in "training" activities, directly or indirectly involving several people (members of the linguistic community), and carried out according to modalities that are themselves collectively controlled. What is acquired is not a mental entity but an ability: the ability to use certain signs according to certain rules.

The publicness of language in Wittgenstein's sense is predicated on the normativity of language. This can be seen from the fact that the private-language argument, which supports the thesis of publicness and gives it its content, appeals to the view that the use of words is governed by norms. In fact, the private-language argument can be seen as an application of a general argument *against private conventions*, a private convention being one that I stipulate with myself and being such that, as a matter of principle, I am the only one who can check on its proper application. A private convention is conceptually impossible, for it leaves no room for the distinction between correctly applying the convention and *believing* that one is correctly applying the convention. Thus the very notion of correct application turns out to be empty, and therefore one cannot even speak of a convention having been established. In the special case of language, a private *semantic* convention is impossible, for it does not allow one to discriminate between correct and incorrect uses (of a word, say). But there is no meaning, there has been no institution of meaning, and there cannot be any responsibility to meaning, unless it has become possible to discriminate between uses that are correct and uses that are not. Thus it is clear that the private-language argument is effective only if *semantic values are normative in nature*, for otherwise the general argument against private conventions would not apply to the case of language.[34] In the private-language argument the use of words is seen as subject to normativity of some kind, normativity that can be respected or violated. Therefore, Witttgenstein's view of the publicness of language depends on the assumption of normativity. If we give up the assumption, the idea of publicness, or at any rate Wittgenstein's idea of publicness, lacks justification.

Thus, if we set aside Frege's Platonism, we are left with a notion of publicness heavily relying on the idea of semantic normativity. An interpreted public language is not a collection of entities lying there for individual speakers to access, to a greater or less extent. Rather, it is a collection of interrelated *norms* for the use of sounds and marks in a wide variety of contexts, which are regarded as *binding* for all speakers of (what we call) a given language, though they may be obeyed to a variable extent. To say that semantics is the study of public languages is to insist on the normative dimension of use, which is conceived to be prior to individual uses rather as the law may be said to antecede its applications; it is *not* to point to a special ontic region open to the semanticist's examination. It follows, first, that much in the notion of publicness is going to depend on how semantic normativity is conceived: different notions of normativity will engender different notions of publicness. Second, from this viewpoint a theory of competence may be judged to be irrelevant to the concerns of semantics only if it has no place for the normative dimension of use, for example, if no account is taken of the fact that individual competences are subject to social checks and are consciously responsible to semantic authorities. As will be seen, this is not my view.

'Cat' Refers to *Cats*

As we saw, there are people (call them 'objectivists') who believe that the reference of many words is ultimately independent of the speakers' beliefs, discriminating abilities, and actual use.[35] The word 'cat' refers to cats (only to cats and to all cats) even if most speakers are confused about the biological identity of cats and cannot decide, in borderline cases, whether or not they are dealing with a cat. Moreover, the word 'cat' refers to cats even if one speaker may use it to refer to cedars, another to refer to the union of cats, lions, and panthers, and a third only to refer to Siamese cats (not to Angora cats or tabbies). And the word 'cat' *always* refers to cats, not just when it is used by people who are knowledgeable about cats but even when used by the guy who calls lions and panthers 'cats' or by the other fellow who calls only Siamese cats 'cats'. Were the latter speaker to assert that 'All cats have black circles around their eyes', we would say (and should say) that he has a false belief about cats, not that he has a true belief about cats *in his sense of 'cat'*.

We also saw that these philosophers do not simply wish to point out the inadequacy of certain discriminating abilities (for example, those relying on perceptual features) or to contrast individual competence with social or collective semantic standards, even though some of them do occasionally present arguments to either effect:

We all know full well that something might share all the usual perceptual features of a kind of plant and animal, but nevertheless fail quite definitely to *be* of that kind: we all have had our run-ins with silk flowers, wax figures, and fancy mechanical toys. (Rey 1983, 246)

[Cases] like that of *tomatoes* ... may *be* (metaphysically) clear cases of fruit (check the dictionary!) even though people may be (epistemologically) confused about them. (Rey 1983, 248)[36]

The meanings of many terms ... are what they are even though what the individual knows about the meaning or concept may be insufficient to determine it uniquely. (Burge 1993, 318)

However, this is not their main point. If it *were* their main point, it would seem that we are simply being sent back once more to the issue of semantic normativity: a word's reference is not something that an individual speaker can in any way determine, for it depends on socially established norms; in the case of natural-kind and natural-substance words, such norms tend to include an appeal to tests and other sophisticated identification procedures, which the ordinary speaker is in no position to carry out (they are the privilege of *experts*).

But this is not so. Even objectivists who make the community (with its experts) responsible for determining reference do not set up the contrast between individual competences and the standard exactly along those lines. Take the view, sometimes labeled "social externalism" (Bilgrami 1992), put forth in Burge's influential article "Individualism and the Mental" (1979). Burge is not making the platitudinous point that individual use may deviate from community-established standards; indeed, for him it would be *incorrect* to say that Sam, who only calls Siamese cats 'cats', has a deviant concept of cat or that he means by 'cat' something different from what he ought to mean, for in his view, the contents of an individual speaker's competence are to be individuated on the basis of expert opinion. Sam may be mistaken in his beliefs about cats, and his behavior involving the word 'cat' may be unorthodox, yet, his notion of a cat is the expert's notion. Thus, in spite of his false beliefs and extravagant behavior, he manages to refer to cats with 'cat' no less than the most expert zoologist.[37]

Social externalism has a problem: it flatly contradicts our intuitions concerning semantic deviance. For a social externalist, one *cannot* use 'cat' to refer to cedars or only to Siamese cats: the word 'cat', no matter who is using it, refers to cats, only to cats, and to all cats. It is, of course, appropriate to say that one who asserts 'Cats taste sour' is making a mistake. However, her mistake is *about cats*; her statement expresses a (catastrophically erroneous) belief about cats. The reference a word has in an individual speaker's use is independent of her intentions, even as they manifest themselves in pointing gestures or in any other pattern of behavior commonly taken to express referential intentions. All the familiar cues we customarily rely on to identify use do not count: use should be described on the basis of objective semantic value. I find such consequences hard to swallow. But anyway, Burge's view of 1979 yields a *communitarian* picture of reference: the reference of words is determined by the community through its experts (to the point of determining the actual content of individual competence, in spite of individual beliefs, intentions, and behavior). Therefore, social externalism does not make the theory of competence irrelevant to the concerns of semantics, for after all, it is communitarian or expert competence that matters for reference.[38]

By contrast, other objectivists believe that even communitarian standards are ultimately irrelevant to the determination of reference. As we saw, one conclusion Putnam draws from the Twin Earth thought experiment is that 'water' in Twin Earthian English referred to XYZ, and not to H_2O, even before 1750, that is, even when the whole Twin Earthian community, with all its experts, would have been unable to tell the difference between the two liquids (indeed, the community's standards at that time would have *forced* the application of 'water' to the Earthian stuff as well). Twin Earthians were referring to XYZ with 'water' even before 1750, for their use of 'water' was grounded in objective interactions ("causal connections") with a liquid that was, and always had been, XYZ. Such objective interactions are what really matters, for both standard (communitarian, semantic) reference and individual reference.

This form of objectivism (which includes all forms of causal externalism) does not reduce to normativism. For norms, whatever they are, derive from the community. But with objectivism the community has no special authority on reference: it could be dead wrong, both collectively and distribuitively, on the reference of 'water'.[39] Causal externalists cannot be depicted as *really* pointing to the contrast between individual competences and semantic values as socially established norms. One can think, for a moment, of objecting that causal-externalist views that assign a special role to *baptisms* and other dubbing ceremonies are indeed forms of normativism, where the norm is set by the initial baptism. The objection would go like this: The community lays down the semantic norm by establishing that certain trees (and all other trees that have the same nature as *those* trees) are to be called 'elms'. Then whether something is to be called an elm depends not on individual or even communitarian criteria but only on whether the norm applies, that is, on whether the object in question has the same nature as the paradigmatic elms. However, this won't do. For norms must be *applicable*: there must be someone in a position to enforce the norm.[40] But by hypothesis, it is possible that nobody in the community can tell whether the norm applies. Worse than that, the most competent members of the community may be wrong on whether the norm applies. However, norms on whose application the community is unable to decide, whatever else they are, are not communitarian norms.

Anyway, baptisms are no longer very popular among objectivists, and rightly so, for the reference of a word cannot be made to depend on a single baptismal ceremony. Take the case of natural-kind and natural-substance words. Suppose that it turns out that the first people to use the word 'gold' were causally connected with instances of copper and intended to baptize copper with the sound 'gold', knowing perfectly well what they were doing (gold they actually called 'shnuff'). Still, 'gold' would not refer to copper.[41] However, once "multiple grounding" is admitted, that is, once it is recognized that words derive their reference from being causally connected with objects of a certain kind on many successive occasions involving different speakers, different circumstances, and so forth, then baptismal ceremonies are no longer singled out for normative import with respect to other referential practices, such as pointing out a person by uttering her name, calling a person by her name (and answering such a call), finding a person by knowing of her name, and so forth. Two consequences appear to follow: (i) The normative import of dubbing is lost, without being replaced by any other norm-establishing practice; the burden of setting the semantic norm is distributed among a wide variety of referential practices. (ii) Reference is really and fully determined only if such practices converge, for instance, in the case of natural kinds, only if the individuals involved in the relevant referential practices really belong to one kind (Devitt and Sterelny 1987, 72).

What, then, is the difference with respect to the notion of referential competence? Isn't it the case that, even for reformed objectivists, individual referential practices are what really matters for the determination of reference? No. The difference appears to be this: For an objectivist, reformed or unreformed, the determination of reference is unaffected by epistemological factors: neither conscious knowledge nor discriminating abilities really matter. In contrast, in the picture I have been presenting, an individual's referential competence is transcended only by the semantic norm. In other words, Sam does refer to Siamese cats (and only to Siamese cats) with the word 'cat', and the only sense in which we can say he is wrong (for 'cat' does *not* refer only to Siamese cats) is that people who are regarded as more competent than he do not use the word that way. In the objectivist picture, on the other hand, 'cat' denotes cats, never just Siamese cats, not because more competent speakers say so but because most significant referential practices are related to (what are in fact) *cats*, that is, to animals of a certain kind, sharing a common nature: it is this common nature that determines the reference of 'cat' in all cases, whether or not it is correctly recognized by even the most competent speakers.

The difference is easily made evident if we go back, once more, to Twin Earth. From my viewpoint, there is simply no reason one could say that the Twin Earthian word 'water' did not refer to H_2O as well before 1750, as there was at that time no speaker, no matter what her semantic authority, whose referential competence would have discriminated between the two liquids. Indeed, a speaker who *had* discriminated between them in a systematic way would have been making an unjustifiable, incomprehensible mistake. For causal objectivists, be they single-grounders or multiple-grounders, 'water' in Twin Earthian only referred to XYZ even before 1750, because the stuff involved in referential practices *was* XYZ, not H_2O. Notice, however, that if one adheres to the idea of multiple groundings, the objectivist view is hard to sustain in this case. For suppose that a group of Twin Earthians had visited Earth before 1750. Then the use of 'water' (in Twin Earthian) to refer to either XYZ or H_2O would even have become *grounded*, unless we assign pride of place to referential practices connected with the acquisition of a word. But it is not at all clear that the same arguments used to downplay the role of individual baptisms in determining reference cannot be turned against the privileged role of acquisitions (which are, after all, just early referential practices as opposed to later practices).

As there are problems both with individual baptisms and with multiple groundings, the " 'Cat' refers to *cats*!" reflex has recently produced theories that dispense with intentional acts altogether and try to make it into a scientific *law* that 'cat' refers to cats, a law based on the fact that most of the time and for most of us, it is cats that occasion cat thoughts.

Of course, not only cats are responsible for cat thoughts: meows and purrs and pictures of cats may also cause them. Moreover, cats may fail to produce cat thoughts, for example, if we mistake a cat for a hat. However, pictures of cats would not occasion cat thoughts if cats didn't, while the converse does not hold (this is called 'asymmetric dependence'). And as for mistaking cats for hats, that's not typical. This, in very sketchy form, is Fodor's theory of 1987 (see also 1990).

On Fodor's theory, before 1750 'water' in Twin Earthian refers to both liquids, XYZ and H_2O, for clearly if XYZ causes water thoughts, so does H_2O, and vice versa, as XYZ and H_2O share the same cognitively relevant properties.[42] Fodor tries to show that this is not so, by exploiting his clever notion of asymmetric dependence. He claims that (for the Twin Earthians) the relation between H_2O and water thoughts depends on the relation between XYZ and water thoughts, but not the other way around. The reason is that an intentional relation to *local* samples of "water" is built into the conditions of the Twin Earth thought experiment: "It's part of the story ... that [Twin Earthian] speakers intended ['water'] to apply to all and only stuff of the same (natural) kind as paradigmatic local samples" (Fodor 1990, 114–115). Therefore, in possible worlds where XYZ and H_2O can be distinguished by Twin Earthians, they would not apply 'water' to H_2O, whereas they would still apply it to XYZ (for they *mean*, and always meant 'water' to refer to their own local stuff). So, there are "nearby worlds," worlds close to Twin Earth, were you get the XYZ-'water' connection without the H_2O-'water' connection, but there are no nearby worlds were you get the H_2O-'water' connection but not the XYZ-'water' connection. According to Fodor's definition, it follows that 'water' in Twin Earthian means XYZ and not H_2O.

However, it seems clear, first of all, that a purely causal theory, such as Fodor's purports to be, cannot appeal to intentional relations. Intending to refer to local samples is not a purely causal connection between a speaker and such samples. The whole point of the causal theory is that "aboutness" must be articulated "in nonsemantic and nonintentional terms" (Fodor 1987, 98). Even though *Putnam* characterized the connection between speakers and samples in intentional terms, Fodor cannot help himself to the characterization without turning his own theory of the connection into an intentional, and therefore not a purely causal, theory.[43]

But, second, even if we grant Fodor (as we should not) such an appeal to intentional relations, his argument does not go through. His main point is that though there are no worlds (close to Twin Earth) where H_2O causes water thoughts but XYZ doesn't, there are worlds where the converse is the case, that is, where XYZ causes water thoughts but H_2O does not, namely the worlds where the two substances are distinguishable. Why does XYZ, but not H_2O, cause Twin Earthian water thoughts in such worlds? Because Twin Earthians now realize that their own local stuff is, and presumably always was, XYZ, and they always *meant* the word to apply to the local stuff. Even before 1750, their water thoughts included an intentional connection to the local stuff. However, if this is taken seriously, that is, as making a difference to the contents of Twin Earthians' minds, it appears to violate the conditions of the thought experiment, for the whole point of the thought experiment is that the relation of Twin Earthians to XYZ (like the relation of Earthlings to H_2O) is objective, a mere fact, with no mental correlate whatsoever to distinguish it from a relation to H_2O. Such an objective difference suffices, according to Putnam, for 'water' in Twin Earthian to have a different reference from 'water' in English, although *nothing* in the speakers' minds corresponds to such a difference in reference. The reason that Twin Earthians who have mastered the distinction between XYZ and H_2O would decide to reserve the word 'water' for XYZ is that they have examined the samples everywhere about them and found them to be XYZ, and the reason they would single out *those* samples for examination is not any discriminating specification in their minds but simply the fact that they *are there*. This is the only sense in which locality of application may be said to be built into the original connection: the Twin Earthians know that the relevant samples are those that are *there*. If the whole Twin Earthian community had been unknowingly transported to the Earth (and vice versa), the Twin Earthians would have been examining samples of H_2O and would presumably have decided to reserve the Twin Earthian word 'water' *for H_2O* (the Earthlings would have decided to reserve *their* word for XYZ). They would have been mistaken, but nothing in their water thoughts could have prevented such a course of events.

That 'water' on Fodor's theory really refers to both H_2O and XYZ is significant, for it reveals a somewhat hidden feature of his conception. As many have remarked, Fodor's causal theory is shot through with difficulties connected with the very notion of *cause*: "to say that the symbols of the language of thought refer to what causes them, without specifying a context which may determine which causal connections are relevant, is to say nothing at all" (Casalegno 1997, chap. 13), for the notion of cause is "both context bound and interest dependent" (Putnam 1992, 47).[44] With such criticism I fully agree. I conjecture that if Fodor tried to better articulate the relation between tokens of 'water' (or tokens of WATER, a symbol in the language of thought) and the external world, his theory would get closer to a theory of referential competence. For after all, if one looks at the basic motivations behind the theory, one sees that Fodor wants a *cognitive* theory of reference, that is, a theory that would connect our use of words (or the instantiation of symbols in the language of thought) with our experience of the world out there, not with its mere existence in our vicinity. It is, I believe, in vain that one looks for some quasi-physical connection unencumbered with cognitive factors such as recognition procedures, or that one tries to "factor out" such cognitive processes by appealing to an absolutely general, and therefore empty, notion of cause. One ought to "go cognitive" all the way and pay attention to the different procedures involving the application of words to objects and actions as recognized in perception or as targets of searching activities triggered by language.

For those who are still under the spell of the " 'Cat' refers to cats!" slogan, I have two remarks. First of all, I agree: 'cat' refers to cats, 'spoon' refers to spoons, and so forth. That is to say, most speakers regularly use 'spoon' to refer to objects of a certain shape and use, to spoons, in short. ('Spoon' would not refer to spoons if all speakers used it to refer to chairs.) What is it for a speaker to use the word 'spoon' to refer to spoons (rather than to forks, say)? Typically, it is to come back with a spoon in one's hand when one is asked to fetch a spoon; it is to draw a picture of a spoon, that is, of an object of certain shape, when requested to do so; it is to answer questions such as 'Are there any spoons in the drawer?' on the basis of whether or not there are spoons in the drawer; and so forth. This is all quite trivial, as it should be. There is nothing mysterious in the notion of using a word to refer to *x*s: it is just shorthand for a variety of performances, some of which I just mentioned as examples. Do they have anything in common? Yes, all of them are concerned with both spoons (or pictures of spoons) and the word 'spoon'. Anything else? No, there is no unique (albeit speaker-relative) relation of reference connecting the word 'spoon' with spoons. Or rather, there is such a relation, and it is defined by the family of performances just exemplified. After Wittgenstein, nobody put this better than Hilary Putnam himself:

Referring ... is using words in a certain way (or ... in any one of a variety of ways). It may well be that a certain referring use of some words would be impossible if we were not causally connected to the the kinds of things referred to.... But that is not to say that ... the referring *is* the causal connection.... Wittgenstein ... suggests that the illusion of intrinsic intentionality, the illusion that reference is a mysterious something that exists while we think and about which nothing can be said, is due to the fact that we pay attention only to our subjective experience and not to the technique of using the word.... If we cannot survey all the referring uses of words, then there is a sense in which we don't have a *theory* of "the nature of reference" at all. (Putnam 1992, 165–167)

Putnam goes on to suggest that we think of reference in terms of family resemblances, as Wittgenstein would have us: "Referring uses don't have an 'essence'; there isn't some one thing which can be called referring. There are overlapping similarities between one sort of referring and the next, that is all" (1992, 168–169).

My second remark is for real toughs who are not impressed by any of this because their metaphysical-realist intuitions are too strong. " 'Water' on Twin Earth," they still would like to say, "refers to XYZ, for the word was introduced to name *that* stuff, and that's what the damn stuff *is*, deep down, not H_2O!" To this I would reply that if we are left with a theory that makes reference irrelevant for both cognition and communication and in which reference has no role to play in the application of words or in any other use of language *except* the determination of the "objective" truth conditions of sentences, which, however, may forever elude the whole community of the speakers of the language, then such a theory of reference can hardly be of great interest for semantics, which, after all, deals with language as used by human beings.

Truth Conditions and Model-Theoretic Semantics

Within the tradition of philosophical semantics, it is usually held that a sentence's meaning is identical with its truth conditions and that the meaning of a word is its contribution to the truth conditions of the sentences in which it occurs. Such claims may be interpreted both as *grounds* for semantic objectivism and as *deriving* from it.

In the former case, the argument may be more or less the following: Intuitively, to understand a sentence is to know under what conditions it would be *true*; it is *not* to know how one would go about verifying the sentence or to be able to construct a mental model corresponding to the sentence or anything else of a cognitive nature. There are plenty of sentences that we understand, although we do not have the faintest idea of how we could verify them. As to mental constructions and other mental procedures, aside from their mysterious and speculative nature, it is not clear that their operation is conceptually essential to understanding: a speaker who, for some reason, were unable to carry out the allegedly required constructions would nonetheless understand a sentence if she knew its truth conditions. Now, truth conditions involve *truth*, an objective relation between a sentence (or a proposition) and the real world. Therefore, if semantics is to be relevant to understanding language, it must explicate a sentence's semantic value in terms of such objective relations, in total independence of epistemological or cognitive factors.

On the other hand, the identification of sentential meaning with truth conditions may be regarded as a corollary of objectivism. Here the argument could be the following: Meanings are public (or they are norms or they are determined by nature, etc.). Therefore, they must be uniformly explicated by theoretical propositions that make no reference to anything subjective or idiosyncratic, such as cognitive procedures, mental contents, and the like. The clauses of a Tarskian truth theory or the theorems of a Montague-style model-theoretic (MT) semantic theory are good candidates for theories that provide such an explication, for they rely only on truth and reference understood as objective notions, connecting language and the world independently of cognitive intermediaries.

In such frames of mind, semantic objectivism is seen as being of a piece with Tarskian semantics and its heirs, in particular, MT semantics. This much reinforces its claims, for, after all, Tarskian semantics, and more particularly MT semantics, is by far the most precise and wide-ranging theory dealing with meaning in natural languages. In the present section I by no means intend to diminish such merits. Rather, I would like to dissociate MT semantics from philosophical objectivism, showing that the kind of information provided by the theorems of MT semantics is not easily interpreted as information about the objective relations between language (a particular language) and the world. Indeed, in a sense, such theorems do not involve the objectivist notions of truth and reference *at all*.

Let us go back for a moment to the argument in chapter 1 concerning semantic interpretation. There we saw that MT semantics *without* meaning postulates does not "give the meaning" of a sentence, for the semantic values of the descriptive constants are left undetermined (except as regards their logical types). We also saw that MT semantics *with* meaning postulates does not succeed in "giving the meaning" of a sentence either, for it does not manage to render the full content of a speaker's competence: the meaning postulates, though they restrict the admissible interpretations, cannot reduce them down to just one (the one in which 'book', 'table', 'cat', etc., have the meanings that a competent speaker knows they have). Thus MT semantics does not really answer the question 'What is the meaning of sentence S?' not even when taken together with a complete set of meaning postulates. In this sense, it is not a theory of meaning for natural language.

So what *is* MT semantics? It is *a theory of the semantic effects of composition*. What MT semantics says, the kind of information it provides, concerns how composition affects meaning: what the effect is of combining certain constituents in a certain way. *In principle*, MT semantics has nothing to say concerning the constituents' meaning; however, it has a lot to say concerning the semantic contribuition of syntactic structure. MT semantics is *functional* semantics: the meaning of a linguistic expression is (expressed as) a specific function of ultimately unspecified constituent meanings. Alternatively, it could be presented as a theory of meaning for syntactic classes of linguistic expressions that does not distinguish among individual members of the same class.

In a few cases the characterization of a syntactic class or, if one likes, of a syntactic structure essentially involves a particular *word*. Thus MT semantics may deal with the class or the structure [Necessarily S], where S is a sentence and 'necessarily' is the *word* 'necessarily'. Or it may deal with the structure [only NP], where NP is any noun phrase and 'only' is the word 'only'. As the theory is a theory of the semantic contribution of structure and in these cases structure is characterized by individual words (as opposed, for example, to the case of the structure [NP VP], where no individual word occurs), one may say that in these cases the theory accounts for the semantic contribution of individual words (though in specified contexts), that is, it explicitly "gives the meaning" of this or that word ('necessarily', 'only', etc.), limited to such contexts. As I said, this happens only in a few cases. In the general case, the characterization of a syntactic class does not involve individual words. Consequently, whatever information is provided concerns not words but classes of words.

How are the semantic effects of composition represented? In the general case it is done by showing how the semantic value of a complex expression can be computed from the semantic values of its constituents. Let $\alpha(\beta_1, \ldots, \beta_m)$ be the structure that combines constituents $\beta_1, \ldots, \beta_m$ according to modality of combination α. Typically, a statement of the theory relative to such a structure will take the form

(1) $V_M[\alpha(\beta_1, \ldots, \beta_m)] = \Phi(V_M[\beta_1], \ldots, V_M[\beta_m])$,

where 'V_M' is the semantic value in model m and Φ is a specified function of the appropriate kind (that is, defined over a domain that includes objects of the types of the semantic values of $\beta_1, \ldots, \beta_m$). The idea is that Φ is determined only by α, that is, by the relevant kind of syntactic combination. Thus the semantic value of the whole expression, or rather *class* of expressions, $\alpha(\beta_1, \ldots, \beta_m)$ is computed by an algorithm that depends only on the expression's structure.

In general, semantic values are abstract entities, mathematical constructs that bear no relations to anything intuitively semantic. Clearly, if there is any cognitive reality to the principle of compositionality, and throughout this book I assume that there is, the ability to compute the semantic value of a complex expression from the values of its constituents is an ability we do possess. We do understand such expressions as 'in the park', 'confusingly explained', and 'drove to Pittsburgh', and we would not understand them if we were not acquainted with their constituents. However, compositional rules of the form (1) may be said to go proxy for such ability rather than to explicate it. We have no theory of structural competence as a module of semantic competence; we have no reason to suppose that compositional rules of form (1) are cognitively real or that the abstract entities assigned by the theory as the constituents' semantic values are related in any way to mental entities. In other words, rules of form (1) have no cognitive significance (nor, of course, do they claim to have any), although we have reason to assume that they emulate cognitively real computations.

Aside from lacking any cognitive significance, rules of form (1) are in general not related to semantic intuitions of any kind. The connection with semantic intuitions is through the notion of truth conditions. In fact, in the special case in which $\alpha(\beta_1, \ldots, \beta_m)$ is a sentence, the theory's statement of its semantic value can ultimately be given the form of a statement of its truth conditions, that is, the following:

$\alpha(\beta_1, \ldots, \beta_m)$ is true in model M iff $R(V_M[\beta_1], \ldots, V_M[\beta_m])$

Here R may have one of several forms, depending strictly on both α and the β_is. For example,

$\beta_1\hat{}\text{and}\hat{}\beta_2$ is true in M iff β_1 is true in M and β_2 is true in M

Here β_1, β_2 are sentences, $\hat{}$ indicates concatenation, and 'and' is the *word* 'and'.

$\beta_1\hat{}\beta_2$ is true in M iff $V_M[\beta_1] \in V_M[\beta_2]$

Here β_1 is a singular noun phrase, and β_2 is an intransitive verb phrase.[45]

Statements of truth conditions are usually taken as the intuitive benchmark of a theory of this kind: the theory is regarded as a *semantic* theory because it assigns truth conditions to sentences, and it is considered a *correct* semantic theory to the extent that such assignments are intuitively plausible. Indeed, all semantic statements in a MT semantic theory tend to be looked at as contributing to statements of the above kind, that is, to statements of the truth conditions of sentences.[46]

The connection between semantic intuitions and statements of truth conditions is usually motivated by reference to the already mentioned tradition, stemming from Frege and Wittgenstein's *Tractatus* (1922), according to which to know the meaning of a sentence is to know the conditions under which it would be true.[47] However, we saw that statements of truth conditions in MT semantics do *not* really instruct us about the conditions under which a sentence is true. For in order to know under what conditions the sentence 'There is a book on the table' is true, one ought to be told what the words 'on', 'book', and 'table' apply to, and MT semantics does nothing of the kind. This is to say not that statements of truth conditions are therefore informationally empty but that they only provide us with *conditional* information. *If* we know the semantic values of $\beta_1, \ldots, \beta_m$ (in model M), *then* we know (that is, we can compute) what it is for $\alpha(\beta_1, \ldots, \beta_m)$ to be true (in M). For example, if we know what it is for S_1, S_2 to be true, then we know what it is for S_1 & S_2 to be true. Such conditional statements cannot be regarded, however, as directly informative of the conditions under which a sentence is true, and they are not even *indirectly* informative, for the theory *never* tells us what the semantic values of the ultimate constituents are.

On the other hand, I said that statements of truth conditions can be tested against our semantic intuitions, assessed for plausibility, and so forth. This appears to mean that such statements are compared with our intuitions of the meanings of sentences, and evaluated as to whether or not they accurately represent such meanings. But how can this be if such statements are not statements of the meaning of any sentence, accurate or otherwise? Against *which* intuitions are statements of truth conditions tested?

Some people believe that the intuitions in question directly involve *truth*, or more precisely, truth as correspondence. On such a view, to test a statement of truth conditions against our semantic intuitions is to wonder whether the sentence occurring on the left-hand side of such a statement would indeed be true just in case the specified conditions obtain. Suppose, for example, that in the attempt to capture the meaning of the word 'only' we stated the truth conditions for sentences of the form 'Only NP VP' to the effect that, for example, 'Only John went to the party' comes out true (in a model) just in case John went and nobody else did (in that model).[48] In the view I am discussing, to evaluate the proposed truth conditions is to wonder whether those are exactly the conditions under which 'Only John went to the party' is true. How is this effected? Here people who believe in intuitions of truth as correspondence may point (more or less vaguely) to some sort of mental picturing or modeling or imaging:[49] we (sort of) picture to ourselves a situation in which only John went to the party and (sort of) check whether it is likewise a situation in which he went and nobody else did, and conversely. Now, there is no reason to deny the heuristic role of such mental picturing. However, it seems equally clear that it cannot be taken too seriously (can one really picture to oneself a situation in which *nobody other than John* went to the party?). There is no one-one correspondence between sentences and pictures, mental or otherwise.

Some may then insist that our intuitions of truth are *primitive* (as becomes a primitive, irreducible notion such as truth): we somehow simply *know* what it is for a sentence to be true, or not true, in a situation in which such and such is the case (that is, in which the specified conditions obtain). This is, of course, mysterious, but my point is not that it is mysterious. What I want to urge is that it is not clear how such an account would be different from an *inferential* account. Suppose that we say that statements of truth conditions are checked against our inferential intuitions: what we do is to evaluate whether the right-hand side would license the left-hand side, and vice versa. For example, in the party case we would check whether, given the premise that only John went to the party, we would intuitively accept the double conclusion that he went, and that nobody else went; and conversely, given the two premises that he went and that nobody else did, would we conclude that *only* he went. This, I surmise, is what we actually do in general, although pictures (mental or material) may help in some cases. Is this any different, mystery aside, from saying that we evaluate whether the left-hand side is *true* in any situation where the right-hand side is the case, and vice versa, on the basis of our immediate, irreducible intuitions about being true in a situation? If not, then I would stand for the less mysterious formulation.

One objection that might arise, but should not be accepted, is the following. Surely, one might object, nothing is gained by reading the truth conditions inferentially, for the notion of inference is itself parasitic on the notion of truth. To say that S_2 can be inferred from S_1 is simply to say that S_2 is *true* if S_1 is. However, such theoretical matters are out of place here: we are not deciding which is more primitive between truth and inference. The issue is which *intuitions* are relevant in evaluating truth conditions. It doesn't seem that intuitions about inferential relations are, as such, parasitic on intuitions about truth as correspondence (or intuitions about truth in general). In other words, it does not seem that whenever we wonder whether S_2 follows from S_1, what we *really* and *consciously* do is to wonder whether S_2 is true in case S_1 is, which question we would then proceed to answer by relying on our intuitions of truth as correspondence. In many cases at least, questions about inferential relations are straightforwardly decided without appealing to intuitions of truth (or, for that matter, to any other intuitions). In other cases, we may use all sorts of heuristic strategies, including recourse to mental pictures or even, for those of us who are sophisticated enough, model-theoretic methods. But there is no general, inherent dependence of inferential intuitions on separate intuitions about truth or about conditional truth.[50]

Another objection is that we have intuitions of truth-in-a-situation that do not easily reduce to inferential intuitions. For example, we might be led to assert a sentence (such as 'More than half of the passengers have been rescued') on the basis of a long and cumbersome linguistic description, a newspaper article, say. In such a case, inferences can, of course, be assumed to have taken place; however, the notion of inference here is no less mysterious than the notion of truth. The answer to this objection should be twofold. First, we are not discussing in general the conditions under which one might be led to assert a sentence; we are discussing only the evaluation of statements of truth conditions in MT semantics. Such statements, though often complicated, do not involve newspaper articles or other forms of unregimented linguistic description. Second, experience with the mechanization of inference in artificial intelligence has shown that there is nothing particularly mysterious about natural inference: it is just standard inference with a lot of premises, many among which must be retrieved from world knowledge and background knowledge in general (often expressed in the form of meaning postulates).[51] Thus the assertion of a sentence on the basis of a linguistic description, no matter how long and convoluted, can indeed be regarded as based on inference; in fact, no other reasonable account has been put forward so far.

Aside from such objections, there is a case that obviously resists an inferential account. It cannot apply to statements of truth conditions for atomic sentences, such as, say, (2):

(2)   'John runs' is true (in M) iff $V_M[\text{John}] \in V_M[\text{runs}]$.[52]

For, evidently, the right-hand side does not contain any sentence or sentences that might or might not license the sentence occurring on the left-hand side. It is with these cases that partisans of an objectivist reading of truth conditions feel most at home, for, they urge, such statements are grounded in the intuition that 'John runs' is *true* in all models in which the *reference* of 'John' is a member of the *reference* of 'run' (a set of individuals, in this case). As truth conditions for atomic sentences are, in a sense, the basis of the whole construction, it is clear, they would conclude, that the (objectivist) notions of truth and reference loom large in MT semantics. It would be unfair to reply that, indeed, atomic truth conditions are not to be tested against our semantic intuitions as more complex truth conditions are, for they are just theoretical tools whose point is to help generate more complex truth-conditional statements, so they are on a par with *non*-truth-conditional statements of the theory, as far as their relation to intuitions is concerned. Clearly, statements of atomic truth conditions are *not* on a par with, say, assignments of semantic values to prepositional phrases; we *do* have intuitions concerning the plausibility of the former. The issue is, Do such intuitions really involve the objectivist notions of truth and reference?

The answer, I believe, should be that to make intuitive sense of statements like (2), we probably need, among other things, referential intuitions of some kind, though not necessarily the objectivist's notion of reference. The reasoning behind the acceptance of (2) appears to be something like the following: If 'John' applies to a certain object, and 'run' picks out certain objects, and the object to which 'John' applies is among them, in such circumstances we would say that 'John runs' is true, wouldn't we? In such reasoning, objective relations supposedly connecting lexical items to the *actual* world are not involved, first of all, because the actual world itself is not involved. In fact, truth enters MT semantics as truth-in-a-model, not as plain truth or truth in the actual world. Models are theoretical entities; causal connections between lexical items and such entities are out of question.[53] True, (2) derives its plausibility from the fact that truth-in-a-model and reference-in-a-model are somehow conceived on the pattern of simple truth and simple reference (as is clear from the reasoning underlying the acceptance of such atomic statements). That the analogy is tenable may, of course, be doubted, and this would amount to denying that statements like (2) have *any* intuitive plausibility (they could only be justified by their theoretical role).[54] But anyway, second, to make (2) plausible, we don't need the idea of a lexical item *objectively* referring to an individual or a class (the " 'Cat' refers to cats!" reflex); *any* of the intuitions connected with our referential practices will do. The important (and relatively controversial) idea captured in atomic truth conditions such as (2) is the extensional analysis of predication: the idea that predication can be reduced to set-theoretical membership. *How* reference is conceived is relatively unimportant if what is at stake is the *intuitive* plausibility of (2). This can also be seen from the fact that intuitions concerning the particular lexical items involved in statements such as (2) play no role whatsoever in determining their plausibility, contrary to what happens in the inferential case. When we assess the truth condition for 'S_1 and S_2', our intuitions concerning the specific inferential properties of 'and' are crucial; similarly with 'only', 'necessarily', the quantifiers, etc. Not so with the atomic cases: here, it does not make any difference whether we are dealing with John or Paul, with running or driving or being human; only logical types matter. One would imagine that if objective reference were involved, intuitions about the particular referential attachments of individual lexical items would make a difference.

Let me summarize. MT semantics is not a theory of meaning; it is a theory of the semantic effects of composition. Such effects are explicitly and informatively stated in theoretical statements that assign semantic operations to compositional structures. Statements having the form of assignments of truth conditions to sentences play a special role, for it is essentially through such statements that the theory is checked against our semantic intuitions: the only reason we call the theory a *semantic* theory is that it is in touch with semantic intuitions through assignments of truth conditions. The relevant intuitions, however, do not involve truth as correspondence: they are *inferential* intuitions, that is, intuitions about inferential relations among sentences. Noninferential intuitions play some role in evaluating statements of atomic truth conditions; however, once we adhere to the extensional analysis of predication, any intuitions stemming from our referential practices will serve to confirm such statements.

To the extent that the *data* of MT semantic theory are inferential intuitions, it may be regarded as a partial theory of inferential competence. The theory together with a "complete" system of meaning postulates may be regarded as a complete theory of (an idealization of) inferential competence. Both 'complete' and 'idealization' must be taken with a grain of salt. For, on the one hand, we saw that even a large dictionary contains but a selection of inferentially relevant information; on the other hand (as we also saw) it may be doubted that the notion of an idealized competence makes any sense at this the lexical level. But this is a different matter (see chapter 2).

Semantic Normativity

Deviance and Normativity

The notion of semantic normativity has made frequent appearances in the last chapter. We saw that Wittgenstein's notion of the publicness of language is predicated on an assumption of normativity: semantic values are norms for the use of words. We also saw that what is regarded as the possible inadequacy of individual competence can be described as deviance from semantic *standards* (that is, again, norms for the use of words) or from idealized patterns of use (which play the role of norms). The behavioral phenomenon of *deference*, giving up one's pattern of use and replacing it with another speaker's pattern, can also be described, in normative terms, as presupposing recognition that certain speakers are better acquainted with the semantic standards, or maybe even that they *implement* the standards by their linguistic behaviour. Keil's experiments can be read as showing that both older children and adult speakers acknowledge the role of domain experts in setting standards for the application of natural-kind words and are prepared to defer to them (even though such an attitude does not directly influence their own use of the words).

We also saw that semantic normativity looms large in objectivistic theories. In Burge's anti-individualism or social externalism of 1979, the experts' use of words sets the standard for all speakers; indeed, it determines their concepts, whatever their use of the corresponding words. In Putnam's theory of 1975c, the norm is established by the association of natural-kind and other words with certain objects out there, an association mediated by such intentional acts as ostensive definition. Once the association has been established, *nature* takes care of the semantic values:

"What makes something gold is having the same nature as the paradigms" (Putnam 1983b, 73). Therefore something is to be called 'gold' if and only if it has such a nature.

I noted that Burge's theory has trouble with our intuitions of semantic deviance. Burge's Bert, who, believing that arthritis can afflict the muscles and not only the joints, complains of arthritis in his thigh, nevertheless shares the expert's concept of arthritis. It appears that on this account one cannot have a deviant concept of arthritis. Consequently, either there are no deviant uses of words, or uses and concepts are radically divorced (that is, a person can, indeed must, share the expert's concept of x even though his use of 'x' is deviant).[1] Is Putnam's view any different in this respect? Prima facie, it would seem not: we already saw that Putnam believes that the word 'elm', as used by himself, refers to elms (not to beeches as well) even though he cannot discriminate between elms and beeches and therefore, one would imagine, may frequently call beeches 'elms'. On the other hand, Putnam appears to explicitly allow for deviance: "Extension may be determined socially, in many cases, but we don't assign the standard extension to the tokens of a word W uttered by Jones *no matter how* Jones uses W. Jones has to have some particular ideas and skills in connection with W in order to play his part in the linguistic division of labor" (1975c, 246). Thus it would seem that there can be deviant uses of W by Jones, namely, if he lacks such particular ideas and skills—essentially, if he lacks the stereotype associated with W. Putnam himself manages to refer to elms with 'elm', for he does associate the word with the right stereotype. If he thought that elms were sea mammals, he would not be referring to elms with 'elm'. Or so one gathers. Deviance is possible if it is big enough.

Conceding that there are cases of deviance is certainly better than making it impossible altogether. Nevertheless, even such a view is not entirely plausible. Putnam says he refers to elms with his use of 'elm', *and yet he calls beeches 'elms'*, dates friends under elm trees yet keeps waiting for them under beech trees, etc. It would seem more plausible to say that Putnam's inferential knowledge and referential abilities concerning 'elm' largely converge with those of more competent speakers, but they are not *quite* standard: he often refers to elms with 'elm', but he equally often refers to other deciduous trees. More competent speakers would do better than him: they would more consistently refer to elms[2] with 'elm'.

Objectivistic views tend to deny deviance by having the semantic standard penetrate the individual speakers' use. Independently of what an individual speaker knows, can do, and actually does with words, the semantic values of the words he employs are fixed by some external agency, be it the expert (Burge) or nature itself (Putnam), *and the very content of the speaker's use* is to be described in terms of such objective semantic values. Thus Bert's concept of arthritis is just the expert's, and 'elm', as used by Putnam, refers to elms. This view of the relations between individual competences and the semantic norm may be regarded as one extreme: the norm constitutes the content of individual competences (unless they are *too* unruly). The opposite extreme is taken by philosophers who reject the normativity of language, like Chomsky (1992, 1995), or radically downgrade it, like Bilgrami (1992).

The more radical view is Chomsky's: for him, neither the idea of publicness nor the idea of normativity has any role to play. Chomsky has the following comment on the case of Bert: "To say that Bert has not mastered the concept *arthritis* ... is simply to say that his usage is not exactly that of the people we rely on to cure us.... Reference to a presumed 'public language' with an 'actual content' for *arthritis* sheds no further light on what is happening between us" (1992, 219). Thus, there is nothing but different uses, though some of them may be more authoritative than others. Notice that for this view, semantic deviance is as impossible as it was for externalism: there can't be any deviance, for *there is no norm* to deviate from.

There is no public language for Chomsky: only likenesses among individual speakers. When we say that a given linguistic expression, such as 'John is painting the house brown', is *the same* for Peter and Tom, we are saying this in the sense "in which we might say that their circulatory or visual systems are the same: they are similar enough for the purposes at hand" (Chomsky 1992, 219). How, then, is communication possible, if there are no shared structures? Chomsky remarks that, interestingly, nobody raised the corresponding question for the phonetic level: nobody wondered whether we shouldn't postulate a "public pronunciation" to account for the success of communication. Anyway, Chomsky's answer is straightforward:

Successful communication between Peter and Mary does not entail the existence of shared meanings or shared pronunciations in a public language ... , any more than physical resemblance between Peter and Mary entails the existence of a public form they share. (1992, 215)

It may be that when he listens to Mary speak, Peter proceeds by assuming that she is identical to him, modulo *M*, some array of modifications that he must work out.[3] Sometimes the task is easy, sometimes hard, sometimes hopeless. (1992, 215; also 1995, 48)

Thus for Chomsky, speaking the same language is on a par with being near or looking like: it is a gradable relation whose subsistence depends on interests that "may vary widely" (1992, 215; see also 1995, 49).

Bilgrami's view is not identical with Chomsky's. First of all, as we saw (chapter 4, n. 51), Bilgrami comes out in favor of a form of publicness. Indeed, his externalistic option is essentially motivated by the need to provide a foundation for the publicness of language (1992, 200). Moreover, although he rejects Burge's strong normativity, he makes some room for a weaker, actually, much weaker, form of normativity. In his view, semantic norms do not determine semantic values, nor do they affect the content of use; rather, they are technical rules governed by the goal of smooth communication. Observance of the semantic norms is just a precondition for easy communication: *if* you want to be easily understood, speak like others do (Bilgrami 1992, 111).

On the other hand, Bilgrami rejects "the very idea that there are norms that govern the use of terms" as "Ersatz Platonism" (1992, 97): "You will bring Plato's domain of forms down to earth and call it 'Society'" (1992, 92). Like Chomsky, Bilgrami thinks that the idea of normativity is simply dispensable: we are not obliged to refer to the semantic norm in order to describe anything. Even in Bert's case, says Bilgrami, "it does not matter if we ... say that he is quite correctly using *his* term 'arthritis'" (1992, 97).

Bilgrami's criticism is essentially aimed at Burge's idea that meanings are constituted by the semantic norm: the idea that Bert shared the expert's concept of arthritis from the beginning (and not just after he has been corrected). He has two arguments against Burge. First of all, that Bert defers to the expert does not show that he shared his concept from the beginning. We are not obliged to have Bert describe the correction by the words "I thought I had arthritis in my thigh, but ...," that is, as a correction of a wrong *belief* about "real" arthritis rather than of a wrong meaning (a deviant meaning). That we do *say* such things doesn't prove anything. Bert might have said "I thought 'arthritis' meant so-and-so, but ...." Therefore, we have no reason to think that Bert had the expert's concept all along. *Consequently*, Bilgrami says, we have no reason to call Bert's unreformed behavior 'mistaken': "One could only be in a position to say he was making a mistake if we followed Burge and looked to the way Bert's community used the term 'arthritis' and attributed that concept to him" (1992, 87).

Why is it that we can only say that Bert was making a mistake if we attribute the expert's concept to him? It would seem, on the contrary, that his mistake just *consisted in* not possessing and not using the expert's concept. This is how Bilgrami's reasoning goes: If Bert does not share the expert's concept but has a deviant concept of arthritis by which the word may denote an affliction of the muscles, then his utterance may well be true; there is no reason to say he was making a mistake. If, on the other hand, Bert has the expert's concept, so that even on his use, the word 'arthritis' only designates an affliction of the joints, his utterance of 'I have arthritis in my thigh' is indeed false (actually, inconsistent).[4]

However, it appears that Bilgrami cannot avail himself of this argument, for he just made the point that we are not obliged to describe Bert's correction as involving a false belief rather than the wrong meaning. According to him, we are entirely free to say that "Bert had a certain concept before he was corrected by the doctor, and, afterwards, came to have a different concept (now perhaps the same as the doctor's, if he is fully informed)" (1992, 80). Therefore, it is not true, by Bilgrami's own lights, that we can only attribute a mistake to Bert if we ascribe to him the expert's concept. On the other hand, the reason why Bilgrami doesn't want to say that Bert was mistaken is quite clear: like Chomsky, he has no use for semantic deviance. For him, Bert's use must be just one use of 'arthritis' among others, not a mistaken use.

Bilgrami has a strong case against Burge: clearly, we are not obliged to ascribe to Bert the expert's concept just because of his deferential behavior. On the other hand, Bilgrami's contention that *nothing* is wrong with Bert, that there is no reason to say he is making a mistake (unless we accept Burge's view about which concept of arthritis he possesses) is itself highly counterintuitive. More competent speakers would find reason to *correct* Bert, not just to oppose their linguistic practices to his. Therefore, I would like to say (against Burge) that Bert's notion of arthritis differs from the expert's *and* (against Bilgrami) that he had a false belief. Moreover, against both Burge and Bilgrami, I would like to call Bert's use of 'arthritis' (partly) *deviant*. Can I do all that? I can, thanks to the idea of convergence.

Let us start with the evaluation of Bert's belief. Belief attribution is done partly on the basis of explicit linguistic behavior, and such behavior, as Burge (1979, 89–92) quite rightly points out, is interpreted literally unless there is reason to do otherwise. When Bert complains of arthritis in his thigh, using these very words, we take his words at face value; we do not normally wonder whether he by any chance meant neck by 'thigh' or inflammation by 'arthritis' or whatever. What is it to take Bert's words at face value? As Chomsky says, it is to take them as if they were *our* words, thus not so much in their standard sense but rather in *our* sense (which, as we will presently see, we regard as responsible to standards). Allowing for differences among individual competences, we take Bert to mean *more or less* what we mean by those words; we take his competence and linguistic behavior to converge with ours. Therefore we attribute him the belief that arthritis can afflict the thigh, which belief we do not share. Of course, we identify the belief through Bert's words, which we are reading as if they were our words. Can we ascribe to Bert notions (of thigh, arthiritis, etc.) that converge with ours and yet attribute to him a belief we do not share? Of course we can: convergent does not amount to identical. Having convergent notions of arthritis means sharing a number of beliefs (not necessarily all beliefs) and applying the word to by and large the same phenomena (not necessarily exactly the same phenomena), which are the conditions of Burge's thought experiment.

Attributing to Bert a belief we do not share is, in general, not enough to ascribe to him a notion different from ours. If we differed from Bert on whether our colleague John did not come to the meeting because of his arthritis, such a difference would not induce us to ascribe to Bert a different notion of arthritis. In this case it does, though, for the belief on which we differ is significant enough. Thus Bert has a convergent but significantly different notion of arthritis (which means that there is much we agree upon, alongside considerable differences).

Now, the belief we have attributed to Bert is not simply a belief we do not share: it is a belief we have reason to judge false. The reasons we regard it as false may vary: if we are medical doctors, we probably have an argument to that effect; for most of us, it is just that we have been told so, directly or indirectly, by reliable sources, experts. Actually, it is not simply that we believe that arthritis cannot afflict the muscles; we believe that *the experts* believe it cannot. Therefore, Bert's notion does not just differ from our notion; as far as we know, it differs from the expert's notion. But a notion significantly different from the expert's notion we call 'deviant', more or less deviant, depending on the extent of the difference.

Bilgrami wanted to buttress his radically antinormativistic view by showing that we can only take Bert to be mistaken if we go along with Burge and ascribe the expert's concept to him. However, we found a way of saying that Bert is mistaken *and* that his notion of arthritis is (partly) deviant; in fact, he is deviant *because* he is *badly* mistaken.[5] This in itself certainly does not show that Bilgrami is generally wrong about semantic norms; it merely shows that we can find fault with Bert's use of 'arthritis' without having to assume *Burge's* idea of semantic normativity. I now want to address the issue of normativity as such and see whether there is room for a notion stronger than the one Bilgrami thinks he can afford but weaker than the very strong notion assumed by the objectivists.

Normativity, Correctness, and Communication

In a sense, objectivism can be read as a form of reification of the semantic norms: the norm according to which a word ought to be used is turned into the semantic value the word has in the use of every speaker, independently of *how* it is *actually* used. What are Burge's concepts, for example, but hyposthasized semantic norms? By using a word, 'contract', or 'arthritis', or 'sofa', I ipso facto have the corresponding concept, so that I can, for example, refer to contracts, cases of arthritis, and sofas even if as a matter of fact I don't (I call armchairs 'sofas', for example). That is, by using words of a public language, governed by experts, I manage actually to speak as I ought to speak.

If it were as simple as this, however, the objectivists' theory would be an ultimately harmless form of Platonism. But the normativity of language that gets reified in the objectivistic conception of reference is not the kind of normativity that actually obtains in a linguistic community; it is instead, as we will see, an extreme idealization of such normativity.

At the other extreme, the philosophers who have no place, or a very limited place, for normativity (and consequently no place for deviance either) do account for the variety of individual uses and competences, but they have some trouble explaining (or explaining away) our intuitions of normativity. For it seems that not all uses of lexemes are on a par: some are more authoritative, some less; there are dictionaries, encyclopedias, and experts (both for given domains and for the lexicon in general); we correct each other's use of language all the time; each one of us is aware of knowing the meaning of many words "only in part" or "up to a point," in a vague or confused way (as Burge [e.g., 1979, 83–84] rightly urged upon us). A theory of semantic behavior should save such phenomena, if it is at all possible. Moreover, we saw that the idea of the publicness of language, to the extent that it does not coincide with a particularly rampant form of Platonism, is inextricably bound up with normativity: to say that an interpreted language is public is to identify it with a collection of norms for the use of marks and sounds that are regarded as binding for the speakers of a given community.[6] Thus, no normativity, no publicness: an implication that Chomsky would welcome, but many others would not.

Bilgrami, though an enemy of normativity, is fully aware that we feel that there is a connection between speaking a language and speaking *correctly*, or according to the norm. He is prepared to go along with such intuitions to a very limited extent: he agrees that speaking "like others do" (abiding by the norms, in this sense) makes communication *smoother*, but he denies that it makes communication *possible*; most of all, he has no patience with the alleged constitutive connection of meaning and correctness. "The entire notion of correctness is entirely secondary to the desire and intention to communicate without causing strain, which underlies the notion of meaning" (Bilgrami 1992, 111). There are indeed semantic norms, but (1) observing them is not necessary for communication to take place, and (2) were it not for our intention to communicate easily, they would have no role whatsoever to play. Both claims (but particularly the second) are open to challenge, at least in the sense in which Bilgrami appears to understand them.

To show that compliance with semantic norms is not necessary for communication, Bilgrami relies on Davidsonian-sounding examples: "I have said 'The gavagai is too loud' and found that a friend of mine (who had never heard the sound 'gavagai' before) turned the volume of the radio down." This shows that "one may use a term which is not in accord with any regularity and yet be understood." Therefore, the claim that "norms attach to particular terms and they assess usage for correctness and incorrectness on particular occasions" is much stronger than is needed to account for successful communication (Bilgrami 1992, 112).

We are all quite familiar with communicative events of the gavagai/ radio type. Clearly, a speaker can occasionally manage to get his meaning across using inappropriate words, meaningless words, or sentences where certain words are simply missing. An interesting example is provided by the language of the Belgian cartoon characters called the Schtroumpfs (the Smurfs in English translation), where many nouns and verbs are replaced by the single sound 'schtroumpf' and its pseudomorphological varieties. In spite of this, most of what they say is perfectly intelligible to the reader.[7] Another example is the so-called Cloze test. Originally intended to measure readability of written texts, it consists in suppressing, for example, one out of every *n* words in a text and then having a reader fill in the gaps, that is, recover the deleted words (Taylor 1953).[8] Not surprisingly, normally competent readers succeed in filling in most of the gaps correctly.

What does all this show? One natural interpretation has it that in such cases the linguistic context provides enough information to predict which word *should have appeared* in the place of the inappropriate, nonsensical, or missing word. Perhaps explicit reintegration of the appropriate word is deemed unnecessary: what matters is that the context suffices to have the reader or hearer form the intended semantic interpretation of the whole sentence. I believe few would say that such cases show that 'gavagai' *can mean* radio, or that the blank or the dots '. . .' in a "clozed" text can mean this or that. The blank simply means that *a word* was supposed to be there; which word we can easily guess, given the context. Similarly with 'gavagai': the example shows that 'gavagai', like any other word, can be used as a dummy in a sentence intended to be about a radio. Such a sentence can be understood even if it contains a dummy word.

Thus, saying that the example shows that 'gavagai' can mean radio or that it can be used to mean radio would amount to a misdescription. On the other hand, it can easily be conceded that compliance with the semantic norms is not necessary for communication, in the sense that it is not necessary to observe *all* norms *all the time*. It does not follow that no norms "attach to particular terms" or that norms do not "assess usage for correctness or incorrectness." That norms may be violated does not entail that there are no norms (norms are not physical laws). What does it mean to say that norms do not assess usage for correctness? It appears to mean either that there are no such assessments, but this is simply false, or that they are not justified: usage may not conform to the relevant norm and yet be correct. One thinks of the 'gavagai' case: the word was not used in conformity with any norm on the occasion of Bilgrami's example, but nevertheless it did serve the communicative purpose it was put to. So, using it was correct, or anyway not incorrect. To insist that, in spite of its effectiveness, it was indeed incorrect looks circular (one would be assuming that to be correct is to conform to a norm). There is no correctness, it might be concluded, over and beyond communicative efficacy: it is correct to use word *w* in context *c* on occasion *o* if and only if doing so is communicatively effective. However, this is playing with loaded dice, for whether using word *w* (in *c* on occasion *o*) is communicatively effective depends on whether most or all other words in *c* are used *normally*. One cannot make up a communicatively effective sentence using all words in any old way or as dummies.[9] Consequently, the "pragmatic" notion of correctness is parasitic on a different notion: *w* may be used correctly (that is, effectively) in context *c* on occasion *o* only if other words in *c* are used correctly (that is, normally or convergently). Bilgrami does concede this point: he agrees that "if there was not by and large regularity and stability in our linguistic usage we would not generally be understood at all and would not be counted as linguistic agents" (1992, 112). It is not clear, then, why he wants to deny that normativity affects individual words (what else would it affect?) and that normativity inspires judgments of correctness and incorrectness.

Bilgrami also claims that the whole *point* of normativity is smoothness of communication: if we did not speak like other people, communication, though possible, would be much harder. So, let us try to imagine a linguistic community functioning along Bilgrami's lines, that is, a community where each speaker conforms to semantic norms and standards only to the extent that he wants to be easily understood by other members of the community. That would be a community where each speaker could have (and plausibly would have) *two* languages, from a semantic standpoint: one that he would use to communicate with other people and another that he would use whenever such a need does not arise, as when he is just thinking to, talking with, or writing for, himself. Within such a community the function of the semantic norm could be compared to that of the rules of etiquette: one abides by them if one is invited to dinner by the Duke of So-and-So, whereas in his own home, a person can eat with his hands if he likes. Notice that we ought not to imagine here the plausible situation in which each speaker uses *some* words idiosyncratically. Perhaps each of us has his own little private code, including invented words or public words with idiosyncratic meanings (I certainly do). We must picture a situation where *the whole lexicon*, including verbs, prepositions, articles, and so forth could be (and plausibly would be) semantically idiosyncratic. Such a situation would be comparable to one in which everyone possessed a second language, but with a difference: in real life, the possession and use of a real second language is supported by a community speaking and writing that language. Not so with our imaginary situation.

Now, first of all, such would be an utterly diseconomical situation. Why have two languages when one suffices? Why associate phonemes with two disjoint sets of semantic values when one is enough? Why using the sound 'cat' both for cedars (in private) and for cats (in public)? Second (this is more speculative, I admit), such a situation would probably involve an overwhelming memory load on a speaker's mind. I have no idea of the cognitive mechanisms by which participation in a relatively uniform linguistic community may support an individual speaker's semantic memory; however, it is natural to think that being confirmed in our use of words by other people's uses reinforces semantic memory, thereby making even noncommunicative use of a language substantially easier. By contrast, a community that worked according to Bilgrami's theory, even if possible in principle, would be unlikely in point of fact; evolution would have disposed of it.

At this point, one may object that surely Bilgrami does not want each speaker to possess a second semantic language alongside the one he uses for communication: what he wants to say is, that we speak as others do *in order to* be understood more easily (*not* for other reasons). We *do as a matter of fact* speak more or less like everybody else in the community not because we consciously acknowledge a semantic norm, nor because the semantic values of the words we use are determined by the norm (whether or not we acknowledge that they are and how they are), but simply because we are pursuing certain aims. The answer to this objection begins with a question: what happens when we are *not* pursuing such aims? It would seem that in such cases, at least, the semantic norm should play no role. If, however, it happens that even in such cases a speaker keeps conforming, that is, even when he is talking to himself, he is still using 'cat' to refer to cats, etc., so that the semantic values are as a matter of fact *always as if* they were governed by the aim of communication, then it is unclear what is gained by holding that conformity to the norm is related to the purpose of communicating smoothly. For the point of the opposition between normativity and ease of communication was to show that uniformity of semantic values is not required by *the use of language as such*. If it now turns out that the use of language is characterized by consistent conformity, even when communication is out of question, then there's no point left to the opposition.

A few minor remarks can be added. First, it appears that we use language, particularly the lexicon, not just with the *intention* of using it as everybody else in the community does but under the *assumption* that we are using it as everybody else does. Such a presumption may be a delusion (and to some extent it is, as we will see). Nonetheless, it does signal what might be called the anthropological role of normativity. A community in which each speaker *intended* to make normal use of the lexicon for the sake of communication while taking for granted the heterodoxy of her own ordinary uses would be quite different from ours: it would be a community where communication would be perceived as a costly and demanding enterprise, as it would be for a hobo (or maybe for one of us) going to dinner at the Duke's.

The anthropological relevance of normativity is also indicated by the fact that we are prepared to correct our uses of language when they turn out to be deviant but not just to be understood more easily. We recognize that language *is* governed by rules, that there *are* standards and authorities. Again, this could be a delusion, yet a community that did not share such a delusion would behave differently. It would be like a community where the laws are obeyed *only* to avoid punishment and never out of habit or because it seems right to do so or for a thousand other reasons. It would be a community where one decides in each single case whether one should conform to the standards, depending on the likely effects on communicative efficacy, and where one *never* conforms if communicative efficacy is out of question. It seems clear to me that such a community would be different from ours.

Normativity without Norms

Actually, the idea of semantic normativity has such deep roots that it easily engenders an extremely idealized picture of the semantic norm: the kind of picture that underlies the objectivists' normativism. In that picture each term of a language is associated with one well determined standard, one semantic norm, that is identical with the term's meaning. In Burge's case, such a unique norm is fixed (or anyway ratified) by the expert. With Putnam, the metaphysician, the standard is set by nature and somehow made available by the expert.

Now, it is important to realize that the recognition of widespread semantic normativity does not entail the existence of *one* norm. That there are standards, authorities, and hierarchies does not entail that there is a unique standard or a supreme authority (a "dictator," in Gärdenfors's [1993] sense), be it a Big Dictionary or Plato's legislator (*Cratylus* 388e ff.).[10] The lexicographer's experience is instructive in this respect. A dictionary is surely a good example of a socially accepted semantic standard: it is to the dictionary that we make appeal in many cases of semantic uncertainty, conflict, or lack of information. However, dictionaries are often *wrong*, mistaken.[11] With respect to what are they mistaken? Better dictionaries, in some cases. But not necessarily: some mistakes may be common to all the best dictionaries of a given language. Dictionaries may be mistaken with respect to other authorities, which may be regarded as superior in individual cases, for example, encyclopedias, treatises, flesh-and-bone experts. None of these, however, is *the* final authority, least of all the human expert, whose limitations (of memory, competence, awareness) are obvious. Forgetting such limitations amounts to a confusion: the expert is not, and should not be identified with, Plato's legislator. The expert knows more about camels than we do. The legislator has absolute competence with the word 'camel' and what it applies to. Burge's expert, in contrast with Plato's legislator, is *an* authority, not *the* authority. In a real-life linguistic community there are no final semantic authorities, and there are no guarantees that the optimization procedures that we all occasionally perform and that some, for example, lexicographers, systematically perform will issue in a unique, absolutely certain result. In Michael Dummett's words, "The paradoxical character of language lies in the fact that while its practice must be subject to standards of correctness, there is no ultimate authority to impose those standards from without" (1991, 85).

People who are fond of formalisms will perhaps remark the following: if the relation 'being more authorative than x on word a', as defined over a linguistic community, is asymmetric, transitive, and connected,[12] there's *bound* to be a final authority on a, at least in principle. However, even in principle, the relation need not be connected: it is conceivable that several people may be equally competent with a (and, by the way, this does not imply that they must *agree* on a). Moreover, in practice such hierarchies of semantic authority are not easily reconstructed. Where should I go for a check on a mathematical word as defined by what is regarded as the best dictionary of Italian? Well, go to a mathematician. What if he disagrees with the dictionary? Should I rest content with his alternative definition? Well, not necessarily. So what then: a better mathematician? What does this mean exactly?

I don't want to overemphasize this kind of trouble. However, having done some lexicographic work myself (Palazzi and Folena 1992), I tend to be impatient with the idea that the optimization of lexical semantic competence is a matter of course. Granted, in many cases the several semantic authorities (experts, encyclopedias, etc.) do converge in determining a semantic norm. However, such convergences are often partial: they do not rule out uncertainties on borderline cases, partial conflicts, etc. For most practical purposes (for example, for the needs of an "average speaker"), they more than suffice. However, they are far from singling out the kind of norm that social externalists are talking about. As for the fixation of a norm by way of fixing the reference, as in some forms of metaphysical externalism, I must stress that such events are extremely rare: perhaps only the names for newly discovered species or for some artifacts (and, in the past, the *scientific* names for species) are introduced by way of something like a baptismal ceremony. With most words of a natural language we have neither baptismal ceremonies nor procedures for retrieving them. We have only uses, some more authoritative, some less.

The qualification 'some more authoritative, some less' is important, for it highlights some disagreement with Bilgrami (and Chomsky). They are right in pointing out that each speaker's use of language is exactly what it is, no matter what the expert (or the real world) thinks about it. It is quite possible to use the sound 'arthritis' to denote an affliction that may concern the muscles and to use 'cat' to refer to cedars. To object "But *really*, 'cat' denotes cats and only cats" amounts to turning a semantic norm into a mysterious relation of reference—a semantic norm that we saw to be not as well defined as an externalist would like it to be. On the other hand, an *inclination to convergence* is indeed rooted in our use of language. Language is *used as* a norm-governed system, which tends to shape its actual use and the use of each word by each individual speaker. We do not necessarily use 'cat' the way the expert does, but we think we do, essentially, and we are prepared to change our ways if we are told we do not.[13]

Thus the normativity of language does not reduce to the fact that there is a hierarchy of competences; there's also the fact that the hierarchy is implicitly, and often explicitly, recognized by individual speakers. Such a recognition not only determines our propensity to defer; it also underlies our use of language as a vehicle for undertaking *commitments*, in Brandom's sense (1994, esp. pt. I, chap. 3). When a speaker uses the word 'elm', he normally intends his assertions to be evaluated on the basis of the prevailing standards of use for the expressions he is employing; if he doesn't, he must make it clear by introducing such qualifications as 'in my sense of "elm" '. He may not as a matter of fact share the expert's concept (that is, his competence may not be identical to the expert's), but he accepts being judged on that basis. Thus if someone utters 'All swans are white', she intends her utterance to be evaluated by everybody else on the basis of the standard senses of 'swan' and 'white' (and 'all' and 'be'). That, in a sense, *there are no* such standards does not keep this principle from actively influencing our linguistic practices. For example, a person normally accepts (and is regarded as socially obliged to accept) the consequences of his assertions taken in the sense in which semantically authoritative speakers take them, independently of whether such a sense coincides with the sense he intended them to have or even with the sense that an accurate examination of his linguistic habits would determine them to have.

Given all this, saying that, in a sense, there are no standards may look like an overstatement. It is not: it simply amounts to repeating that, in general, there is no unique, well-defined set of bits of knowledge and/ or abilities that is *the* standard for the use of a word (in the sense that anybody using that word *must* possess such knowledge and abilities *if* he is to use the word competently). That such is not the case has been argued throughout this book.

Weak Normativity and the Private-Language Argument

One may wonder whether the notion of semantic normativity I have been defending, weaker than the objectivists' though stronger than Bilgrami's, is enough for the needs of Wittgenstein's private-language argument. The argument needs a notion of correctness of use in order to go through, and not only that, it needs the distinction between a speaker's use *seeming* correct to her and its *being* correct. My view of normativity, according to which there are authorities (though no final authorities) and standards (though no absolute standard) makes room for both: one may believe that one's use of a word conforms to the use of more competent speakers, whereas, as a matter of fact, it doesn't; correctness is here interpreted as convergence with the linguistic use of speakers who are generally regarded as competent. This is not, of course, *absolute* correctness: there is no such thing, for there are neither absolute standards to comply with nor absolute authorities to exemplify and enforce such standards. But neither does the argument require such absolute correctness.

It may be objected, however, that this is entirely beside the point, the point being whether individual competence has been defined so as to be compatible with the argument's conclusion. Is individual competence, in any sense, *private*? For surely, in the present view, a speaker whose competence underlay a radically nonstandard use of language would nonetheless be speaking a language, although her use of language would hardly be intelligible to other speakers. Notice, however, that her deviance would be entirely open to view: it would be clear from her linguistic practices, both referential and inferential, whether and to what extent she deviates from other speakers' use (or, if one wishes, from standards). The problem with Wittgensein's private language is that it is supposed to have been set up so that it is not open to assessment as to whether its expressions are being used correctly (for their meanings are supposed to result from private attachments to inner states): in a private language, the "real" meanings of the expressions used by the speaker are, by hypothesis, hidden to the public. By contrast, I introduced the notion of individual competence in such a way that it does not make sense to suppose that linguistic practices do not reflect competence. In fact, a person's competence is just the complex of knowledge and abilities (such as discriminating abilities) that make it possible for that person to use language the way she uses it. Consequently, competence is by definition manifested in use (except to the extent to which use may be affected by slips of the tongue, occasional failures of memory, etc.). Therefore, it does not make sense to wonder whether a person may perchance mean by w something other than what her use of w publicly exhibits her to mean.

But then, one might insist, suppose that the deviant speaker is "opting out," so to speak, that is, suppose that she is declaring herself not responsible to the social hierarchy of competences. Wouldn't she still be speaking a language on the present view, and wouldn't that be her own private language? The answer is that her opting out would be utterly irrelevant: it would not, and could not, keep other speakers from assessing her use of language and regarding it as deviant. The notion of correctness could, and would, still apply to her use of language, even if she refused to defer. If she claimed to be speaking correctly in her own way or according to her own standards, *this* response would fall under the private-language argument: other speakers would see no reason to regard her as speaking a language at all, and they would insist that *she herself* has no such reason.

What if she saw herself, and required other people to look at her, as a Fodorian well-functioning machine? This is indeed an unassailable defense. However, her behavior would not count as speaking a language from Wittgenstein's standpoint, for the notion of being right that would apply to such behavior would not be analogous to the notion of being right that we customarily apply to linguistic behavior (for a Fodorian machine, "being right" admits of no alternative) (see Marconi 1995b).

6

Referentially Competent Systems

I want a theory *of what it is to attach a camera.*
B. C. Smith (1991, 275)[1]

There are performances that stand in a *criterial* relation to understanding, in Wittgenstein's sense. For example, if a person can summarize a text, we say that he has understood it, whereas if he cannot, we doubt that he understood. If a person can answer questions concerning the topics a text is about and her answers appear to be based on the information contained in the text, we say she has understood the text, whereas if she cannot answer, it is legitimate to raise doubts about her understanding. If a person can correctly translate the text into another language, we say that she understood, but if she cannot and yet does know the second language, we are inclined to say that she did not understand. Such are the "paradigmatic" cases in which we say that somebody understands a text in a natural language. Wittgenstein would say that our use of such words as 'understanding' and 'to understand' is intertwined with such performances and the ability to carry them out. Understanding is not identical with summarizing or answering questions or translating. However, we probably learn how to apply the concept of understanding by learning how to assess such performances.

Inabilities of Natural-Language-Understanding Systems

Today we have artificial systems that can carry out such tasks as the above with different degrees of success.[2] They are called 'natural-language-understanding systems' precisely because they are capable of one or another among such performances.[3] However, in spite of the fact that these systems can carry out the very performances on the basis of which we normally say of a human being that she understands a language, many would say that such systems do not really understand natural language.

Of course, the present systems are not as good as human beings at carrying out such tasks: their translations are often clumsy, their summaries unintelligent, the questions they can answer relatively few in number. Moreover, the existing systems can (usually) carry out only one or another among such tasks: in contrast with human beings, they are either translators or question-answering devices, or automatic abstractors. Finally, the range of texts that each system can process is strongly restricted, lexically at any rate. To overcome such limitations, more is required than just building huge lexical databases or integrating complex systems into one big system: we need to solve problems (some of which have not even been clearly formulated so far) from metaphoric uses of language to pragmatic competence and contextual knowledge.

However, I surmise that it is not essentially because of such difficulties that natural-language-processing systems are said not to really understand natural language. To realize this, imagine we have been successful in building a very sophisticated "understanding" system of the standard type. Such a system would have an adequate syntactic analyzer, a vast lexical database, and a semantic interpreter capable of compositionally constructing fully analytic semantic representations: they would be as explicit as we need them to be for the system to carry out all the inferences that could plausibly be attributed to a competent, or even very competent, speaker. From 'There are four elephants in the living room' the system would infer that there are four large animals in the living room, that there are four elephants in the house, that there is an even number of elephants in the living room, that there are higher mammals (to be more precise, proboscideans) in the living room; it could even infer that the living room's furniture is likely to be badly spoiled. In short, the system's inferential competence would be satisfactory to the highest degree.

Why would we say, even of such a system, that it does not really understand the language it can process? There is a classic answer to this question, based on Searle's "Chinese room" thought experiment. According to Searle, the reason we would (and should) say that the system does not understand language is that any such system is a mere symbol-manipulator: it does not know what the symbols *mean*. For those who don't know, Searle's thought experiment, in a simplified form, is as follows (see Searle 1980, 1982). Imagine yourself locked in a room with two windows. Through one window you are handed over a batch of marks that look like writing. It is indeed Chinese writing, but you don't know any Chinese; to you, it is just a lot of meaningless squiggles. However, you are also given instructions (in English, which you understand) directing you to match the marks coming through the first window with other marks, equally unintelligible to you, which you are supposed to pass out through the other window. After a while you become extremely skilled at following the instructions so that your mark matching gets very fast. However, you still do not understand what is going on. Now, it turns out that the first set of marks were questions (in Chinese), and the instructions directed you to match them with the appropriate answers (the marks you had been passing out through the other window). You did not know Chinese, and do not know any more of it by virtue of having become skilled at mark matching: you can indeed handle the marks at great speed according to the rules you have been given, but you still don't understand them. For Searle, a computer implementing a natural-language-understanding system is exactly in your position: it can manipulate symbols (which it identifies by their shapes) according to rules so as to emulate a question-answering session or, for that matter, any other linguistic performance; however, it does not understand the symbols it manipulates any more than you, locked in the room, understand Chinese.

Notice that from Searle's standpoint, my description of the ideal system would be incorrect.[4] For I said that the system can carry out inferences, indeed, that the system is inferentially highly competent. If this is interpreted as involving only the system's ability to grind out certain strings of symbols whenever it is fed certain others, then Searle would have no objection. But if it is taken seriously, that is, as asserting that the system *shares* some of *our* linguistic abilities, namely, our inferential competence, then Searle would remark that nothing of the sort is the case. Strictly speaking, it would not even be correct to say that the inferences in our example concern sentences in which the word 'elephant' occurs. The system can indeed manipulate strings of symbols, including a symbol that materially coincides with the English word 'elephant'. Such a symbol, however, is devoid of meaning for the system: emphatically, it does not mean elephant (that is, it does not mean what the English word 'elephant' means). Whatever conclusions the system can infer are not in themselves about elephants: they are strings of symbols, meaningless for the system, that we (the system's users) interpret as pertaining to elephants.

I am not going to discuss Searle's view in full. Here I will just point out one thing that I find essentially wrong with it and one that I find essentially right. What I find essentially wrong is Searle's *opposition* of competence and the ability to manipulate symbols, as if "genuine" knowledge of meaning were obviously bound to be other than symbol-manipulating ability. True, the Chinese-room thought experiment is intended to make us *feel* that one can effect all sorts of manipulations of marks without ever achieving genuine understanding. However, even if we grant that the manipulating abilities of the man in the room fall short of linguistic competence, still they are abilities to effect *a certain kind* of manipulations. Pointing out the inadequacy of such manipulations is surely not enough to discredit the connection between linguistic competence and the ability to use certain marks and sounds. Quite a few years ago Putnam remarked that "the account according to which understanding a language *consists* in being able to use it ... is the only account now in the field" (1979, 199). Nowadays other views have become popular. According to some of them, understanding a language is being able to map it onto a system of mental representations.[5] What we call 'being able to use the language' is at best a symptom that genuine understanding has taken place. It is, however, neither a necessary nor a sufficient condition of understanding. I am not sure that such alternative accounts are really inconsistent with the account in terms of use. Certainly, displaying an ability to use a language has a lot to do with *ascription* of understanding. I doubt that any system, natural or artificial, that *really* exhibited a degree of ability in the use of language comparable to the ability *we* possess would be *seriously* denied understanding. The fact is that we are the only such systems around: all the other systems are radically inadequate *as language users*, or symbol manipulators, quite independently of whether they "really" understand language in any other sense (in the cognitivists' sense, for example). Thus it is somewhat futile to inveigh against the identification of understanding with symbol-manipulating ability, as it is quite clear that the abilities displayed by artificial systems (even idealized systems, like the one we are imagining) are inadequate, even from the standpoint of such an identification. The genuine problem is not whether knowledge of meaning can be "reduced" to symbol manipulation but what kind of symbol-manipulating abilities would count as knowledge of meaning or understanding of language.

Searle is quite right that the ability to perform the syntactic transformations he imagines the man in the Chinese room to be executing would *not* count as semantic competence. In fact, the man in the room is associating linguistic expressions with other linguistic expressions according to rules.[6] That the ability to (correctly) make such associations is insufficient for semantic competence was made clear in chapter 1: a meaningless linguistic symbol cannot be made meaningful by being connected, in any way whatsoever, to other uninterpreted symbols.[7] Therefore, Searle's argument is effective against the several views, ranging from certain forms of structuralism to ideas of early artificial intelligence, according to which meaning can emerge from purely intralinguistic connections and semantic competence can be identified with the ability to trace or retrace such connections.

Searle, however, believes that nothing can be done to enhance a system's competence as long as the system remains, essentially, a program, for any program, no matter how sophisticated, will be nothing but a symbol manipulator, a "syntactic" device, in Searle's somewhat tendentious terminology, and no symbol will ever acquire meaning by virtue of being subjected to syntactic manipulations of any kind. This is because of Searle's *general* opposition of symbol manipulation and understanding. So Searle's answer to the question 'Why doesn't the system really understand language?' is simply 'Because, like all computer programs, it is just a symbol manipulator.' As I am unconvinced by Searle's opposition (though I recognize that the system's manipulations are, indeed, inadequate), let us go back to the question 'What is it exactly that the system cannot do but that *we* can?'

Some philosophers would say that the system does not know the *truth conditions* of the sentences it deals with; in this sense it does not understand them. However, we saw that at least in one sense of 'knowing the truth conditions', this cannot be the problem (chapter 4, pp. 105–114). If knowing sentences' truth conditions amounts to being endowed with adequate statements of truth conditions for a language such as English, as provided by a standard model-theoretic account of the language complete with meaning postulates, then the system can be supposed to know as much. In fact, is there anything we know and can do by virtue of understanding such statements but that the system could not do? On the one hand, if we knew the truth conditions of all the sentences of English (in the model-theoretic sense), we could draw all the appropriate inferences, but so can the system. On the other hand, the system would not know, by virtue of having mastered such truth conditions, what words such as 'book', 'table', or 'on' apply to, but neither would we. We saw that a model-theoretic semantic system emulates structural competence and expresses inferential competence, which is exactly what we are imagining the system to possess.

But it would also not be right to say that the system doesn't know a sentence's truth conditions in the sense that it cannot establish, for each situation σ, whether the sentence is true or false in σ. For if situation σ is described in language, the system can indeed determine whether a sentence is true or false in σ. This is exactly what systems do that (like the system we are considering) can answer questions relative to a text's topic: such systems determine whether certain sentences (corresponding to the questions) are true or false in the situations described by the texts they have processed. As we have assumed that there are no limitations, either lexical or syntactic or discursive or of any other kind, to the texts the system can process, we conclude that the system can indeed determine whether a given sentence is true or false in any situation that can be described in the language the system can interpret.

On the other hand, the system cannot establish whether a sentence is true or false in a situation that is not given to it through language. For example, it cannot determine whether a sentence is true or false in the real world, it cannot verify the sentence, unless the "real world" is given to it through a linguistic description. If you place the system in a room and require it to evaluate the sentence 'There are at least four seats in this room', the system won't do it.

A related inability can be highlighted by focusing on the reference of words. There is a sense in which the system does know the reference of 'elephant': it knows that the word refers to elephants, that is, to large mammals, proboscideans, living in Africa or India (or zoos), etc. Thus it would be incorrect to say that, for all the system knows, its conclusions might be about flamingos rather than elephants. The system can very well tell elephants (mammals, proboscideans, etc.) from flamingos, which are birds, waders, pink or white (not grey, like elephants), etc. On the other hand, the system cannot *recognize* elephants in the real world or in a photograph, just as it cannot *verify* a sentence about elephants. Lacking such recognitional abilities, the system is referentially incompetent. It is, I believe, such incompetence that underlies our feeling that natural-language-understanding systems are only metaphorically such, for they do not *really* understand natural language. If the views that were put forth in this book are even remotely on the right track, a referentially incompetent system cannot be regarded as semantically competent.

Which Recognition Abilities Are Relevant?

It follows that in order to have a genuinely competent artificial system, a system that could really understand natural language, we ought to build a referentially competent system, that is, a system capable of applying words to the real world. We saw that, *pace* Wilks, this involves some degree of recognitional ability (chapter 3, pp. 64–66). However, we must be more precise on two points (at least). First of all, what degree or amount of recognitional ability counts as referential competence? Suppose that we take it as established that *some* degree of recognitional ability is a *necessary* condition of referential competence. Is *any* degree of recognitional ability a *sufficient* condition of referential competence? Second, any view that connects semantic competence with the ability to recognize referents and verify sentences is open to the charge of *verificationism*, the discredited theory according to which to know the meaning of a sentence is to be able to verify it. Thus the second question is, Does the view that referential competence involves recognition and verification abilities entail verificationism?

Concerning the first question, we already saw that several social and cultural factors are relevant in determining which type and amount of recognitional abilities are regarded as significant for semantic competence (see chapter 3, pp. 65–66). We also saw that there is no principled reason for excluding sophisticated recognition abilities from referential competence and that, on the other hand, the distinction between naive and sophisticated abilities does not coincide with the distinction between purely perceptual recognition procedures, based on macroscopic criteria, and recognition procedures that make use of complex tests and artificial instruments (see chapter 4, pp. 91–92). For example, the diagnostic ability of a trained physician, though extremely sophisticated and based on a complex training, does not necessarily involve the use of artificial devices. The conclusion should be that *any* recognition ability can count toward referential competence and that which abilities *do* count, in the sense of being socially acknowledged as significant or even crucial, cannot in general be predicted but should be investigated in each single case.

However, something more can be said concerning the special relevance of macroscopic recognition criteria. Clearly, a normal speaker's application of words such as 'cat' or 'water' or 'gold' is based on very rough identification criteria, not on DNA or chemical or spectrographic analysis. However, as it is often pointed out, such macroscopic recognition criteria are conspicuously fallible. They make us identify hydrogen peroxide as water, iron pyrites as gold, plastic imitation wood as wood, and under certain conditions even porcelain cats as cats. Of course, not only does 'cat' not refer to porcelain cats nor 'gold' to iron pyrites, but speakers know that they don't. Psychological research (e.g., Keil 1986, Neisser 1987b) has emphasized that adult and even very young speakers are quite aware that superficial, perceptual criteria are insufficient for guiding the application of many words. One might thus be led to the conclusion that genuine referential competence cannot be reduced to the ability to apply macroscopic criteria. There are at least two ways in which referential competence could be defined *in contrast with* macroscopic recognition ability:

First, one could appeal to Putnam's division of linguistic labor, holding that a normal speaker's referential competence is parasitic upon the expert's competence. *Genuine* referential competence is the expert's privilege; my own competence concerning, say, 'gold' or 'gorilla' consists of my ability to apply superficial identification criteria plus my knowledge of where to turn for more adequate identification. The trouble with this suggestion is that it makes speakers incompetent who are not (and should not be) so regarded. Take the friend of manatees, mentioned in chapter 3: she is extremely skilled at recognizing manatees, but she may have no idea that there are people (certain zoologists) who are supposed to be even better than she at telling manatees from other sea mammals. Or take a speaker who, having a very sharp eye, knows exactly how long one meter is (he can evaluate lengths with great precision): he may be ignorant of the fact that there are metrologists. Or again, consider a speaker who, like most people around us, has an average ability to recognize brass but doesn't know that there are metallurgists. By the present criterion all these people should be considered referentially incompetent, or anyway less competent than other speakers who know about the professional articulation of our society. This looks counterintuitive to the extreme.

Second, a prima facie more plausible, though vaguer, suggestion would be that the ability to apply words, referential competence, is really based on the interaction of a plurality of factors, prominently including *inferential* competence. For example, our application of the word 'cow' may initially rely on macroscopic criteria. However, if something looking like a cow were to lay an egg or proved to be able to breathe underwater or could run faster than a leopard, we would hesitate to call it a cow, for we *know* that cows don't do such things. Similarly if it turned out to have the internal anatomy of a reptile or no internal anatomy at all but just a lot of wiring. This suggestion is surely correct in that it underscores two facts. (1) Macroscopic criteria are defeasibile even within normal competence (even not-so-expert speakers usually know that, for many words, such criteria are not entirely reliable). (2) Inferential competence plays a role in many referential performances.[8] However, the examples also show that the essential burden of providing *candidates* for identification is carried by our recognition procedures based on macroscopic criteria. It appears that, though there is no sharp line to be drawn here, it is the ability to apply such criteria that is commonly regarded as relevant to *linguistic* competence. Thus, imagine the following case. Tests of impaired lexical competence are often based on the recognition of pictures. For example, subjects may be shown pictures of common artifacts or animals and asked to name them. Suppose that a subject has been shown a picture of a cat and has uttered the word 'cat' in response. Suppose that afterwards she is informed by the experimenter that what she was shown was in fact a picture of a very skillfully manufactured *porcelain* cat, so that her response had been incorrect (for porcelain cats are not cats). The subject might well wonder what she was being tested *on* and would be surprised to learn that her *linguistic* competence had been at stake. She would probably object that there was nothing wrong with her performance from a linguistic viewpoint: she had shown herself to possess the kind and amount of ability expected from a normal speaker if he is to be regarded as competent on a word like 'cat'.

The moral is this: normally, semantic competence is ascribed to a speaker on the basis of his ability to apply superficial recognition procedures in ordinary circumstances. The reason is that, in ordinary circumstances and most of the time, such procedures are indeed reliable. That they are not *always* reliable, and that even ordinary speakers know that they are sometimes not, is no reason for not identifying the basis of referential competence with the ability to carry out such procedures. If referential competence required that one could apply words according to the standard in all circumstances and without exception, nobody, not even the expert, would turn out to be competent. But even requiring *more* than the ability to carry out superficial procedures would be misguided: first, because it would make most speakers incompetent; second, because it would ignore the adequacy of such superficial procedures in most cases and in ordinary circumstances.[9]

The conclusion is as follows. As in the case of inferential competence, it is impossible to establish a priori what amount or degree of recognitional ability counts as referential competence. Depending on social and natural factors, the amount and nature of the recognitional ability regarded as relevant or even necessary to linguistic competence varies widely from word category to word category and even from word to word within the same category (consider 'common cold' versus 'sickle-cell anemia'). An artificial system that were made referentially competent in the sense in which a normal speaker is would have to be taught different abilities in different cases. However, for many common words, recognitional abilities based on superficial properties appear to constitute a significant core of referential competence.

Verificationism

Now for the charge of verificationism. Notice first of all that it is not my intention to *identify* semantic competence with the ability to verify sentences. The question is, at most, whether verification abilities are relevant to understanding. I believe they are, in the following limited sense: as far as words such as 'cat', 'yellow', or 'walk' are concerned, the inability (under normal circumstances) to verify simple sentences in which they occur would be regarded as evidence of semantic incompetence. This, of course, does not mean that the same should be said of such words as 'although', 'eight', or 'function'.[10] Nor does it mean that recognition (and verification) abilities are a *sufficient* condition of semantic competence. One standard objection to verificationism is based on the fact that there are lots of sentences we seem to understand, although we have no idea of how to go about verifying them: sentences like 'God exists', 'Positrons are made of quarks', 'Aristotle liked onions', to borrow some of Fodor's examples (1981, 216). This objection is irrelevant to the view I have been defending. I do not hold that understanding a sentence is or requires knowing how to verify it. Understanding a sentence is a complex process that draws from both structural and lexical competence. Lexical competence, in turn, is partly inferential and partly referential. For *some* sentences, the ability to verify them is a necessary condition of linguistic competence in the sense specified above. But note that for many sentences, the process by which they are validated does not directly involve "the real world" or "experience" or perception. Neither 'Positrons are made of quarks' nor 'Aristotle liked onions' would be validated by being directly correlated with perceptual input. This does not mean that such sentences only *appear* to be about the real world (but are really about, say, our database). Being about the real world is an intricate and obscure notion that certainly does not reduce to being verifiable by appeal to perceptual input. Fodor (1981, 219) may well be right that being about the real world is a holistic notion, meaning that a proposition may be said to be about the world because of a very roundabout itinerary through many layers of our knowledge, both theoretical and perceptual. Thus the relation of understanding and verification is as follows: (1) Not all sentences that may be said to be about the real world are therefore to be verified in perception. (2) Verification is not necessarily verification in perception. (3) Understanding is neither identical to, nor does it require the availability of, a method of verification in any sense. (4) Yet for some sentences, the ability to verify them is a necessary condition of understanding.

It could still be objected that even within such limitations, the ability to verify a sentence is at most a *symptom* of understanding; it cannot be a necessary condition. The argument runs as follows. Most cases of understanding are cases of understanding *in absentia*: in most cases, the texts and speeches we understand (daily newspapers, novels, our friends' accounts of their own feats) are not about the scene we have under our eyes at the moment of understanding. In all such cases, verification is simply impossible. Yet there are also cases of understanding *in praesentia*. Examples are reading the instructions for a household appliance while looking at the machine and its controls, obeying an order such as 'Take the book in front of you and read the first line on p. 28', listening to a person who is telling us about his medical condition. But such cases, though frequent, are not the most frequent. To account for natural-language understanding is essentially to account for understanding *in absentia*: verification simply does not come into the picture.

Moreover, Johnson-Laird (1983, 246) has plausibly argued that understanding fictional discourse is not essentially different from understanding nonfictional discourse: the distinction, all-important as it is in other respects, is irrelevant from the standpoint of language processing. A fortiori, *in absentia* understanding, one can say, cannot differ in kind from understanding *in praesentia*.[11] So even in the case of understanding *in praesentia*, the possibility of verification cannot be crucial.

However, the argument as it stands fails to draw the (obvious) distinction between not being in a position to verify a sentence and being unable to verify it. Right now I am not in a position to verify the sentence 'There are six people sitting in the next room', but it would clearly be inappropriate to say that I am unable to verify it or that I don't know how to verify it. The clearest cases of understanding *in absentia* seem to be of this type: they are cases in which one is not in a position to verify whatever is asserted but would know how to do it (of course, one is usually unwilling to). The same purpose would be served by a distinction between the *ability* to verify a sentence and the *possibility* of verifying it: I may have the ability without there being the objective possibility, or vice versa. What we lack in the case of *in absentia* understanding is the possibility of verification, but this proves nothing concerning our possessing the ability to verify or the role it plays in understanding.

But if what matters (when it does matter) is not actual verification but the ability to verify, why should we want an artificial system to carry out actual verifications? The answer is simple: it is the only way to effectively show that the system does possess the required abilities. Until we face the problem of actual verification, we will tend to have systems that construct semantic representations (of single sentences or whole texts), which are nothing but formulas of a more or less formal language, themselves in need of interpretation. The only way to build a system to which we would grant genuine semantic competence is to build a system that can actually verify natural-language sentences. Of course, understanding, even understanding *in praesentia*, neither consists in nor requires actual verification, but there is no better evidence of understanding than actual verification.

The Inertness of Images and Kant's Schematism

Let us go back to the artificial system and wonder what would be required for it to be referentially competent. First of all, the system must be able to perceive—typically, to see the real world, just like us (Harnad 1989, 15). For an artificial system, the beginning of referential competence is to be found in artificial vision.

I must avoid a possible misunderstanding. There is a naive picture of the relation of perception to semantic competence that keeps coming back, in spite of Wittgenstein's attempts at dispelling it (1953) and of Putnam's more recent criticism (1981). In this naive view, part of semantic competence is represented by a certain store of mental images associated with words, such as the image of a dog, of a table, of a running man. Thanks to these images we can apply to the real world words such as 'dog', 'table', and 'run'. This is done by comparing our images with the output of perception (particularly of vision). Sometimes the picture may be supported by reference to prototype theory, although the theory does not license it, as we saw (chapter 1, pp. 22–28). Now, the point is not that we lack mental images: there are good reasons to believe that we do have something of the kind.[12] The point is that in the naive picture, the use of the images in relation to the real world or the perceptual scene is left undescribed. In Putnam's words, "One could possess any system of images you please and not possess the ability to use the sentences in situationally appropriate ways.... For the image, if not accompanied by the ability to act in a certain way, is just a picture, and acting in accordance with a picture is itself an ability that one may or may not have" (1981, 19). In other words, in the naive picture the whole explanatory burden is carried by the relation of comparison between an image and the perceptual scene, which relation (or process or whatever) is itself unexplained. This is partly true even of sophisticated accounts of the connection of language and perception such as Jackendoff's (1992), which makes recourse to Marr's models as highly structured "pictures" attached to (some) individual words. In chapter 4 (pp. 80–81) we saw that 3-D models do not include the procedures for matching them with the output of vision. Even 3-D models in themselves just sit there, like all other pictures.

One wonders why in this case the picture that "holds us captive" (Wittgenstein 1953, sec. 115) is so strong. Perhaps one tends to think of the mental connection between language and perception on the pattern of the connection, in dictionaries, between words and the pictures meant to illustrate them. You have the entry corresponding to the word 'dolphin', containing all sorts of information including a "definition" of 'dolphin', and then you have a picture of a dolphin (a line drawing or maybe a photograph), and the idea is that, thanks to the picture much more than to the linguistic description that the entry may contain, the word acquires perceptual content, so that you will be able to recognize dolphins, you'll know what to look for when required to look for a dolphin, you won't make mistakes of a certain kind when asked to count the dolphins in an aquarium, and so forth. All of this is indeed true (to some extent), not because the connection between the word 'dolphin' and the picture of a dolphin somehow brings about the ability to apply the word to the output of perception or because the picture contains instructions for its match with perceptual outputs, but because *we* know how to use such pictures. Thus, imagine an artificial system endowed with a list of words ('dog', 'cat', 'dolphin', 'armchair', 'car', etc.) each of which has a pointer to a digitalized picture (of a dog, a cat, and so forth). Imagine further that the system were endowed with artificial vision, in the sense that it can process light signals all the way up to Marr's $2\frac{1}{2}$-D sketches. Still, the system could not decide whether or not the perceived scene contains a dog unless it were also endowed with procedures to match the pictures in its catalog with $2\frac{1}{2}$-D sketches. Illustrated dictionaries have no such procedures: *we* do. Pictures in dictionaries do reinforce, or even create, referential competence relative to the words they are attached to; they can do so because we can interpret pictures (or at any rate, the kind of pictures customarily used in our culture for such purposes) and match them with the output of visual processes. Illustrated dictionaries *presuppose* such a general ability; they do not generate it.

Interestingly, Kant saw more clearly than some modern theorists that the interface of language and perception has to be procedural in nature.[13] Such an insight is embedded in his doctrine of the schematism in the *Critique of Pure Reason*. The doctrine is intended to solve many different problems at the same time,[14] which makes it difficult and at times confused. Prominent in Kant's own presentation is the problem of explaining how pure concepts, which do not include anything empirical, could apply to the phenomena: how can we, for instance, *perceive* causal connections in nature? We need to postulate an intermediary, "some third thing, which is homogeneous on the one hand with the category, and on the other hand with the appearance, and which thus makes the application of the former to the latter possible" (Kant 1929 [1781], B 177, A 138). Such an intermediary is the *schema*. Though they are created by productive imagination, schemata are not images: they are methods, or as Kant says, "universal procedures" (Kant 1929 [1781], B 179–180, A 140) for associating images with concepts.[15] Thus schemata are procedural in nature: they are not pictures but methods for the generation of pictures.

Kant's discussion of why this has to be so is complicated by his need to give a uniform treatment of two kinds of schemata: those attaching to mathematical concepts, intended for application in pure intuition, and those attaching to empirical concepts, such as the concept of dog (Kant's own example). Here I will disregard the complication, for I am mainly interested in what Kant has to say concerning the relation of concepts to intuitions in the case of empirical concepts.[16] Kant's reasons for regarding schemata as procedures are most clearly formulated in his discussion of mathematical examples. The essential reason is that images lack generality, so they are constantly exceeded by the concepts for which they are intended to go proxy. The clearest example Kant gives resumes a time-honored discussion:[17]

No image could ever be adequate to the concept of a triangle in general. It would never attain that universality of the concept which renders it valid of all triangles [*welcher macht, dass dieser für alle . . . gilt*], whether right-angled, obtuse-angled, or acute-angled; it would always be limited to a part only of this sphere. (Kant 1929, B 180, A 141)

Another example is related to numbers:

If five points be set alongside one another, thus, ... , I have an image of the number five. But if, on the other hand, I think only a number in general, whether it be five or a hundred, this thought is rather the representation of a method whereby a multiplicity, for instance a thousand, may be represented in an image in conformity with a certain concept, than the image itself. For with such a number as a thousand the image can hardly be surveyed and compared with the concept. (Kant 1929, B 179, A 140)

Here the problem is that what can count as the image of a certain number does not count as the image of *any* number.[18] In the previous case, the problem was that what can count as the image of a certain subclass of triangles cannot count as an image of the concept of a triangle. In both cases, images are clearly inadequate to figuratively represent the concepts they are intended to so represent: each individual image is exceeded by the concept it is meant to represent. Only a procedure can be endowed with the required generality: what can act as an intermediary between a pure concept (such as that of triangle) and intuition is the general procedure by which we construct images of triangles (or perhaps better, triangular images) in intuition. According to Kant, this is no less true in the case of empirical concepts:

The concept "dog" signifies a rule [*bedeutet eine Regel*] according to which my imagination can delineate the figure of a four-footed animal in a general manner, without limitation to any single determinate figure such as experience, or any possible image that I can represent *in concreto*, actually presents. (Kant 1929, B 180, A 141)

Here too the concept exceeds in generality both the object of experience and its image. Therefore, we must think of an empirical concept as "always stand[ing] in immediate relation to the schema of imagination, as a rule for the determination of our intuition, in accordance with some specific universal concept" (Kant 1929, B 180, A 141). Empirical concepts are applied in intuition by being associated with a method for "determining" intuitions.[19]

So Kant emphasizes that images cannot mediate between concepts and intuitions, because of their lack of generality. It is not because of an *image* of a dog that we can recognize dogs: what if a particular dog does not fit the particular image? This is certainly part of the reason why the interface between language and perception must be procedural in nature, but it cannot be the only reason, for no image can fit perception (not even its own copy in perception) unless it is specified what it is for an image to *fit* something. Images do not include their own application. Kant, I believe, did not see this side of the problem because, although he also meant his account to hold for empirical concepts, he was concentrating on mathematical schemata as intermediaries between mathematical concepts and constructions in *pure* intuition. In pure intuition, five points may count as an image for the number 5: the issue of such an image's fitting *empirical* intuition (that is, operating as an intermediary in the application of the concept of five to a group of five objects or, in other words, playing a role in counting objects in perception) simply does not arise.

Actually, however, both sides of the problem have a common root. Images are things, not rules. Thus they cannot connect anything to anything else (in particular, they cannot connect themselves to the output of perception or compare themselves to other images or generate other images with themselves as a pattern). On the other hand, as they are things, images are *particular* things (there are no other kinds of things). Consequently, they are different (in some respect) from most other images of the same kind or "falling under the same concept." Therefore, if to "fit" something else, in particular, another image, it is required that an image be exactly like it, then no image can fit most other images of the same kind. Of these two difficulties, the former is more basic, for, to repeat, even if an image were exactly like another (in some relevant sense), still a method of comparison would be needed by way of which it could be *found* to be exactly like it.

Artificial Vision and Artificial Competence

Systems of artificial vision as described by Rosenfeld (1988) do not literally contain images, not even digitalized images. Classes of objects the system can recognize (for example, tables or cubes) are identified with classes of shapes, which are themselves interpreted as relational structures, that is, labeled graphs where the nodes represent object parts and the arcs represent relations between parts: a node is labeled with an ideal property value or a set of constraints on such a value, whereas an arc is labeled with a relation value or a set of constraints on such a value. For example, a table is identified with a class of shapes expressed by a relational structure whose nodes represent parts of the table (top, legs) and whose arcs represent relations between two parts. Node and arc labels are not absolute values but constraints on possible values. The problem of recognizing a table in a scene is then the problem of "finding subgraphs of the scene graph that are close matches to the object graph, or that satisfy the constraints defined by the object graph" (Rosenfeld 1988, 286). The scene graph is the result of a sequence of processing stages. In the first stage, the image provided by a sensor is digitalized, that is, converted into an array of numbers "representing brightness or color values at a discrete grid of points in the image plane" (Rosenfeld 1988, 266) or average values in the neighborhoods of such points (elements of the array are called 'pixels'). In the second stage (segmentation), pixels are classified according to several criteria, such as brightness or belonging to the same local pattern (for example, a vertical stroke). In the third stage (resegmentation), parts of the image such as rectilinear strokes, curves, angles, etc., are explicitly recognized and labeled. In the fourth stage, properties and relations of such local patterns are identified, both their geometric properties and relations and, for example, the distribution of grey levels through a given local pattern, color relations between two patterns, etc. The scene graph's nodes are the local patterns with their properties, and its arcs are the relations among local patterns with their values. To recognize a table in a scene is thus, as we saw, to find a subgraph of the scene graph that satisfies the constraints associated with the table graph. In practice, recognition is complicated by several factors: it is hard to make recognition invariant with respect to different illumination conditions, and three-dimensional vision raises many additional problems. In what follows, I will disregard these kinds of problems (though they are, of course, far from trivial) in order to focus on others.

From my viewpoint, the content of an artificial system's referential competence relative to the word 'table' can be identified with the relational structure associated with the class of tables, together with the matching algorithm that applies it to the analyzed scene.[20] If a system were endowed with competence of this kind, plus a minimal amount of structural semantic competence and inferential competence, it could verify sentences such as 'There is a vase on a table', 'There is a vase on the table', 'There are two small chairs in front of the table', etc.

Verification would go like this.[21] The sentence 'There is a vase on a table' would be subjected to traditional natural-language processing and would issue in a semantic representation. Such a representation would specify at least the following:

1. The sentence's logical structure as expressed, typically, by a first-order logical formula; in this case, something corresponding to $(\exists x)(\exists y)(\text{vase}(x)\ \&\ \text{table}(y)\ \&\ \text{on}(x, y))$.

2. A certain amount of inferential information attaching to the individual words (such as information about a vase's function, the hyponymical connection between 'table' and 'furniture', information about typical contexts of both kinds of objects, etc.). Lexical ambiguities (including the ambiguity of 'on') should be resolved at this level, to the extent that they can be resolved on the basis of the system's inferential and structural competence. The residual ambiguities would be recorded in the form of different possible "senses" (that is, inferential sub-networks) relative to each individual word, with pointers, indices, indicating cross-associations among senses.

3. Pointers to structural descriptions, that is, to the relational structures associated with words in the system's catalog of shapes. Of course, such information is available not for all words but only for words that have a visual content, that is, a characteristic shape.

Verification of the sentence in the scene (which I imagine to have been processed by the system's visual module) would be based on such a semantic representation. In one example (Meini and Paternoster 1996), the system would first carry out object recognition, that is, it would try to locate one or more vases and one or more tables in the scene's graph, using the structural descriptions associated with 'vase' and 'table'. Suppose that it succeeded, and suppose further that only one vase and one table were recognized (it is easy to see how the complications resulting from multiple recognition would be dealt with). The system would then proceed to establish whether the spatial relation between the relevant scene subgraphs could be described by 'on', relying on the spatial constraints associated with (the selected sense of) 'on'. In case of success, the system would regard the sentence as verified in the scene. Notice that the algorithm is determined by the sentence's logical form as given under (1) above: one can say that the system is reading the sentence's truth conditions as verification conditions. Inferential information recorded under (2) above would be used in case of failure at any stage in the verification process. Thus suppose that the scene does contain a vase, which is, however, so filled with flowers that its shape is not identifiable. Knowing that vases are typically used to contain flowers, the system could try to recognize flowers or a vase-full-of-flowers or both.

There is no doubt that all or most of this is extremely hard to actually carry out, except in the most favorable of cases. However, before looking at the obvious complications, let us see whether there are objections of principle to the suggestion that semantic competence could reasonably be ascribed to such a system, integrating natural-language processing and artificial vision.

The Robot Reply

A classic objection is Searle's answer to what he labeled "the robot reply." Searle himself formulated, examined, and dismissed the robot reply, one of the possible reactions to the Chinese-room thought experiment. It goes like this:

> Suppose we put a computer inside a robot, and this computer would not just take in formal symbols as input and give out formal symbols as output, but rather would actually operate the robot in such a way that the robot does something very much like perceiving, walking, ..., anything you like. The robot would, for example, have a television camera attached to it that enabled it to "see," it would have arms and legs that enabled it to "act," and all of this would be controlled by its computer "brain." Such a robot would ... have genuine understanding and other mental states. (Searle 1980, 420)

So the robot reply is in line with my present suggestion: though it does not explicitly spell out *why* the computer-robot would genuinely understand language, it clearly implies that artificial perception (and action) would make a difference, the difference being that artificial perception would endow the system (the complete system, of course) with referential competence.

Searle's answer to the robot reply is, essentially, that the Chinese-room thought experiment still applies. Suppose that I am in the room, inputting Chinese symbols and rules for their manipulation, and suppose further that,

> unknown to me, some of the Chinese symbols that come to me come from a television camera attached to the robot and other Chinese symbols that I am giving out serve to make the motors inside the robot move the robot's legs or arms.... I know none of these other facts. I am receiving "information" from the robot's "perceptual" apparatus, and I am giving out "instructions" to its motor apparatus without knowing either of these facts. I am the robot's homunculus, but ... I don't understand anything except the rules for symbol manipulation.... The robot has no intentional states at all.... And furthermore, by instantiating the program I have no intentional states of the relevant type. (Searle 1980, 420)

There is some confusion here: who is supposed to be the equivalent of the computer inside the robot: me inside the room, or me and the robot inside the room? It appears, me inside the room, but part of the room is really, unknown to me, the robot. So let that be the situation. Searle's point is that just as images from the camera come to me (inside the room) in the form of *just another bunch of Chinese scribbles*, so televised scenes and other perceptual contents are just more symbols to the computer, and the rules attaching words, for example, to perceived elements are just rules for the manipulation of symbols, like all others. The computer inside the robot is still aware only of uninterpreted symbols and rules for their manipulation. It doesn't see scenes and attach words to their constituents. It just inputs symbols and manipulates them according to syntactic rules (the symbols are of different kinds, to tell the truth, though Searle is rather hasty on this). Similarly, Searle would say, my integrated system is just another symbol manipulator: pointers to procedures for the analysis of scenes, object graphs, scene graphs—all this is just a lot of meaningless symbols.

The obvious reply is, can't we give the same description *of our own* cognitive structure and performance? "If [one] still regard[s] the computer-plus-sensory-transducers as merely a syntactic device, then surely *we* are only syntactic devices too, since light just produces code at the retina and sound only produces code at the cochlea" (Harnad 1989, 15). Where should we expect, for example, the referential significance of lexical units to come from if not from their being connected with such "code"? Searle's answer appeals to the "causal powers" of the brain: referential significance, like all other intentional properties, is produced by the brain (how, we don't know). However, as such an answer is totally devoid of explanatory power, it should be interpreted as little more than a restatement of the thought experiment's conclusion: no matter where it comes from, referential significance *cannot* come from a symbol's being connected with other symbols; witness the Chinese-room thought experiment.

So eventually it all comes down to whether it is correct to describe the televised scenes and other perceptual contents as just more Chinese scribbles. Why should they be so described? Why can't we say that the man in the room is seeing *images*, as we do when we watch TV?[22] The reason is that Searle believes that *the system* (the computer) does not identify the visual input as visual, and the reason for this is that there cannot be any difference in kind between linguistic data, visual data, and any other data accessible to a computer: once more, they are just symbols, all of them. That the visual input has a different cause than the linguistic input (it is produced by an artificial vision module interacting with the actual scene) does not make any relevant difference to the input itself, nor does it attach a special intentional content to it from the computer's standpoint.

Why does it make a difference *for us*, allowing us to identify visual input as such? How are *we* supposed to identify visual input as visual, except by its being input *of a certain kind,* coming through a certain channel? This is information that the system too may be supposed to possess: the system, for example, surely can discriminate between, say, scene graphs and words. They are symbols of different forms, bearing the mark of the different channels through which they have been taken in. What is it to be *visual* input, aside from having been (recognizably) generated by a certain kind of process? Searle's answer would be that it is being the kind of input that *we* experience as visual. Such an answer appears to depend on an a priori decision not to regard the notion of vision as generalizable beyond human experience. It is like deciding that flying is what *birds* do: whatever other creatures or devices may do does not count as flying (unless they are biological replicas of birds). I doubt that we are really inclined to make such a decision in the case of vision: for example, when one speaks of artificial vision, one does not feel that one is using 'vision' metaphorically. But anyway, as Wittgenstein pointed out (1958, 57–58), one does not really *argue* with such decisions.

Limitations of Artificial Competence

Let us now go back to the referentially competent system for immediate complications. A system of the kind we designed is essentially a shape-recognition system. However, the part of the lexicon whose application is entirely governed by shape recognition is strongly limited, in several ways and for different reasons. Here I will merely hint at some of the problems one has to face when really trying to articulate the notion of referential competence.

First, a general remark. One may be tempted to say that for *all* words, external appearance (not to say visual appearance) is at best a necessary condition for application. Something may look like a *cat* and yet (as more accurate examination would determine) not be a cat; two people may only be pretending to be *fighting,* even though their simulation would deceive any observer; an object may seem to be *floating* on water, while really being supported from below or suspended from above; and so forth. However, such a generalization would be both false and misleading. It would be false, for there are objects whose external appearance does not deceive us, except perhaps in highly nonstandard circumstances: something looking like a spoon *is* a spoon (though it may not be *used* as such, but this is a different matter). Even if the thing turned out to be a living creature spying on us and our food habits, it would still deserve to be called 'spoon' ("evil spoons from Mars"). Similarly, there may be fake cats and fake pistols, but there are no fake chairs: even a chair made of cardboard, and therefore so fragile that nobody could really sit in it, would still deserve to be called 'chair' (and it is indeed called so, for example, by set-designers in the movie industry). Second, the generalization would be misleading: it would make us obfuscate the very different roles that external appearance plays in the application of different words. This is exactly what I want to focus on. Therefore, in the examples that follow I will disregard difficulties of recognition related to imitation, simulation, and other forms of contrast between appearance and reality. We don't want the referentially competent artificial system to be smarter than most of us, anyway.

There are words that, though they are used to designate physical objects (and are therefore different in this respect from words such as 'nevertheless' or 'entail'), are not applied on the basis of external appearance. We do not see or otherwise perceive that x is an *uncle* or that y is a *contract* or that x is the *owner* of z. One sees that x is a man, which is a necessary requirement for being an uncle, but men who are uncles do not look like anything particular: they may be very young or very old, fat or thin, tall or short. Even sophisticated biological tests would be of no avail. Our referential competence with 'uncle' reduces to our competence with 'man': one sees that someone is a man and may *know* that he is an uncle. Thus it would be wrong to say that our referential competence with such words is empty. However, strictly recognitional abilities play a very limited role in it. To apply such words, a system of the kind we designed would have to make ample recourse not only to its inferential competence but also to what may properly be called 'factual knowledge'.

If words such as 'uncle' or 'owner' represent one extreme (there is no such thing as looking like an uncle or an owner), the opposite extreme is represented by words such as 'block', 'chair', 'pencil', 'can', which are applied to objects whose appearances may vary as to size and color but have a high degree of geometric constancy. Practically all

Figure 6.1
What a chair looks like.

Figure 6.2
The typical observatory.

chairs look very much like figure 6.1 (where the phrase 'look very much like figure 6.1' can, with some effort, be given a geometrically precise meaning). Still, even within this category one may want to distinguish between cases in which different materials can make a significant visual difference in spite of geometric constancy and cases of overall visual constancy. The visual appearance of a stuffed Louis XVI chair is rather different from that of a metal and plastic office chair, although the geometric structure is the same in both cases. By contrast, all pencils look very much like one another.

In between, we find a continuum of cases, which may be thought of as organized according to the extent to which the phrase 'looks like an x' is appropriate. Take words such as 'observatory', 'theater', 'restaurant'. These are applied to objects whose appearances may vary widely. However, the words are associated with stereotypical aspects, knowledge of which is part of referential competence. Thus the typical observatory looks like figure 6.2, although there have been and are observatories that don't much look like figure 6.2. Many verbs may be like the noun 'observatory' in this respect: although there are many visually distinct ways to *dive* or to *carry* something, there probably are visually stereo-typical ways of diving and carrying (the knowledge of which is part of referential competence).

Further along the continuum, we find words with which not one but several typical aspects are associated: words for "superordinate con-cepts" such as 'toy', 'weapon', or 'clothing'. In dictionaries, such words are often illustrated by what have been called 'enumerative illustrations' (Hupka 1989, 711): tables that show different kinds of toys, weapons, or clothing. Clearly, 'looking like a toy', though not meaningless, is less appropriate than 'looking like a chair'. Perhaps there is no such thing as the characteristic aspect of a toy. There are, however, typical toys (dolls, balls, puppets, toy cars, etc.), each of which has a characteristic aspect. Therefore, it would be a mistake to say that competence with 'toy' or 'weapon' is purely inferential in that it reduces to knowledge of the definitional *functions* of toys or weapons. It would be more appropriate to say that referential competence with 'toy' is indirect, in that it necessarily relies on referential competence relative to 'ball', 'doll', and other words that are inferentially connected with 'toy'.

Such superordinate words raise a general problem for the con-struction of a referentially competent system. Suppose that we want the system to be able to verify a simple sentence such as 'There is a toy on the table' in a given scene. Intuitively, one would think that to verify the sentence, we human beings go through the following steps: first, we look at the table top; second, we identify whatever objects are on it; third, we decide whether any of them can be described as a toy. It is hard to accept that we may instead start with a list of toy types (ball, doll, puppet, skates, train, etc.) and proceed to determine whether any such object is on the table. However, that would be the only procedure open to the system as we imagined it to be designed: to verify the sentence 'There is a toy on the table', the system would have to verify at least one sentence in a finite list constructed from the inferential meaning of 'toy', that is, it must verify either 'There is a doll on the table' or 'There is a ball on the table', etc. As far as I know, today's vision systems can (under certain conditions) recognize objects in a scene starting with the objects, but not starting with the scene (Rosenfeld 1988, 287–288). They can determine whether and where in a scene a given object is located starting with the object's definition ("top-down recognition"), but they cannot determine which objects are present starting with a scene's analysis ("bottom-up recognition"). In order to solve problems of this kind, the system ought to have a different architecture.[23]

Still further along the continuum we have words such as 'tool', applying to a wide variety of objects of very different sizes and shapes that do not naturally fall into a relatively limited number of subclasses (or less so than weapons and clothing, etc.). Such words are often said to have a purely functional semantics: a tool is (primarily) "any instrument of manual operation,"[24] that is, any object operated by hand for a purpose. Therefore, there can't be any such thing as "looking like a tool." Nevertheless, there are typical tools (hammers, screwdrivers, scissors, and so on), that is, there are subclasses of tools that are "good representatives" of the category (in the sense of prototype theory) and whose members have a characteristic aspect. All this is part of our competence concerning 'tool'. Thus even 'tool' does not have a purely inferential semantics. The difference from words such as 'uncle' should be clear: there are no good representatives of the category 'uncle' (or 'owner').

There are words that most of us are quite competent with referentially, that are applied to objects possessing a characteristic aspect, and that are applied (mostly) on grounds of visual information; nevertheless, such words present a problem for an artificial system such as the one we designed, for the associated characteristic aspect, the 3-D model, let's say, is clearly insufficient to decide application. Take the word 'box'. The problem with 'box' is not simply that there are prismlike boxes, cylindrical boxes, cubic boxes, and more, but that it is essential to a box to be a container. A parallelepiped of solid wood, size $25 \times 10 \times 5$ cm, is not a box. A parallelepiped of the same size that has a groove parallel to its base is not a box either. Whether an object is recognized (correctly in normal cases) as a box depends on many factors, most of which are not available to a mere shape recognizer. Many common words are like 'box' in this respect: 'desk', 'ball' (as opposed to 'sphere'), 'dish', 'lever', 'antenna'. Among the factors governing their application, two can easily be singled out. On the one hand, they apply to objects having a characteristic aspect, which, however, is not captured by their 3-D model. Thus a dish has a typical aspect different from a disk's, but the 3-D model of a dish is just the model of a disk. From this viewpoint, the problem raised by such words is just the roughness of our shape recognizer: the referential procedures it can (realistically) be assumed to use do not have the right granularity. So this can be seen as a technical difficulty. On the other hand, that something, a metal stick, is recognized as a lever largely depends on *contextual* factors: where it is located, what function it may be presumed to play. Now functions or possible functions are not something one *sees*, although there are *visual cues* to function, that is, relatively stable associations between certain visual features of the object itself or the place it is located and the object's presumable function. A disk on a table set for a meal is presumably a dish; a thin metal stick on a roof-top is probably an antenna; a sphere in a child's room is probably a ball. This is were the inferential associations embedded in a sentence's semantic representation become relevant: they can be exploited to decide application in cases in which application is partly governed by such visual cues. However, I should note that in many cases, identification of an object's context is extremely hard for an artificial recognizer, even when it depends on purely visual factors. Think of the identification of a table set for dinner, or of Wittgenstein's locomotive cabin (1953, sec. 12), or of a child's room.

Many verbs of motion have a strongly referential component: competence with them requires that one be able to visually identify situations and activities that, in turn, have a typical appearance, a physiognomy. In some cases (such as those of 'knock' or 'kick') the stereotypical scene may be unique, in others (such as those of 'jump', 'swim', or 'run') there may be a limited variety of visual stereotypes. Even in the simplest cases, however, the ability to apply such words requires the ability to identify complex patterns of motion in complex situations. For today's systems of artificial vision, such abilities are definitely out of reach. So there is a sizable part of a normal speaker's referential competence that cannot realistically be attributed to an artificial system. This is, in a sense, a "technical" problem, not one of principle; however, its size is so great that one hesitates to present it as a *mere* technical problem (that is, one that is likely to be solved in a few years, given the present rate of technological progress).

Is the artificial system we designed referentially competent, though minimally, in spite of all such limitations? Is it therefore *semantically* competent? Even though my own instinctive answer tends to be positive, this may be one of those cases in which a difference of degree becomes a qualitative difference: many would say that the system's competence is so poor anyway that it cannot pass for referential competence in the sense in which *we* may be said to be referentially competent. So I will not push the point any further. What I have established is that reflection on what would be needed to enhance an artificial system's referential competence is likely to cast much light on both the semantic variety of the lexicon and the structure of human semantic competence.

Notes

Introduction

1. I later discovered that a similar picture had been proposed by C. I. Lewis in the 1940s (Lewis 1943–1944), though not as a theory of competence but as a theory of intension (as opposed to extension). Lewis made a distinction (within intension) between an expression's *linguistic* meaning, the network of definitional and other relations between that expression and other expressions, and its *conceptual* meaning, or the mental criterion by which we choose to use or not to use the expression for objects and circumstances we may be confronted with. Lewis thought that conceptual meaning was necessarily connected with *images*: it is only thanks to imagination that linguistic expressions can be connected with objects (as applying to them) before such objects are actually present. However, conceptual meanings cannot *be* images, for images do not have the required generality (see the discussion of this point in chapter 6). They should rather be identified with Kant's schemata (see again chapter 6). Such interesting views could not survive the rejection of all forms of verificationism and operationalism in the 1960s.

Chapter 1

1. "Semantics without an adequate treatment of the lexicon is no semantics at all" (Bonomi 1987, 69).

2. 'Aristotle' in "Über Sinn und Bedeutung," the others in "Über Begriff und Gegenstand" (both in Frege 1980a). See also "Comments on Sense and Meaning" (Frege 1979, 119, 120, 123, etc.) and "Logic" (Frege 1979, 139–140).

3. "Logic" (Frege 1979, 126).

4. "Logic in Mathematics" (Frege 1979, 225).

5. Actually, even this is not a "fact" in the *Tractatus*'s technical sense, and even this cannot be said: it shows itself.

6. "Wittgenstein's 'simples' were to have the useful property of being non-composite, and were to combine with this the agreeable property that they could be treated as if they had a certain kind of complexity" (Pears 1979, 202).

7. The belief that such a correspondence between grammatical and semantic categories holds for a natural language such as English is part of the belief that English is a "logically perfect" language in the sense of Kaplan 1970. The other part is belief in the correspondence of syntactic structure and semantic composition.

8. As far as I know, in modern times Wittgenstein was the first to remark that there is no reason to assume that words are all alike in semantic function: "Think of the tools in a tool-box: there is a hammer, pliers, a saw, a screw-driver, a rule, a glue-pot, glue, nails and screws.—The functions of words are as diverse as the functions of these objects" (1953, §11). Putnam's ideas on the semantics of natural-kind words can be read as pointing to a semantic distinction within one and the same grammatical category (common nouns). More recently, Johnson-Laird underscored the "non-uniformity of intensions" even within the same grammatical category (1983, 195–197).

9. See for example, Harman 1975.

10. Field (1977, 401) objected that even Tarski's account of the meaning of logical connectives can be looked upon as essentially translational: to say that '$\sim p$' is true (relative to an interpretation) if and only if 'p' is not true (relative to that interpretation) tells us nothing, one might say, about the meaning of '$\sim$' that is not revealed by saying that '$\sim$' in the object language is to be translated into the metalanguage as 'not'. There are, however, other ways of phrasing the truth condition that would give an impression (at least) of being more informative, for example, "'$\sim p$' is true (under an interpretation) just in case 'p' is false (under the same interpretation)." Nothing can be made to correspond to such a formulation in the case of nonlogical words.

11. Thomason 1974, 49.

12. Philip Johnson-Laird has insisted on the need for explicit instructions at the lexical level: "One would want to know what information is in the 'body' of the function corresponding to the intension of [a] predicate, that is, what has to be computed in order to specify the individuals possessing the property. This problem is finessed in model-theoretic semantics, which merely posits the existence of such functions without indicating how they would work" (1983, 172–173).

13. See this chapter, pp. 17–18.

14. It was pointed out long ago that the difference between 'They got married and had a child' and 'They had a child and got married' is not accounted for by the truth-conditional semantics for 'and' (Strawson 1952, 80). More generally, see Grice's remarks on the cleavage between the (standard) semantic rules for the connectives and their "total signification" (1975; 1978; 1989, chap. 1, pp. 8–9).

15. That $a = b$ is seldom analytic, for it is seldom a priori, had, of course, been noted by Frege at the very beginning of "Über Sinn und Bedeutung" (1980b, 56).

16. Church 1951a, 1951b.

17. This was, however, somewhat anticipated by Carnap himself (see 1956b, 181).

18. Johnson-Laird 1983, 232, 258–259; Marconi 1989, 76–77.

19. *Pace* Putnam 1975c for the sake of this particular argument.

20. Such stipulation is subject to the formation rules for the language, the "semantic rules" for the connectives and quantifiers, and the Tarskian taxonomy of logical types for the descriptive constants, which Carnap inherits: unary predicates have sets of individuals as their extensions, etc.

21. Carnap himself did not have possible worlds; he had *state descriptions*, that is, sets of atomic sentences and negations of atomic sentences such that for each atomic sentence of the language, either the sentence is in state description D or its negation is (but not both). Possible worlds, as they are used in the standard semantics of modal logic, differ from state descriptions in several ways: for example, state descriptions as they are constructed by Carnap share the same individuals, whereas in the case of possible worlds, it is a separate stipulation that they do. However, nothing hinges on these differences in the present context.

22. In Montague's work (1974c, 263) meaning postulates are constraints on *admissible models* (interpretations) for a language. This makes a difference, for in Montague 1974c each interpretation comes with its own set of possible worlds. In Carnap there is no distinction, for the set of state descriptions is assumed to be fixed, given a language, as it is determined only by the structure and vocabulary of the language. It begs the question to say, like Katz (1986, 194), that "meaning postulates do not describe meaning at all. They state an extensional condition but not one reflecting meaning relations," so "the name 'meaning postulate' is a misnomer." Katz is assuming that intensions cannot be meanings, as they are constructed from extensions. Meaning postulates do state "an extensional condition," but one holding (at least) in all possible worlds: thus they concern intensions, not extensions.

23. We can define analyticity either directly, as we did above, or through a redefinition of L-truth, taking L-truth to be the *explicatum* of analyticity, as Carnap himself did (1956c, 225–226).

24. Brandom calls such inferences "materially good," as opposed to 'logically good' (Brandom 1994, 168).

25. 'Competence' is inherently ambiguous, for on the one hand, we use it for *any* degree of ability in the use of language, and on the other hand, we often restrict it to *socially adequate* ability. Thus we might say, that a given speaker is incompetent means not that he has no command at all of a certain fragment of the lexicon but that his command is insufficient for certain purposes (which may vary). In what follows, such an ambiguity will be left to take care of itself in most cases. However, in chapter 5, I will address the issue of the hierarchy of competences, that is, of the effects on individual competence of the fact that semantic competences are not regarded as equal.

26. "The main purpose of semantic representation is to provide a level at which sound inference can take place" (Thomason 1991, 7).

27. Realistically, the object language is a fragment of a language such as English.

28. It does not make any difference for the argument whether I assigns intensions (rather than denotations) to the descriptive constants of the language.

29. "The use of a language would ideally involve not only the determination of the collection of *all* models of the language (a determination sufficient for the *logical* notions …), but also the specification of a particular, *actual* model" (Montague 1974a, 209).

30. This can be understood in several ways: the "informational content" of (8), the "cognitive or informational input" provided by (8), what a competent speaker comes to believe when he believes (8), etc.

31. I heard this remark from Terence Parsons at the Karlóvy-Váry Conference on Meaning (September 1993). His paper was called "Theories of Meaning and Truth for Natural Languages."

32. So the matter is not simply that "pure" truth conditions (without meaning postulates) do not suffice for genuine semantic interpretation, as Bonomi (1987, 62–66) seems to put it. Even truth conditions *with* meaning postulates do not suffice.

33. Partee refers to R. Grandy "and others." Similar difficulties were highlighted by H. Putnam (1983a) in his well-known "model-theoretic argument" against metaphysical realism.

34. Such consequences of the Löwenheim-Skolem theorem were originally pointed out by Quine (1969) and Putnam (1983a). Lakoff (1987, 235) remarked that Putnam's argument does not depend on a restriction to first-order languages, for Putnam's point is that truth (for example, of meaning postulates) underdetermines reference (of their constituent expressions). Thus the argument in this form is not a corollary of the Löwenheim-Skolem theorem; it only depends on the general features of semantic interpretation in the model-theoretic sense (including compositionality).

35. "With symbols defined only in terms of more symbols, their meanings are ungrounded. The problem is rather like trying to learn Chinese from a Chinese-Chinese dictionary alone, without any prior knowledge of Chinese" (Harnad 1989, 15; see also Harnad 1990).

36. This interpretation is correct, I believe; however, it is slightly misleading in that it can be taken as the statement that meaning postulates have no semantic import. This is not so. The point is that meaning postulates are insufficient to represent lexical meaning, not that they are vacuous. An example of an overstatement of this point is the following quotation from Haiman: "Given the three Ooga Booga words 'nooze', 'thung', and 'slimp' and the information that 'nooze' is the converse of 'thung', which, in its turn, is a hyponym of 'slimp', we clearly know nothing about any of them. One of them (it does not matter which) must be named by ostension" (1980, 333). I would say that we know, about the three words, exactly what we have been told and what follows from it. This is clearly not enough to recognize a slimp or to obey an order involving a thung (if there be any such); on the other hand, it is enough to assert that all thung are slimp. Perhaps the following analogy may be enlightening: It is correct to say that an electric typewriter can't write, can't write at all, until it is plugged in. However, it would be wrong to conclude that the machine, or its wiring, plays no role in its writing, or in its writing ability.

37. Katz also holds that "meaning postulates do not describe meaning at all," for "they state an extensional condition but not one reflecting meaning relations" (1987, 194). Therefore, the method of meaning postulates does not reconstruct semantic inferences for what they are, that is, inferences based on meaning: they are reconstructed as first-order deductions like any other. However, here Katz is patently ignoring the fact that meaning postulates do state "an extensional condition," but

one holding *in all possible worlds.* Therefore, inferences involving one or more meaning postulates are not just first-order inferences, as they involve a modalized premise. If one wishes, this is what characterizes them as "depending on meaning." One may, of course, be dissatisfied with Carnap's (or Montague's) treatment of meanings as intensions; one may not, however, simply ignore it. See n. 22 above.

38. Nor, of course, do they claim to be. The issue of grounding is essentially absent from these theories.

39. "Cognitive representations of categories clearly contained more of the information needed to respond to category members which had been rated good examples of the category ... than to respond to category members which had been rated bad examples. In other words, cognitive representations of categories appeared to be more similar to the good examples than to the poor examples" (Rosch 1975a, 225).

40. Wittgenstein's idea that (at least some) category words are used not on the basis of a set of necessary and jointly sufficient conditions for their application but on the basis of *family resemblances* among the items to which they are applied (Wittgenstein 1953, §§66–69) was clearly on Rosch's mind when she thought out prototype theory. See Rosch 1987.

41. "I ... must admit that I was ambivalent from the start about whether I thought of 'prototype' simply as a placemaker indicating the center of a 'Wittgensteinian' category or whether I thought of it as an actual something, for example, a mental code to which the category name might refer" (Rosch 1987, 155). Actually, she had made it clear already in 1978 that "for natural-language categories, to speak of a single entity that is the prototype is either a gross misunderstanding of the empirical data or a covert theory of mental representation.... Prototypes do not constitute a theory of representation for categories" (Rosch 1978, 40–41).

42. See Lakoff's discussion of several misinterpretations of prototype theory (1987, chap. 9).

43. The latter identification *could* be based on texts like the following: "There is a depth meaning of superordinate categories [such as *bird* or *vehicle*] not specifically coded in terms of words or pictures, but ... the depth meaning is translated into a format in preparation for actual perception which differs slightly for words and pictures. *The fact that less time is required to prepare for pictures suggests that pictures may be closer to the nature of the underlying representation than are words*" (Rosch 1975a, 226; italics added).

44. Examples are Reiter 1987, 151 ff., and Lakoff 1987, 169 (Lakoff notices, however, that Putnam's stereotypes are "not exactly" prototypes).

45. Frames are sometimes described as representing *only* stereotypical knowledge (see, for example, Johnson-Laird 1986, 107; Allen 1987, 321). My presentation here is more standard (see Barr and Feigenbaum 1981, III C7, pp. 216–219; Rich 1983, 230; Winston and Horn 1984, 311 ff.).

46. According to Putnam, what is metaphysically necessary (such as being H_2O for water or having a certain genetic code for tigers) is not thereby either epistemically necessary or required for semantic competence (1975c, 240), and contrapositively, what is required for competence (the features that make up the stereotype) is not

therefore metaphysically necessary (1975c, 250). Only a tiny fraction of the information included in a typical frame would be regarded as (metaphysically) necessary by Putnam. Most of it (*both* possible values *and* default values) would be considered by him as relevant to the stereotype. A lot he would regard as *neither* necessary *nor* stereotypical, for it is neither metaphysically necessary nor socially required for a competent use of the word.

47. In the case of Putnam's stereotypes, it may be doubted that all the information involved is defeasible. Could a tiger, a genuine tiger, not something looking like one, turn out not to be a feline? Perhaps not. That a feature is part of the stereotype associated with word '*w*' surely does not make it into a necessary feature of the *w*s, but perhaps *some* necessary features *may* be included in the stereotype, although they would not be included *because* they are necessary.

48. See for example, Keil 1987, 186.

49. An alternative: such conditions won't work, won't give the meaning, for difficult metaphysical reasons that Putnam once explained.

50. A good approximation of Nobody is George Lakoff. Surely Lakoff does not make the mistake of reifying prototypical effects: indeed, he is steadfast in denouncing any attempt in that direction (1987, 136–152). However, he does "roughly" identify Putnamian stereotypes with frames (1987, 116), and he suggests that "the Minsky-Putnam proposals appear to be capable in principle of accounting for the same range of prototype effects as [his own] propositional ICMs [idealized cognitive models]" (1987, 116). Propositional ICMs, like all ICMs, "are *cognitive* models," and the entities they contain are *mental* entities (1987, 285). ICMs are structures "consisting of symbols" (1987, 284), but such symbols are partly "directly meaningful" and partly "understood indirectly via their relationship to directly understood concepts" (1987, 284). Directly meaningful constituents of ICMs include "basic-level categories" (such as the concepts correponding to classes of medum-sized objects: OAK, COW, CHAIR, etc.) and "image schemata" (such as CONTAINER, PATH, UP-DOWN, CENTER-PERIPHERY) (1987, 267). They are directly meaningful by being "directly understood in terms of preconceptual structures in experience" (1987, 291). ICMs are *embodied* (1987, 206, 267). This is why D. Lewis's well-known criticism of "markerese" as just another uninterpreted formalism does not apply to them. Those among their constituents that are directly meaningful are such because "they are directly and repeatedly experienced because of the nature of the body and its mode of functioning in our environment" (1987, 268). Whatever the viability of Lakoff's own notion of an ICM and no matter how obscurely grounded the direct meaningfulness of ICMs, it seems clear that frames and stereotypes are being equated with "directly meaningful" mental structures, the ICMs, at least as far as their ability to account for prototype effects is concerned. This is not exactly Nobody's theory— ICMs are not prototypes; indeed, there are no prototypes—but it comes close.

51. Default inference is irreducible to standard inference not, of course, in the sense that one cannot account for default inference within the framework of model theory but in the sense that a theory in which default inference is carried out requires nonstandard semantics, such as one of several semantic proposals that have been put forward for so-called nonmonotonic logic.

52. Standard criticisms of versions of prototype theory have been put forth by Osherson and Smith (1981) and by Armstrong, Gleitman, and Gleitman (1983).

53. Barsalou (1987) and others have shown that the "graded structure" of concepts is "unstable": different subjects disagree with one another in their rankings of instances as to how typical they are with respect to a given category, and even the same subject disagrees with himself at different times. Such instability appears to be connected with both the strong influence of the context in determining how typical instances are and the use of different criteria in judging typicality. However, as Barsalou himself points out, this only excludes the hypothesis that concepts have graded structures that are both permanent (within individual subjects) and universal (between subjects). Prototype effects are not challenged; indeed, graded structure can be regarded as "the most important variable in predicting performance on a wide range of categorization tasks" (Barsalou 1987, 102–103).

Chapter 2

1. "Where exactly does one stop? And, more important, why does one stop? Is there a theoretical basis for deciding exactly what belongs in a dictionary?" (Haiman 1980, 329).

2. Actually, the dichotomy does not specifically involve true sentences. We could very well say that a sentence is analytic if and only if its truth *or falsity* depends only on the meanings of words, whereas it is synthetic if and only if its truth value depends on how the world is. It's just that we are not used to calling a sentence such as 'Tables are mammals' 'analytic'. But we might.

3. More accurately, any set of sentences of a language *L* that collectively (logically) entail the analytic sentences of *L* is a complete set of meaning postulates for *L*.

4. It should be pointed out that strictly, there is no absolutely unrevisable sentence if we are prepared to go crazy. We ought to speak of more or less revisable. Thus mathematical truths are highly unrevisable, for mathematics is a tightly knit theory (in contrast to botanics, for example), and it pervades all science.

5. In a similar vein, Bierwisch and Kiefer (1970, 79, n. 20) note that some a priori truths such as 'The sum of the angles of a triangle is 180 degrees' are not central in terms of semantic competence.

6. "Ignore the analytic-synthetic distinction, and you will not be wrong in connection with any philosphic issues not having to do specifically with the distinction. Attempt to use it as a weapon in philosophical discussion, and you will consistently be wrong" (Putnam 1975a, 36).

7. Putnam 1975a, 39. See also Putnam 1983c, 89 n.

8. For example, skeptical doubts about mathematical entities (as expressed by such questions as 'Are numbers real?') would be interpreted as questions whose answers were rather trivially determined by the "rules of language" (*internal* questions) or else reduced to *external* questions (that is, questions about the appropriateness of adopting a certain language), which do not admit of a clear formulation. Thus a positive

answer to the question about the existence of numbers as an internal question immediately follows from '5 is a number', which is itself an *analytic truth* of the language to which '5' and 'number' belong. As an external question, on the other hand, the question about numbers involves notions such as that of an "ideal," nonmaterial reality, which cannot be couched in "common scientific language" (Carnap 1956a, 209; compare Horwich 1992, 103).

9. I believe that here Horwich is reading Quine's later indeterminacy arguments into the paper of 1951 (1953). I can find no such behavioristic overtones in "Two Dogmas." Notice, however, that much later Quine himself insists on "the distrust of mentalistic semantics that found expression in 'Two Dogmas'" and on his early reading of Watson's *Psychology from the Standpoint of a Behaviorist* (which "chimed in with [his] predilections") (1991, 265–266).

10. The "second dogma" of empiricism is the doctrine according to which a statement's cognitive significance is identical with its empirical content, that is, with the relation that the particular statement has with experience.

11. For Quine's explicit endorsement of Putnam's attenuated version of the analytic/synthetic distinction, see "Reply to Putnam" (1986, 427). The first formulation of Quine's proposal is in 1973, 78–80; that version, however, is partly different from the one he appears to defend in 1986.

12. Notice, however, that even here Quine wanted the analytic truths to be closed under elementary inference: "We would want a recondite sentence to count still as analytic if obtainable by a chain of inferences each of which individually is assured by the learning of the words" (1973, 79–80). It is hard to see how, given the logical truths that Quine wants to count as analytic (for example, double negation and the law of contradiction), the excluded middle would not be obtainable by such a chain of inferences.

13. "All logical truths in my narrow sense . . . would then perhaps qualify as analytic" (Quine 1991, 270).

14. Here 'consequence' is to be understood, so to speak, lexically: consequences follow from other analytic truths by way of principles that we accept because we learned them in learning the relevant words.

15. "Even the unconvinced tend to avoid putting much weight on the distinction, just to be on the safe side; and few are prepared to come out explicitly in favour of it" (Horwich 1992, 95). Horwich also notes that the distinction fares much better among linguists and psychologists.

16. Notice that replacing 'delimitation from other entries' with 'delimitation from other linguistic expressions' in the definition of 'core' would make its characterization perfectly empty. For then any specification would belong to the core. We ought to introduce 'having two kidneys' in the core of 'tiger' in order to delimit 'tiger' with respect to 'animal exactly like a tiger except that it has only one kidney', and so on, for all information on tigers.

17. The motivations for the distinction may be somewhat unusual. According to White, "Lexical and world knowledge must be distinguished lest we lapse into an unenlightened determinism of human institutions," meaning that without the dis-

tinction we would be forced to adhere to a strong version of the Whorf-Sapir hypothesis: any discrimination that is not lexically implemented is cognitively inaccessible. I don't see any argument to that effect. Take a language L in which the distinction of blue and green is not lexicalized (L has one word, 'grue', covering both). Even in L, one could say such things as (the L equivalent of) 'The grue of the grass is different from the grue of the sky'. The semantic holist, who rejects the distinction of lexical knowledge and world knowledge *and* regards all true sentences as partial definitions of the words occurring in them, would take such a statement as introducing a distinction between two senses of 'grue', and she is free to do so. Not every sense must be lexicalized, nor is the holist bound to reject polysemy.

18. Actually, it would seem that no such confusion is involved in the usual formal semantic treatment, where meaning postulates typically have the form of *necessitated* universally quantified conditionals or biconditionals ($\Box(\forall x)(\text{dog}(x) \supset \text{mammal}(x))$), which, of course, do entail their modal-free subsentences ($(\forall x)(\text{dog}(x) \supset \text{mammal}(x))$) without being equivalent to them. Of course, the problem of whether 'Dogs are mammals' *ought to* be (translated into) a meaning postulate is still with us. Natural-language sentences do not wear boxes on their sleeves.

19. That we do have such intuitions and that they are pretty resistant probably formed the gist of Grice and Strawson's early criticism of Quine (Grice and Strawson 1970 [1956]; see particularly 58–62). They may have regarded such intuitions as slightly more uniform across speakers than they actually are.

20. Notice that the intuitions we are discussing here concern semantic import, not analyticity. Consider the following sentences (all from Brandom 1994, 168):

If A is to the East of B, then B is to the West of A.

If this patch is red, then this patch is not green.

If thunder now, then lightning earlier.

They all have a strong analytic flavor (that is, they are perceived as "true by virtue of meaning"), but they would be out of place in a dictionary. The reason is exactly that they are about individuals. Thus not all analytic-sounding sentences are perceived as constitutive of meaning, or definitional, or dictionarylike, etc.

21. Similarly, it might seem that if a piece of information is perceived as contingent, it will automatically be regarded as encyclopedic: isn't the encyclopedia the repository of (mere) matters of fact? It is not so. That water is drunk by people or that ground wheat is baked and eaten is utterly contingent, as it is contingent that we eat by introducing food into our mouths (we could eat through our noses). Nevertheless, information of the above kind does have semantic import: it would not be out of place in a dictionary (where it is indeed to be found, most of the time), in contrast to the information that, say, the river Thames is 323 km long, which would be.

22. This distinction was stressed by Putnam: "We do not want ... to draw the analytic-synthetic distinction in terms of dispositions to use the words 'analytic' and 'synthetic' themselves, nor dipositions to use related expressions, for example, 'have the same meaning' and 'does not understand what he is saying'. ... We should be able to indicate the nature and rationale of the analytic-synthetic distinction. What happens to a statement when it is analytic?" (1975a, 35). What Putnam here says we

don't want to do is exactly what I proposed to do by the above considerations; I fully agree with Putnam that it does not amount to a restatement of the analytic/synthetic distinction.

23. At the end of this chapter I will have something to say concerning the *real* analytic/synthetic distinction (see p. 54).

24. The distinction among syntactic competence, structural semantic competence, and lexical semantic competence is due to Partee (1981, 60 ff.). I am using the notion of semantic competence more or less like Gennaro Chierchia (1992, 290–297), that is, as "an ability to decode the meanings associated with the expressions of a language" (1992, 290). Chierchia does not explicitly distinguish between structural and lexical semantic competence. He sees semantic competence as including both the ability to evaluate entailments and the ability to apply language to the real world (see his examples on pp. 293–294), or in his words, "the ability to evaluate the relation between expressions and states of affairs" (1992, 293). However, he identifies the inferential aspect of competence with the ability to evaluate *logical* implications, which are just a subset of the implications a competent speaker can assess, unless one believes that all semantic inferences (This is a hammer/This is a tool) are really logical inferences in disguise, that is, enthymematic inferences that can be completed by introducing the appropriate meaning postulates (This is a hammer; *Hammers are tools*/This is a tool). That Chierchia does not appear to see this point may be a consequence of his failing to draw the distinction between structural and lexical competence. Moreover, Chierchia identifies the ability to apply language to the world with knowledge of sentences' truth conditions (1992, 295). This is ambiguous, to say the least. It will be seen (chapter 4, pp. 105–114) that what's frequently called 'knowledge of truth conditions' is rather connected with the inferential aspect of semantic competence and with structural competence. Partee was more sensitive to the irreducibility of the referential side to knowledge of truth conditions in that sense, when she wrote, "Language-to-world grounding ... is the part of lexical semantics that has no analog in syntax or structural semantics and where the interconnections among language, thought, and reality are perhaps most complex" (1981, 71).

25. This is what Frege called a judgment's "conceptual content" (1879, §3).

26. More accurately, one has to be able to use the words in conformity with the restrictions packed into the notions of mass noun and factive verb.

27. Notice that even the model-theoretic slogan 'an expression's meaning is its contribution to the truth conditions of the sentences in which the expression occurs' is holistic, given the premise that a sentence's truth conditions are determined compositionally (a premise that is generally accepted in model-theoretic semantics).

28. Fodor and Lepore's own example of being a sibling is unfortunate, for 'sibling' is a two-place predicate. No *individual* has the property of being a sibling. An individual may have the property of being a sibling of *a*, but at least on one reading, this property is not anatomic.

29. I owe this suggestion to Marco Santambrogio.

30. Fodor and Lepore (1992) occasionally use the more common notion of semantic holism, for example, p. x ("The doctrine that only whole languages or whole theories ... *really* have meanings, so that the meanings of smaller units ... are merely

derivative") or, more confusingly, pp. 6–7 ("The doctrine that intentional states, institutions, practices and the like are ontologically dependent on one another"). It is not clear to me whether they take the two notions to be one and the same or how they understand their relation if they believe they are distinct.

31. This assumption is not really required. If holism holds, comprehension, be it compositional or not, is bound to involve a speaker's whole semantic competence. For an expression's meaning is said to depend on the whole language; thus, grasping *e*'s meaning requires grasping the meaning of all other expressions of the language. However, the hypothesis of compositional understanding allows a more precise presentation of this point.

32. It would not be plausible, not even prima facie, to suppose that the meaning of, say, 'yellow' is a function *only* of the structural aspects of the linguistic system.

33. If one admits that the units of a language of thought are interpreted symbols, their interpretation consisting in a connection with the world, this version of atomism reduces to the first version mentioned.

34. A hypostatic theory of meaning is a theory that treats meanings as *things*.

35. This sense of 'molecularism' is different from Dummett's (1976, 72). For Dummett, a molecular theory of meaning is one that represents a speaker's competence as an ability to use *whole sentences* (rather than individual words) of a language. Any theory of meaning, according to Dummett, will have axioms governing individual words, but a speaker's knowledge of such axioms "need not be manifested in anything but the employment of the sentences." There may well be such a thing as knowledge of an individual word, but if molecularism is correct, such knowledge is not directly correlated with any linguistic ability. It should be pointed out, however, that Dummett is also a molecularist in *my* sense: "On a molecular view, there is, for each sentence, a determinate fragment of the language a knowledge of which will suffice for a complete understanding of that sentence" (Dummett 1976, 79).

36. The version that Perry (1994, 125) labels 'lotsism'.

37. Similar, though not identical distinctions are drawn by P. Jacob (1993, 17) and J. Perry (1994, 137–138). For Perry, strong anatomism is expressed by (i), whereas what is required by the molecularist's intuitions is (ii):

(i) $(\forall p)(\exists q)(p$ is shared $\supset \Box(q$ is shared$))$

(ii) $(\forall p)(p$ is shared $\supset \Box(\exists q)(q$ is shared$))$

If necessity is S5 necessity, (ii) is stronger than (6), and (i) is stronger than (5). I don't see any reason for assuming the stronger formulations (why should q be shared even in the possible worlds where p is not shared?). However, I take it that Perry is making essentially the same point I want to make. Jacob's strong anatomism is the same as mine (that is, (5)), whereas his weak anatomism coincides with Perry's (ii). Jacob's overall argument, however, is different from both Perry's and mine.

38. For a similar view of "the inferential component of conceptual competence," see Rey 1983, 259–260.

39. "It is unlikely that any two people will have the same concept of anything since it is unlikely that they have the same beliefs associated with the term which expresses

that concept" (Bilgrami 1992, 11). According to Bilgrami, this is true at the "meaning-theoretic" level, that is, at the level of an individual's overall competence; only a fraction of such competence, however, is effectively involved in identifying the contents that are relevant, for example, in the explanation of actions. Most of your beliefs about water play no role in your water-related behavior as determined by thirst. At such a "local" level, we may be said to share many contents (that is, the same beliefs may be relevant for both you and me on a given occasion, or maybe on several occasions). Although I fully agree that only a fraction of an individual's competence need be involved in understanding language and in other cognitive processes (*which* fraction it is an empirical matter to determine), I don't see that there is any real need for a level at which contents (or meanings) are shared. In chapter 4, I will try to show that issues that appear to requie for content sharing (such as communication) can be dealt with in terms of *convergence*.

40. As Fodor and Lepore rightly notice in the context of a slightly different discussion (1992, 28–30).

41. It may be objected that (7) is too weak: we want *A* and *B* to share "important" or "significant" beliefs about gold and metals, not just any belief whatsoever (such as the belief that there is a lot of gold in South Africa or the belief that metals don't float on water). I hesitate to accept this suggestion, for it would make it hard for an expert (on gold, say) and a layman to share any belief. Notice, however, that even if the suggestion were accepted and (7) were strengthened by requiring that the shared beliefs be among the "important" truths relative to gold and metals, whatever this is taken to mean, this would not entail that there is a certain list of beliefs (the "analytic truths" about gold and metals) that *A* and *B* are bound to share if they share any belief about gold and metals. It would merely entail that some of the beliefs they share must be on the list.

42. This view is sympathetic with Barsalou's suggestion that in general, different information is activated when a concept is constructed in working memory, though there may be ("context-independent") information that is obligatorily activated whenever a concept is constructed for a particular category: "For example, whenever people construct a concept for *skunk*, the activation of *smells* is obligatory; whenever people construct a concept for *diamond*, the activation of *valuable* is obligatory" (Barsalou 1987, 123). It appears that in this context, 'obligatory' means 'constant'. Hence it is an empirical fact whether and which such connections do occur in concept construction.

43. P. Horwich has proposed the following definition of I-analyticity (which, in his opinion, would escape Quine's criticism): "A sentence is analytic in a person's I-language [in Chomsky's (1986) sense] at time *t* iff it is a consequence of that person's language faculty at time *t* that this sentence be taken as true regardless of evidence" (1992, 101). This is similar to the notion put forward in the text, in that analyticity of this kind would be idiosyncratic to each speaker and a merely empirical matter (in fact, Horwich remarks that I-analyticity "will require sophisticated techniques to uncover" (1992, 104), whereas Quinean analytic truths were supposed to be obvious). However, as Horwich does not specify what it is for the language faculty to determine the unassailable truth of an I-analytic sentence, I-analyticity is not distinguished from (what we might call) I-obstinacy. As a matter of fact, when we say

that analytic truth is determined "by the rules of language," we have in mind certain rules and not others (not phonological rules or syntactic rules alone, for example). If my language faculty were weird enough to force me to regard a sentence as true by virtue of its syntactic structure alone, come what may, this would not count as analyticity, not even *sui generis*.

44. Moreover, why should we require that the contribution of 'Roses are flowers' to the system's competence with 'rose' be based on the inferential value of 'flower' rather than on its referential value?

45. Chomsky rightly pointed out that dictionaries are incomplete: they do not record many subtleties that are part of the competence of all or most speakers. Thus, concerning the word 'house':

If I see the house, I see its exterior surface; seeing the interior surface does not suffice.... The house can have chairs inside it or outside it, consistent with its being regarded as a surface. But while those outside it may be near it, those inside it are necessarily not.... The house is conceived as an exterior surface and an interior space (with complex properties). Of course, the house itself is a concrete object; it can be made of bricks or wood, and a wooden house does not just have a wooden exterior. A brown wooden house has a brown exterior (adopting the abstract perspective) and is made of wood (adopting the concrete perspective). (Chomsky 1992, 220–221)

And so forth. The main, though not the only, problem here appears to be that dictionaries do not include (enough) information about semantic compositional effects, that is, about the precise way in which the inferential values of words w and w' combine to determine the inferential value of α (w, w'), an expression in which both words occur. In this respect, a dictionary may be inadequate in two different ways: it may fail to record the particular value a word can take up in a given combination, or though it does record such a value, it may fail to provide the reader with any criterion to select that value (rather than another) in a given combination. Thus a dictionary may fail to indicate that 'see NP' may involve only the surface of NP, or it may specify that 'wooden' can mean *made of wood* but fail to indicate in combination with which words it takes up such a meaning. Defects of the former kind can only be remedied by supplying the missing information; defects of the latter kind may ask for the dictionary to include a system of "pointers" much richer than what can be found at present (usually in the form of information about selectional restrictions and the like). Such a system of pointers would embody Pustejovsky's (1991) notion of *cocompositionality*.

Chapter 3

1. With the usual qualification: meaning postulates written in an "interpreted" language.

2. Or he may mistake a different butterfly for an *A. Clemensi*: "Someone may know, in some reasonable sense, what a guanaco is, and that it is not a llama, and yet be regularly caused to assent to 'That's a guanaco' in the presence of llamas" (Davidson 1991, 195).

3. According to a useful distinction due to Bilgrami (1992, 22–23), in the *strong* version of the thesis of the division of linguistic labor, the content of the layperson's competence is *fully* determined by the expert's competence: every speaker in the community shares the expert's concept of, say, gold or pandas. In Putnam's original and weaker version (1975c), the layperson's concept includes her reliance on the expert's competence but does not coincide with the expert's concept.

4. That is, assuming that the construction of a mental model of a sentence automatically engenders a mapping of the relevant lexical items onto perception in which all the relevant relations are preserved. As a matter of fact, Johnson-Laird is far from explicit or exhaustive concerning the relations between mental models generated in language understanding and models derived from perception. Most of the time, he speaks as if models generated in language comprehension were constructed by the mind, not derived from perception (see, for example, 1983, chap. 11). (Incidentally, this is required to sustain the claim that "the processes by which fictitious discourse is understood are not essentially different from those that occur with true [that is, realistic] assertions" [1983, 246].) But then he sometimes seems to assume that the connection between language and perception (and the world) is ensured by the fact that language is directly mapped onto models derived from perception (1983, 407). This is confusing, for it seems at least prima facie obvious that we very often understand a discourse (which may involve the construction of a mental model of it) *and then* try to relate it to the world as given to us in perception: for example, we read instructions *and then* try to follow them, or we understand an order *and then* try to obey it.

5. Dual theories of meaning were put forward by Field (1977), Loar (1981), McGinn (1982), Block (1986), and others. For an account of the dual aspect (or "two component") picture and a defence of a version of it, see Recanati 1993, chaps. 11–12.

In Putnam's mental experiment of Twin Earth, which will be discussed at greater length in chap. 4, we imagine that there is a planet (Twin Earth) identical to Earth except for the fact that the stuff that fills the lakes, seas, rivers, etc., of Twin Earth is not water (that is, H_2O) but an essentially different liquid whose complicated formula is abbreviated XYZ and whose superficial properties are identical with those of H_2O. Such a liquid, XYZ, is also called 'water' in Twin English. Nowadays speakers on Twin Earth are well aware (thanks to chemistry) that their word 'water' does not refer to the Earthian stuff H_2O, and similarly, Earthians know that *their* 'water' refers to H_2O, not to XYZ. But before 1750, when nobody on either Earth or Twin Earth could have told the difference between the two liquids, an Earthian traveling to Twin Earth would have called the local stuff 'water' believing that it was essentially the same stuff he was used to on Earth (and conversely for a Twin Earthian traveling to Earth). Now, according to Putnam's (and many other people's) intuitions, this would have been a mistake, for even before 1750 the Earthian word 'water' did not refer to the Twin Earthian liquid. If such intuitions are sound, the experiment appears to prove that a word's reference is not determined by whatever a speaker using the word may have "in mind," for before 1750 there was nothing to distinguish what both Earthians and Twin Earthians had in mind in connection with 'water', but nevertheless, the Earthian word and the Twin Earthian word did not refer to the same stuff.

6. Therefore, an individual's referential competence is not to be identified in terms of which objects "out there" the individual associates with certain words. When we speak for example, of an individual's ability to tell cats from cows, cats and cows enter into our *description* of her ability, and they may have partially determined such an ability, *genetically*. The ability itself, however, would remain exactly what it is even if cats and cows ceased to exist, could (in principle) have arisen even if there never had been any cats or cows, and would still be there (even if we would no longer describe it in those terms) if, say, cats changed to the point of no longer being recognizable by the procedures that constitute the ability. Thus many of us are referentially competent with 'centaur' and 'unicorn'.

7. A somewhat similar view on this point can be found in Lakoff 1987, 279–280.

8. On basic-level concepts see Rosch 1975b, 200–201; Rosch et al. 1976. A survey of work on basic-level concepts in Lakoff 1987, 31–54.

9. When I say that there are words we are particularly competent with referentially, that is, words whose application is especially straightforward, I am not, of course, implying that in a language such as English there is a unique set of words that are referentially basic for all speakers, that is, such that all speakers of the language have good referential command of them (perhaps in the sense that one would not be regarded as a competent speaker of that language if he or she did not share referential command of such words). The blind have limited referential competence with color words, but they are not therefore incompetent speakers of the language. More generally, different English speakers (that is, people that we refer to as speakers of "the same language," English) may differ in referential competence in that different sets of words are referentially straightforward for each of them.

10. H. J. A. had extensive infarction extending forward in both occipital lobes, in consequence of a stroke.

11. In application, H. J. A. "made errors when there was a close overlap between the features of the target object and those of the distractor [for example, tiger/zebra, owl/eagle, violin/guitar]" (Riddoch and Humphreys 1987b, 53), that is, he made the kind of mistakes one would expect of a feature-by-feature procedure.

12. On numerals, see McGinn 1981, 174.

13. The variability of the social requirements on individual semantic competence was pointed out by Putnam in "The Meaning of 'Meaning'" in connection with stereotypes for different words: "In our culture speakers are required to know what tigers look like . . . ; they are not required to know the fine details (such as leaf shape) of what an elm tree looks like. English speakers are *required by their linguistic community* to be able to tell tigers from leopards; they are not required to be able to tell elm trees from beech trees" (1975c, 249).

14. Evans thought that this applied to type recognition as well: "What I say about the process of recognition applies no less to the recognizing of something as a dog (the recognition of a type) than to the recognition of particular instances of that type" (1982, 289).

15. Wettstein appears to think that if semantics is interested "in the connection between language and the world, the realm of referents" (1986, 201), then it should

not at all concern itself with matters cognitive. This presupposes that the connection between language and the world should be conceived of as an objective, not as a cognitive, connection. In the next chapter I will discuss this view ("objectivism") at some length.

16. He could distinguish squares from rectangles, detect shapes, discriminate dot positions, point out differences between otherwise identical complex pictures.

17. A parallel case, D. E. L., was described by Hécaen et al. (see Shallice 1988, 199).

18. As far as "concrete" words were concerned. E. S. T. had a generalized problem with abstract words.

19. In a significant number of cases Mme. D. T. could name faces of famous French people (Serge Gainsbourg, Catherine Deneuve, etc.) whom she could not otherwise identify. For example, she couldn't say whether Deneuve was an actress or a singer or a politician, etc.; she rather thought she was a singer but couldn't really tell. However, her performance with proper names did not exactly parallel her performance with common nouns, for in the case of proper names, her overall recall was much impaired (not so with names of objects, as we saw). Thus Mme. D. T. cannot be described as a case of preservation of the recall of people's names, as contrasted with the loss of the ability to categorize or verbally describe them (Brennen et al. 1996, 104).

20. In naming, E. S. T. got 22 percent spontaneously plus an additional 19 percent in response to phonemic cues on the Boston Naming Test, and he got 37 percent without hesitation plus a further 10 percent with some difficulty on the Snodgrass and Vanderwart set. In selecting pictures for abstract words (such as 'boredom'), E. S. T. was only 60 percent correct.

21. I am using 'semantic lexicon' for a collection of mental representations distinct from the representations of both phonological and graphic word forms. Therefore, I am *not* using 'semantic' as it often occurs in the neuropsychological literature, that is, as standing for (representations of) the functional and associative properties of objects, as opposed to specifications of their visual forms.

22. For failure of the recognition stage, see, for example, Warrington and Shallice 1984.

23. Cases of intact inferential competence together with impaired application are hard to come by. One that could be so regarded is the already mentioned case of H. J. A. (Riddoch and Humphreys 1987b), the feature-by-feature recognizer. As we can now see, he had trouble with both application and naming (though he was much better at the former). On the other hand, he was very good (100 percent correct) at giving verbal definitions of object names. Impressively, his definitions included details of the object's appearance. For example, his response to the word 'duck' was, "A duck is a water bird with the ability to swim, fly and walk. It can be wild or kept domestically for eggs.... In the wild it has a wingspan between 15 and 18 inches and weighs about 2 or 3 pounds. Domestic ducks are heavier, up to about 6 pounds perhaps. Wild ducks are multicoloured, mainly brown but with green and yellow breasts. Domestic ducks are white or khaki. (Riddoch and Humphreys 1987b, 1447). The richness of H. J. A.'s definitions may partly explain the relative success of his feature-by-feature referential procedures: he had lots of features to go by.

24. Relatively more frequent and better studied is the inability to name or identify living things (or foods) as contrasted with much greater ability with inanimate objects (Warrington and Shallice 1984 and many others, including Sartori et al. 1994), but the complementary pattern is also reported (Warrington and McCarthy 1983). Similarly with concrete versus abstract: cases in which concrete words are selectively impaired seem to be more frequent (Warrington 1975, Warrington and Shallice 1984, Warrington 1985), but the reverse case is also reported (Kay and Ellis 1987). For a survey of results, see Shallice 1988, 297–304.

Chapter 4

1. See especially chap. 2, pp. 44–45. It was Barbara Partee (1981, 62) who pointed out that knowledge of the semantic compositional rules can be regarded as part of a speaker's competence, at least in principle.

2. By 'pragmatic competence' I mean to hint at the tradition of philosophical pragmatics: pragmatic competence includes the ability to generate and perceive Gricean conversational implicatures, the ability to perform and identify speech acts such as promises and commands, and, more generally, the ability to use language appropriately under given circumstances. The notion of appropriateness is not easily circumscribed; however, I do not regard it as appropriate to say that using the word 'cat' to refer to a cat is a matter of appropriateness. What *is* a matter of appropriateness is selecting the word 'cat' *rather than* 'feline' or 'pussy', depending on the circumstances.

   As far as the interface with syntax is concerned, Ray Jackendoff's work, particularly 1990, is exemplary.

3. On the notion of objective reference, see later in this chapter, pp. 85–86.

4. I conceived this view independently in the mid 1980s (Marconi 1987, 1989).

5. See also *Semantics and Cognition* (Jackendoff 1983, 29–31).

6. For a neuropsychological account of an alternative route to object recognition, see Shallice 1988, 195–198.

7. Jackendoff rightly emphasizes that 3-D models are much more than "statues in the head," for they encode "the decomposition of objects into parts, the geometric systems of spatial axes around which objects are organized, and the relations among the parts" (1990, 33).

8. This discussion will be resumed in chapter 6.

9. This objection is, in spirit, Fregean. Today it expresses Michael Dummett's standpoint.

10. In spite of appearances, this objection can be brought back to the later Wittgenstein's insistence on the connection between meaning and criteria of correctness.

11. Use, of course, does not include the original mention of the word in the baptismal ceremony.

   This viewpoint is inspired by Putnam 1975c and other realistic theories of reference.

12. That is, since about second grade and more steadily since fourth grade.

13. Keil (1986, 137) explicitly connects his picture of the use of natural-kind words with Kripke's and Putnam's accounts. However, he confusingly conflates Kripke's notion of the causal history of the use of a name (the "causal chain" that links present uses to past uses and the initial baptism) with his own notion of the causal history of the *objects* to which a natural-kind word is applied (see Keil 1986, 137, 138). As a matter of fact, he has no use for Kripke's notion: what he wants to say is that our application of a natural-kind word is strongly influenced by our beliefs about the origin and development of candidate referents for the word. Thus if we believe that a certain animal was born from skunk parents and has the "internal structure" of a skunk, we will not categorize it as a raccoon (and call it 'raccoon') even if it looks and behaves exactly like one.

14. Many philosophers, after Putnam (1975c), have insisted on this, for example, Rey 1983, 253; Wettstein 1986, 203; Burge 1993, 118.

15. As Putnam rightly points out (1975c, 237–238), it would not be correct to say that objective reference is "cognitively inaccessible": inhabitants of Twin Earth *could* have discriminated between H_2O and XYZ if they had been duly instructed to perform certain tests and if they had been taught enough chemistry to understand the results of such tests in the appropriate way. It is not that objective reference cannot be cognitively captured. Rather, the point is that objective reference is what it is whether it is captured or not.

16. It may be doubted that even convergence is really necessary for communication: Davidson 1986 contains arguments to the contrary. It appears that much depends on what is meant by 'successful communication'. On the issue of whether any *word* can convey any information the speaker intends it to convey, see the next chapter, pp. 122–124.

17. In a similar vein, Richard Rorty (1979, 285) pointed out that it is not clear how we could come to be assured that "revolutionary change in science has come to an end," that is, that we have reached the final picture of reality; In any case, it is not clear how such a conviction could be supplied by the theory of reference.

18. See also Burge 1993, 319. According to Davidson (1991, 196–197), external factors determine both the content of one's thought and the content of the thought one believes one has, "these being one and the same thought." Thus 'water' for an Earthling is associated with the same content, affected by the same external factors, in all mental contexts. Even in the context of the belief one expresses by '"Water" refers to both the Earthian and the Twin Earthian stuff', the word 'water' only refers to the Earthian stuff, H_2O. Therefore, such beliefs are not simply wrong but inconsistent with linguistic dispositions. Before 1750 people on both Earth and Twin Earth were irrational, not just mistaken (see immediately below).

19. Thus neither could have correctly answered the question 'How do you understand "water"?'

20. For an account (and a defence) of the externalization of mental contents, see Récanati 1993, 214 ff.

21. I argued in chapter 2 that two speakers can share a few beliefs without having to share *all* beliefs.

22. If they are not bookish, like the zoologist I mentioned in chapter 3.

23. I do not mean that there are no distinctions to be drawn here; I simply mean to emphasize continuities between the layperson's competence and the expert's competence. The layperson's competence with some words strongly resembles the competence of certain experts on other words.

24. Rey himself is well aware that this is the opposition he wants (see Rey 1983, 255).

25. "It is a belief in biological essence that seems to grow out of a naive theory of natural kinds that is driving their intuitions" (Keil 1987, 189).

26. See also Malt 1990, 291, 311. According to Malt's experiments, people appear to believe that expert opinion is much more relevant to deciding category membership in the case of natural kinds than in the case of artificial kinds.

27. "The spoken word 'dog' is not a single entity: it is a class of similar movements of the tongue, throat, and larynx.... The word 'dog' is a universal, just as *dog* is a universal.... There is ... no difference of logical status between *dog* and the word 'dog': each is general, and exists only in instances" (Russell 1950, 24).

28. This is how the logical positivists looked at language (see for example, Carnap 1942, 4–8). Peirce's distinction between a linguistic expression as a *type*, on the one hand, and its *tokens*, on the other (1934–1948, 4: 537) is an obvious predecessor.

29. For example, the configuration 'belli' means *goodlooking* in Italian, whereas it means *of the war* in Latin.

30. Frege 1980b, esp. 57–60; Frege 1964, 17; Frege to Husserl 1906 (Frege 1976, 101–102); Frege to Jourdain, undated (Frege 1976, 128); Frege 1956, 301.

31. Frege 1964, 15–16; Frege to Husserl 1906 (Frege 1976, 102); Frege 1956, 301–302.

32. This might be Bilgrami's view: "What makes this publicness of belief and meaning possible? ... The only correct answer to this question lies in externalism. It is only because an agent's meanings and beliefs are, in general, constituted by a world external to the agent that those meanings and beliefs are available to others who live in that world, to others who can experience the same environment" (1992, 200). "A common external world *which we experience*, in general, determines our thought" (1992, 201; my italics). Whether this is enough to qualify Bilgrami's stand as externalist is another matter. Here I am taking his self-proclaimed externalism for granted.

33. If one believed that meanings are just de facto uniform, one ought to regard (i) as informative and therefore a posteriori true.

(i) When I think of Pythagoras's theorem, I think of the same object as you think of when *you* think of Pythagoras's theorem.

However, for Frege (as for us) (i) is true a priori. Consequently, in Frege's view, the uniformity of meanings cannot simply be a fact. (This objection was pointed out to me by Alberto Voltolini.) However, the a priori truth of (i) depends not on the publicness of meanings but rather on a general principle of nonequivocation: there is no reason why both occurrences of 'Pythagoras's theorem' in (i) should not have the same semantic value, whatever that is. In other words, by uttering (i), one does not refer, does not succeed in referring, to two distinct interpretations of Pythagoras's theorem. Such a result can be achieved by uttering sentences like (ii):

(ii)   The meaning that Dario attaches to the words 'The sum of the squares ...' is the same as Aldo attaches to the words 'The sum of the squares ...'.

Contrary to (i), (ii) is both informative and a posteriori true.

34. Actually, the argument is more complex. If there were such a thing as self-managed normativity, then one could think of a private convention. But there can't be any such convention; thus self-managed normativity is impossible. This applies to language only if language is a normative institution. The crucial step is the definition of a private language as one that I (alone) could govern. This appears to assume that language is governed (possibly by me).

35. Objectivist accounts are sometimes limited to natural-kind and natural-substance words (Devitt and Sterelny 1987, 75–76); others extend them much further (as in Putnam's original proposal of 1975c; see also Rey 1983, 254, n. 18; Davidson 1991, 196; Burge 1993). As a matter of fact, even those who believe that objectivism holds unrestrictedly mostly quote natural-kind and natural-substance words as examples (see, for example, Fodor 1987). "One criterion" words, such as 'bachelor', may be excepted (see Putnam 1975c, 244). As the objectivist case appears to be strongest in the case of natural-kind words (aside from proper names and indexicals), I will limit my discussion to them.

36. Here Rey is clearly contrasting individual competence with communitarian standards: "metaphysics" has nothing to do with it (the dictionary is not a book of metaphysics). Interestingly, 'tomato' is mentioned by Dowty (1980, 386–387) as an example of a word used according to incompatible standards (the biological and the commercial), both of which are socially legitimized.

37. I am not discussing the arguments in favor of Burge's view. They are critically reviewed in Bilgrami 1992, 35 ff., 65 ff.

38. I must stress that I am referring to Burge's views of 1979. The picture set forth in Burge 1993 is much closer to causal theories.

39. I mean, of course, that the community's explicit knowledge and discriminating abilities, as well as the actual linguistic practice of its members (including expert members) would in no way point to a differential application of 'water' to XYZ and H_2O. Naturally, if communitarian competence is "externalized," if we say that the community's notion of water is itself grounded in causal interactions with XYZ, then the community "knows" that 'water' refers to XYZ, not to H_2O. But then, so does each individual speaker. Externalization of mental contents tends to trivialize the issue.

40. This, of course, must be kept distinct from the case of a norm that, though applicable in principle, is never applied in point of fact, and from the closer case of a norm that is not applicable for epistemological reasons, in that nobody is ever assured that the circumstances for its application do occur (an example of the latter case would be the following: a community, having being told that water *is* H_2O, is willing to abide by the norm that 'water' is to be applied to H_2O and only to H_2O but

has no way of determining whether a sample of liquid *is* H_2O, for they do not know enough chemistry).

41. On the inadequacy of causal theories (of both proper names and natural-kind words) based on single baptisms and on the need for "multiple grounding," see Devitt and Sterelny 1987, 62–63, 71–72.

42. Stalnaker has shown that if intentional content is conceived in information-theoretic terms, then there cannot be any difference between water thoughts "caused" by H_2O and water thoughts "caused" by XYZ: "The reason that O'Leary's internal cognitive state, as he steps into the bathtub, carries the information that there is water in the tub is that if there weren't water in the tub he would not be in the internal state he is in. But . . . if it were twater—XYZ— . . . in the bathtub, O'Leary would be in exactly the same internal state" (1993, 306).

43. Putnam (1992, 221) has made it clear that his theory is not a causal theory in Fodor's sense.

44. Casalegno 1997, chap. 13, contains an excellent presentation and critical discussion of Fodor's theory.

45. Of course, these are not the statements one actually finds in a Montague grammar, nor would one find there a category such as 'singular noun phrase'. These oversimplified examples are introduced (with no significant loss, I believe) only to make the point about truth conditions in a simple way.

46. 'Contributing' in the following sense: semantic statements that are not statements of truth conditions are intermediate steps in the derivation of statements of truth conditions.

47. "To understand a proposition means to know what is the case if it is true" (Wittgenstein, *Tractatus*, 4.024).

48. This is not meant to contradict presuppositional analyses of 'only' (beginning with Horn 1969), according to which 'Only John went to the party' does not *assert* but *presupposes* that John went. What I say concerning truth conditions involving 'only' should be taken just as an example.

49. An example is Chierchia 1992, 293.

50. Robert Brandom has tried to effect an inferentialist reduction of "the traditional representationalist semantic vocabulary," including 'true' and 'refers' (1994, 283). This he does by treating 'true' and 'refers' as proform-forming operators, so that "all legitimate semantic talk about truth *and* reference [is explained] in purely anaphoric terms" (1994, 306). My view is committed not to the possibility of such a reduction, that is, to the conceptual primacy of inference over truth (and reference), but only to the idea that inferential *intuitions* are not necessarily derived from intuitions of truth.

51. I neglect inference by default. Inference by default, however, is just a special kind of inference.

52. Again, this is not the truth condition for 'John runs' in standard Montague semantics. Yet the real truth condition derives its plausibility from the fact that it can be reduced to a formulation like (2).

53. Thus Chomsky is right to insist that the reference relation R of formal semantics cannot be seen as a relation "between words and things, or things as they are imagined to be, or otherwise conceived" (1992, 223–224). Yet I would not go as far as he goes in denying the relevance of referential intuitions of any kind in assessing the overall plausibility of formal semantics.

54. Such I take to be Chomsky's view (1992, 1995).

Chapter 5

1. Recently (1993) Burge laid down some requirements that a speaker must satisfy in order to share the expert's concept: "The individual must be able to discriminate arthritis from such things as animals, trees, and numbers, and from certain other diseases, in order to have the concept" (1993, 325). Thus semantic deviance is possible if it is big enough, so to speak: if one believes that 'arthritis' is a kind of plastic, he does not share the expert's concept and cannot be referring to arthritis.

2. To what does *this* occurrence of 'elms' refer? To what more competent speakers in our community take to be elms (*not* to what a Peircean omega scientist will take to be elms).

3. This appears to presuppose that each speaker is semantically transparent to herself, that is, that while understanding another may be something one has to "work out," no such problem can arise with respect to oneself. This is a stronger assumption than so-called "first-person authority" ("Each person generally knows what he thinks without appeal or recourse to evidence" [Davidson 1991, 195]), for it involves language: the idea is that I simply know not just what I think but also what I *mean* by a sentence S. The assumption could be seen as contradicting the conclusion of Wittgenstein's private-language argument, but it doesn't. It could be seen as contradicting it, for it would seem that on this assumption, it is not possible for the speaker to be corrected on what *she* means by S: she simply and unconditionally knows. However, the private-language argument shows, or purports to show, that there are no private meaning assignments, not that each speaker's understanding of the expressions of a public language must be subject to public checks. *Whether* she understood S (that is, whether she got it right) is subject to public control; *what* she understood (what she got out of S) is, for Wittgenstein, irrelevant.

4. Bilgrami (1992, 37–38) claims that on Burge's account, inconsistencies are easily attributed to Bert. Burge, on the other hand, insists that there is nothing irrational about the error we are attributing to him. "A belief that arthritis may occur in the thigh appears to be ... uncharitably attributed only if it is assumed that the subject must fully understand the notions in his attitude contents" (Burge 1979, 100), but the point is exactly that Bert does not fully understand such notions. However, what is at issue here is the *sentence* 'I have arthritis in my thigh'. This sentence is said to be false as uttered by Bert (or, for that matter, by anybody else) not because Bert's thigh is all right but because arthritis cannot afflict the muscles. Now, says Burge, Bert does not believe that arthritis cannot afflict the muscles; therefore, he is not being inconsistent or irrational. The problem, of course, is what it means exactly to ascribe the expert's concept to Bert if such an ascription does not entail attribution of the relevant beliefs, that is, the beliefs that single out *the expert's* concept, as against other, deviant notions

(see also Bilgrami 1992, 42). Notice that I am not objecting in general to ascribing to Bert a notion that exceeds his awareness or his capacity of verbally explaining content. Burge (1979, 102) is surely right in opposing the general idea that a person's mental contents should be limited to what he understands. In any case, such an objection would not be available to me, as I made it clear that, in general, the contents of a person's referential competence are not transparent to her. What I am objecting to is ascribing to a speaker a notion whose content is *at odds* with that speaker's explicit beliefs and referential practices.

5. This account does not contradict the view, which can be traced back to Wittgenstein's *On Certainty* (1974), and on which Davidson (e.g., 1974) has repeatedly insisted, that divergences can only be identified against a background of convergence. Indeed, it reasserts such a view in two ways: (1) We can say that we do not share a certain belief only by identifying that belief, which we do by assuming that, ceteris paribus, words occurring in the belief's expression are used convergently (though not identically). (2) We regard another person's notion of *x* as different from our notion of *x* on the basis of some of her beliefs, only under the hypothesis that other notions ascribed to her by the attribution of such beliefs to her converge with our own correponding notions.

6. Externalistic theories of publicness appear to provide grounds for the thesis that meanings are uniform across speakers, rather than for genuine publicness.

7. On the language of the Schtroumpfs, see Eco 1979.

8. The words to be deleted may be chosen mechanically (for example, every fifth word in sequence) or according to a qualitative criterion, depending on what use the test is put to (of course, the difficulty of the task may vary depending on which words are deleted). The test may be used to measure readability of the text or reading comprehension. Whether the recovered word exactly coincides with the deleted word or is a close synonym does not appear to make a difference when the test is used to evaluate readability; it may make a difference when it is used to assess the reader's overall linguistic competence. On the Cloze test, see McKenna and Robinson 1980, Marello 1989.

9. There may be cases in which one manages to get one's meaning across even so, thanks to gestures or special circumstances. In these cases, however, though one is communicating, one is not communicating *by means of words*.

10. Actually, Plato's legislator is a baptizer rather than an expert. Here I am introducing him as an example of a single final authority on the meaning of words.

11. The best known (though probably not the best) Italian dictionary defines 'natural number' as "positive integer." Another highly regarded dictionary of Italian (until the next-to-last edition) had it that 'stipulare' [stipulate] means "redigere un contratto" [to draw a contract] and that a proton is "a nucleus of positive electricity around which . . . the electrons turn, all together forming the atom" (a proton is "an elementary particle that is identical with the nucleus of the hydrogen atom," *Webster's Collegiate*, 10th edition), that *Urania* is a butterfly (it is a moth), that 'sperimentale' [experimental], in contexts such as 'scienza sperimentale' [experimental science], 'metodo sperimentale' [experimental method], means "founded on experience" (instead of "on experiment"). Examples could be multiplied.

12. A relation R defined over a set A is connected if and only if for all x, $y \in A$, either Rxy or Ryx is the case.

13. See Dummett 1978, especially p. 425: "[One who uses the word 'elm'] intends that anything he says should be judged as true or false by reference, inter alia, to the way a tree is held to be recognised as being or not being an elm by other speakers of the language, in particular, by those entitled to claim authority in the matter, for example, lexicographers and botanists."

Chapter 6

1. The remark is part of a comment on Lenat and Feigenbaum's (1991) ambitious artificial intelligence project intended to represent "the sum total of human knowledge" (Smith 1991, 252). Smith is here arguing that Lenat and Feigenbaum's system, which is a frame-based system of the traditional kind, "would never be able to understand the difference between right and left." It could be thought that "attaching a camera" (that is, endowing the system with some form of artificial perception) might solve that particular problem, but such a solution would fall outside the scope of Lenat and Feigenbaum's program. Moreover, much must be made clear before that begins to look like a solution: "how to integrate the resulting images with conceptual representations, and how envisionment works, and how this all relates to the existence of 'internal' sensors and effectors, and how it ties to action." Cameras "are just the tip of a very large iceberg."

2. For a recent survey, see Gazdar 1993.

3. Since the repudiation of Turing's test, the stress has tended to be placed on the way such performances are carried out, that is, on the structure of the programs and the kind of data they have access to. Here I am neither implying that such features are irrelevant to whether a system can legitimately be said to understand language nor restoring some version of Turing's test as having definitional import. I am simply suggesting that one would think we were dealing with natural-language-understanding systems only if they were capable of these kinds of performances.

4. Actually, Searle's stand is even stronger: "[The symbol manipulations] aren't even *symbol* manipulations, since the symbols don't symbolize anything" (1980, 422).

5. Fodor 1975 and Johnson-Laird 1983 are (very different) examples of such views. The former, of course, was already "in the field" at the time Putnam wrote "Reference and Understanding" (1979).

6. That he doesn't even know they *are* linguistic expressions doesn't seem to make a difference: if he were told they are, he would not understand them any better.

7. In chapter 1, n. 36, I also made clear, however, that this should not be taken to imply that inferential connections are informationally empty. I do not agree with Searle (1980, 418) that a computer program displaying some degree of inferential competence would not even possess a *factor* of genuine understanding.

8. That the two sides of competence may support each other was already pointed out in chapter 3, pp. 62–63.

9. The present account is strongly sympathetic with Rescher's idea of "philosophical standardism," according to which ordinary concepts are inherently attuned to the way the world is and works ordinarily and most of the time (Rescher 1994). For a closer analogy with the ideas put forth in the text, see Rescher's "standardistic" analysis of the empiricist criterion of meaningfulness (1994, 74–76).

10. Thus I am certainly *not* assuming that "every nonlogical concept is reducible to sensation concepts" (Fodor 1981, 213).

11. If understanding *in absentia* were qualitatively different from understanding *in praesentia*, then understanding fictional discourse, which is mostly *in absentia*, would differ in most cases from understanding nonfictional discourse, which can be *in praesentia*.

12. Tye 1991 contains a good survey on the issue of mental images.

13. In this paragraph I'll be switching back and forth between the language-perception pair and the Kantian pair of concepts and intuitions. I do not mean to make Kant into a forerunner of the "linguistic turn," nor do I want to say that the differences are irrelevant; I merely want to bring out the common structure of both problems.

14. To mention some, the problem of "subsumption," that is, of how we identify instances of concepts in intuition; the problem of how images can stand for concepts (what we would call 'the problem of mental modeling'); as a specially important case of the last problem, the problem of how constructions in intuition can have the generality required for mathematical proof; and the problem of the constitution of empirical concepts (such as the concept of a dog).

15. Literally, according to Kant, a schema is a *representation* [*Vorstellung*] of such a general procedure. This should not be taken to mean that a schema is itself a *picture* of something (a method or a procedure). 'Vorstellung' is Kant's general term for mental contents (Kant 1929, B 376, A 320). So perhaps Kant is saying that schemata are representations of general procedures in the same sense in which we could say that methods for analyzing scenes are "represented" in an artificial system, meaning that the definitions of such methods are part of the system's competence.

16. Actually, there is a further complication (which I will also disregard): schemata for "sensible concepts," including both mathematical concepts and empirical concepts, must be kept distinct from schemata for "pure concepts of the understanding," that is, for the categories, which latter schemata "can never be brought into any image whatsoever" (Kant 1929, B 181, A 142). Ferrarin 1995 has a very good account of mathematical schematism.

17. Locke (1975 [1690], IV, vii, 9) pointed out the difficulty of entertaining a general idea of a triangle, "for it must be neither oblique nor rectangle, neither equilateral, equicrural, nor scalenon; but all and none of these at once." He saw this as a difficulty inherent in general ideas themselves. Berkeley (1948–1957 [1710], Introduction) saw it instead as marring *Locke's* theory of ideas and abstraction.

18. Here Kant is also trying to solve the problem, which he inherits from seventeenth-century discussions, of how can we mentally operate on entities that appear to transcend our imagination, such as a polyhedron of a thousand faces (Locke 1975

[1690], II, xxix, 13–14) or, as in his example, the number 1,000. His solution is, however, unconvincing: if we cannot really take in an image corresponding to a thousand and yet the schema is supposed to take care of it, how can schemata be defined as (representations of) methods "providing an image for a concept"?

19. There is an obvious difficulty here, as Ferrarin has pointed out: "No pure apriori concept or schema of the dog makes sense" (1995, 159). It appears that in the case of empirical concepts, the schema cannot be conceived as an intermediary between a pure concept and intuition, for there is no pure concept that the schema could so mediate. However, I believe that it is wrong, both exegetically and theoretically, to conclude that with empirical concepts, "a schema . . . is not a method," and that "the task of productive imagination is [in this case] limited to the transformation of the sensible object into its figurative image without any a priori productive counterpart" (Ferrarin, 1995, 159). It is wrong as a reading of Kant, for it is clear from the above quotations that Kant takes the schema for dog to be both a rule for the generation of dog images and a rule for the identification of dogs in empirical intuition. Thus the dog schema is no less a method, or procedure, than the schemata for mathematical concepts. And it is also wrong from a theoretical standpoint, for it is not at all clear how the sensible object could be constituted as such in the first place, unless it can be identified in intuition by the operation of some identification procedure. There is indeed no pure concept of dog from which the dog schema could be produced in imagination. However, the dog schema must *function as* an a priori method, both in the generation of images and in the recognition of empirical instances.

20. One should not for a moment conclude that our own referential competence should be conceived along exactly the same lines. For instance, I am not attributing to the system any form of *partial* referential competence, such as the ability to discriminate uranium with respect to animals and plants, which I claimed we possess. As far as the system is concerned, referential competence is an all-or-none affair: either the system *has* a referential algorithm associated with the word 'uranium' or it lacks it, and if it does lack it, then its direct referential competence relative to that word is simply nil (naturally, the system may have a referential algorithm that is *imperfect* from the standpoint of, say, scientific standards of classification, but that is another matter).

21. Here I am particularly relying upon the description of a module of an integrated natural-language-processing and visual-processing system in Meini and Paternoster 1996.

22. Of course, the question of whether a computer would ever *experience* seeing images the way we experience it (that is, the question of "how does it feel" to be a computer watching TV) is a separate issue. See Harnad 1989, 14–15.

23. People have been trying to use neural nets in tasks of bottom-up categorizing (see Harnad 1993).

24. Johnson's *Dictionary* (1755) as quoted by the *Shorter Oxford English Dictionary*, 1973.

References

Allen, J. 1987. *Natural Language Understanding.* Menlo Park: Benjamin/Cummings.

Armstrong, S. L., L. R. Gleitman, and H. Gleitman. 1983. "What Some Concepts Might Not Be." *Cognition* 13:263–308.

Barr, A., and E. A. Feigenbaum. 1981. *The Handbook of Artificial Intelligence.* London: Pitman.

Barsalou, L. 1987. "The Instability of Graded Structure: Implications for the Nature of Concepts." In Neisser 1987a, 101–140.

Berkeley, G. 1948–1957. *A Treatise Concerning the Principles of Human Knowledge.* In *The Works of George Berkeley.* Edinburgh-London: Nelson. First published in 1710.

Bierwisch, M., and F. Kiefer. 1970. "Remarks on Definitions in Natural Language." In F. Kiefer (ed.), *Studies in Syntax and Semantics,* 55–79. Dordrecht, Holland: Reidel.

Bilgrami, A. 1992. *Meaning and Belief.* Oxford: Blackwell.

Block, N. 1986. "An Advertisement for a Semantics for Psychology." In P. A. French, T. E. Uehling, and H. K. Wettstein (eds.), *Studies in the Philosophy of Mind,* Midwest Studies in Philosophy, no. 10, 615–678. Minneapolis: University of Minnesota Press.

Bonomi, A. 1987. "Linguistica e logica." In A. Bonomi, *Le immagini dei nomi,* 48–72. Milan, Italy: Garzanti. First published in C. Segre (ed.), *Intorno alla linguistica.* Milan, Italy: Feltrinelli, 1983.

Brachman, R. 1979. "On the Epistemological Status of Semantic Networks." In N. V. Findler (ed.), *Associative Networks.* New York: Academic Press.

Brachman, R., and J. Schmolze. 1985. "An Overview of the KL-ONE Knowledge Representation System." *Cognitive Science* 9:171–216.

Brachman, R., R. Fikes, and H. Levesque. 1983. "KRYPTON: A Functional Approach to Knowledge Representation." Fairchild Laboratory for Artificial Intelligence Research, Palo Alto, Calif., technical report no. 16.

Brandom, R. B. 1994. *Making It Explicit.* Cambridge: Harvard University Press.

Brennen, T., D. David, I. Fluchaire, and J. Pellat. 1996. "Naming Faces and Objects without Comprehension: A Case Study." *Cognitive Neuropsychology* 13:93–110.

Burge, T. 1979. "Individualism and the Mental." In P. A. French, T. E. Uehling, and H. K. Wettstein (eds.), *Studies in Metaphysics*, Midwest Studies in Philosophy, no. 4, 73–121. Minneapolis: University of Minnesota Press.

Burge, T. 1993. "Concepts, Definitions, and Meaning." *Metaphilosophy* 24:309–325.

Caramazza, A., A. E. Hillis, B. C. Rapp, and C. Romani. 1990. "The Multiple Semantics Hypothesis: Multiple Confusions?" *Cognitive Neuropsychology* 7:161–189.

Carnap, R. 1937. *Logical Syntax of Language*. London: Routledge and Kegan Paul. First published in German as *Logische Syntax der Sprache*. Vienna, 1934.

Carnap, R. 1942. *Introduction to Semantics*. London: Oxford University Press.

Carnap, R. 1956a. "Empiricism, Semantics, and Ontology." In Carnap 1956b, 205–221. First published in *Revue internationale de philosophie* 4 (1950): 20–40.

Carnap, R. 1956b. *Meaning and Necessity*. Enlarged edition. Chicago: University of Chicago Press. First published in 1947.

Carnap, R. 1956c. "Meaning Postulates." In Carnap 1956b, 222–229. First published in *Philosophical Studies* 3 (1952): 65–73.

Casalegno, P. 1997. *Filosofia del linguaggio*. Firenze, Italy: La Nuova Italia Scientifica.

Chierchia, G. 1992. "Logica e linguistica: Il contributo di Montague." In M. Santambrogio (ed.), *Introduzione alla filosofia analitica del linguaggio*. Rome/Bari, Italy: Laterza.

Chomsky, N. 1986. *Knowledge of Language*. New York: Praeger.

Chomsky, N. 1992. "Explaining Language Use." *Philosophical Topics* 20:205–231.

Chomsky, N. 1995. "Language and Nature." *Mind* 104:1–61.

Church, A. 1951a. "A Formulation of the Logic of Sense and Denotation." In P. Henle, H. M. Kallen, and S. K. Langer (eds.), *Structure, Method, and Meaning*, 3–24. New York: Liberal Arts Press.

Church, A. 1951b. "The Need for Abstract Entities in Semantic Analysis." *Proceedings of the American Academy of Arts and Sciences* 80:100–112.

Davidson, D. 1974. "On the Very Idea of a Conceptual Scheme." *Proceedings and Addresses of the American Philosophical Association* 14. Later in D. Davidson, *Inquiries into Truth and Interpretation*, 183–198. Oxford: Clarendon Press, 1984.

Davidson, D. 1986. "A Nice Derangement of Epitaphs." In R. E. Grandy (ed.), *Philosophical Grounds of Rationality*, 157–174. Oxford: Oxford University Press. Later in E. Lepore (ed.), *Truth and Interpretation: Perspectives on the Philosophy of Donald Davidson*, 433–446. Oxford: Blackwell, 1986.

Davidson, D. 1991. "Epistemology Externalized." *Dialectica* 45:191–202.

Devitt, M., and K. Sterelny. 1987. *Language and Reality: An Introduction to the Philosophy of Language*. Oxford: Blackwell.

Dowty, D. 1980. *Word Meaning and Montague Grammar*. Dordrecht, Holland: Reidel.

Dummett, M. 1976. "What Is a Theory of Meaning? (II)." In G. Evans and J. McDowell (eds.), *Truth and Meaning*. Oxford: Clarendon Press.

Dummett, M. 1978. "The Social Character of Meaning." In M. Dummett, *Truth and Other Enigmas*, 420–430. Cambridge: Harvard University Press. First published in 1974.

Dummett, M. 1986. "A Nice Derangement of Epitaphs: Some Comments on Davidson and Hacking." In E. Lepore (ed.), *Truth and Interpretation: Perspectives on the Philosophy of Donald Davidson*, 459–476. Oxford: Blackwell.

Dummett, M. 1991. *The Logical Basis of Metaphysics*. London: Duckworth.

Eco, U. 1979. "Schtroumpf und Drang." *Alfabeta*. Later published in U. Eco, *Sette anni di desiderio*. Milan, Italy: Bompiani, 1983.

Evans, G. 1982. *The Varieties of Reference*. Oxford: Clarendon Press.

Evans, G., and J. McDowell (eds.). 1976. *Truth and Meaning*. Oxford: Oxford University Press.

Ferrarin, A. 1995. "Construction and Mathematical Schematism: Kant on the Exhibition of a Concept in Intuition." *Kant-Studien* 86:131–174.

Field, H. 1977. "Logic, Meaning, and Conceptual Role." *Journal of Philosophy* 74:379–409.

Field, H. 1978. "Mental Representation." *Erkenntnis* 13:9–61.

Fodor, J. 1975. *The Language of Thought*. Hassocks: Harvester.

Fodor, J. 1981. "Tom Swift and His Procedural Grandmother." In J. Fodor, *Representations*. Brighton, England: Harvester.

Fodor, J. 1987. *Psychosemantics*. Cambridge: MIT Press.

Fodor, J. 1990. *A Theory of Content and Other Essays*. Cambridge: MIT Press.

Fodor, J., and E. Lepore. 1992. *Holism: A Shopper's Guide*. Oxford: Blackwell.

Frege, G. 1879. *Begriffsschrift*. Halle, Germany: Nebert.

Frege, G. 1956. "The Thought: A Logical Inquiry." *Mind* 61:298–311. First published as "Der Gedanke: Eine logische Untersuchung" in *Beiträge zur Philosophie der deutschen Idealismus* 1 (1918), no. 2: 58–77.

Frege, G. 1964. *The Basic Laws of Arithmetic*. Translated by M. Furth. Berkeley: University of California Press. First published as *Grundgezetze der Arithmetik* in 1893.

Frege, G. 1976. *Wissenschaftliche Briefwechsel*. Edited by G. Gabriel, H. Hermes, F. Kambartel, C. Thiel, and A. Veraart. Hamburg, Germany: Meiner.

Frege, G. 1979. *Posthumous Writings*. Oxford: Blackwell.

Frege, G. 1980a. *Translations from the Philosophical Writings of Gottlob Frege*. Edited by P. Geach and M. Black. 3rd edition. Oxford: Blackwell.

Frege, G. 1980b. "On Sense and Reference." In Frege 1980a. First published as "Über Sinn und Bedeutung" in 1892.

Frixione, M. 1994. *Logica, significato e intelligenza artificiale*. Milan, Italy: F. Angeli.

Gärdenfors, P. 1993. "The Emergence of Meaning." *Linguistics and Philosophy* 16:285–309.

Gazdar, G. 1993. "The Handling of Natural Language." In D. Broadbent (ed.), *The Simulation of Human Intelligence*, 151–177. Oxford: Blackwell.

Grice, H. P. 1975. "Logic and Conversation." In P. Cole and J. L. Morgan (eds.), *Speech Acts*, Syntax and Semantics, no. 3, 41–58. New York: Academic Press. Later in Grice 1989.

Grice, H. P. 1978. "Further Notes on Logic and Conversation." In P. Cole (ed.), *Pragmatics*, Syntax and Semantics, no. 9, 113–127. New York: Academic Press.

Grice, H. P. 1989. *Studies in the Way of Words*. Cambridge: Harvard University Press.

Grice, H. P., and P. F. Strawson. 1970. "In Defense of a Dogma." In J. F. Harris Jr. and R. H. Severens (eds.), *Analyticity*, 56–74. Chicago: Quadrangle Books. First published in *Philosophical Review* 65 (1956).

Hahn, L. E., and P. A. Schilpp. 1986. *The Philosophy of W. V. Quine*. La Salle, Ill.: Open Court.

Haiman, J. 1980. "Dictionaries and Encyclopedias." *Lingua* 50:329–357.

Harman, G. 1975. "Meaning and Semantics." In M. Munitz and P. Unger (eds.), *Semantics and Philosophy*, 1–16. New York: NYU Press.

Harman, G. 1987. "(Nonsolipsistic) Conceptual Role Semantics." In E. Lepore and B. Loewer (eds.), *New Directions in Semantics*, 55–81. London: Academic Press.

Harnad, S. 1989. "Minds, Machines, and Searle." *Journal of Theoretical and Experimental Artificial Intelligence* 1:5–25.

Harnad, S. 1990. "The Symbol-Grounding Problem." *Physica* D 42:335–346.

Harnad, S. 1993. "Grounding Symbolic Capacity in Robotic Capacity." In L. Steels and R. Brooks (eds.), *The "Artificial Life" Route to "Artificial Intelligence": Building Situated Embodied Agents*. New Haven: Erlbaum.

Hart, J., and B. Gordon. 1992. "Neural Subsystems for Object Knowledge." *Nature* 359:60–64.

Hausmann, F. J., O. Reichmann, H. E. Wiegand, and L. Zgusta (eds.). 1989. *Wörterbücher: Ein internationales Handbuch der Lexikographie*. Berlin: De Gruyter.

Horn, L. R. 1969. "A Presuppositional Analysis of 'Only' and 'Even'." In *Papers from the Fifth Regional Meeting of the Chicago Linguistic Society*, 98–107. Chicago: Department of Linguistics, University of Chicago.

Horwich, P. 1992. "Chomsky versus Quine on the Analytic-Synthetic Distinction." *Aristotelian Society Proceedings* 92:95–108.

Hupka, W. 1989. "Die Bebilderung und sonstige Formen der Veranschaulichung im allgemeinen einsprachigen Wörterbuch." In Hausmann et al. 1989, 1:704–726.

Israel, D. J. 1983. "Interpreting Network Formalisms." *Computers and Mathematics with Applications* 9:1–13.

Jackendoff, R. 1983. *Semantics and Cognition.* Cambridge: MIT Press.

Jackendoff, R. 1990. *Semantic Structures.* Cambridge: MIT Press.

Jackendoff, R. 1992. *Languages of the Mind.* Cambridge: MIT Press.

Jacob, P. 1993. "Is the Alternative between Meaning Atomism and Meaning Holism Exhaustive?" Paper given at the First European Society for Analytic Philosophy Conference, Aix-en-Provence, France.

Johnson-Laird, P. 1983. *Mental Models.* Cambridge: Cambridge University Press.

Johnson-Laird, P. 1986. "How Is Meaning Mentally Represented?" In U. Eco, M. Santambrogio, and P. Violi (eds.), *Meaning and Mental Representations*, 99–118. Milan, Italy: Bompiani.

Kant, I. 1929. *Critique of Pure Reason.* Translated by N. Kemp Smith. London: Macmillan and Co. First published as *Kritik der reinen Vernunft*, 1st ed., 1781; 2nd ed., 1787.

Kaplan, D. 1970. "What Is Russell's Theory of Descriptions?" In W. Yourgrau (ed.), *Physics, Logic, and History.* New York: Plenum Press.

Katz, J. J. 1972. *Semantic Theory.* New York: Harper and Row.

Katz, J. J. 1987. "Common Sense in Semantics." In E. Lepore and B. Loewer (eds.), *New Directions in Semantics*, 55–81. London: Academic Press.

Katz, J. J., and J. Fodor. 1963. "The Structure of a Semantic Theory." *Language* 39:170–210.

Kay, J., and A. Ellis. 1987. "A Cognitive Neuropsychological Case Study of Anomia." *Brain* 110:613–629.

Keil, F. C. 1986. "The Acquisition of Natural Kind and Artifact Terms." In W. Demopoulos and A. Marras (eds.), *Language Learning and Concept Acquisition*, 133–153. Norwood, N.J.: Ablex.

Keil, F. C. 1987. "Conceptual Development and Category Structure." In Neisser 1987a, 175–200.

Kripke, S. 1972. *Naming and Necessity.* In G. Harman and D. Davidson (eds.), *Semantics of Natural Language.* Dordrecht, Holland: Reidel.

Lakoff, G. 1987. *Women, Fire, and Dangerous Things.* Chicago: University of Chicago Press.

Lehmann, F. (ed.). 1992. *Semantic Networks.* Special issue of *Computers and Mathematics with Applications* 23:2–9.

Lenat, D. B., and E. A. Feigenbaum. 1991. "On the Thresholds of Knowledge." *Artificial Intelligence* 47:185–250.

Lewis, C. I. 1943–1944. "The Modes of Meaning." *Philosophy and Phenomenological Research* 4:236–249. Later published in Linsky 1952.

Lewis, D. 1970. "General Semantics." *Synthese* 22:18–77.

Linsky, L. (ed.). 1952. *Semantics and the Philosophy of Language.* Urbana, Ill.: University of Illinois Press.

Loar, B. 1981. *Mind and Meaning.* Cambridge: Cambridge University Press.

Locke, J. 1975. *An Essay Concerning Human Understanding.* Oxford: Clarendon. First published in 1690.

Malt, B. C. 1990. "Features and Beliefs in the Mental Representation of Categories." *Journal of Memory and Language* 29:289–315.

Marconi, D. 1987. "Two Aspects of Lexical Competence." *Lingua e Stile* 22:385–395.

Marconi, D. 1989. "Rappresentare il significato lessicale." In Viale, R. (ed.), *Mente umana, mente artificiale,* 76–83. Milan, Italy: Feltrinelli.

Marconi, D. 1991. "Understanding and Reference." *Sémiotiques* 1:9–25.

Marconi, D. 1995a. "On the Structure of Lexical Competence." *Aristotelian Society Proceedings* 95:131–150.

Marconi, D. 1995b. "Fodor and Wittgenstein on Private Language." In R. Egidi (ed.), *Wittgenstein: Mind and Language,* 107–115. Dordrecht, Holland: Kluwer.

Marello, C. (ed.). 1989. *Alla ricerca della parola nascosta.* Firenze, Italy: La Nuova Italia.

Marr, D. 1982. *Vision.* New York: Freeman and Co.

McCarthy, R. A., and E. K. Warrington. 1986. "Visual Associative Agnosia: A Clinico-anatomical Study of a Single Case." *Journal of Neurology, Neurosurgery, and Psychiatry* 49:1233–1240.

McCarthy, R. A., and E. K. Warrington. 1988. "Evidence for Modality-Specific Meaning Systems in the Brain." *Nature* 334:428–430.

McGinn, C. 1981. "The Mechanism of Reference." *Synthese* 49:157–186.

McGinn, C. 1982. "The Structure of Content." In A. Woodfield (ed.), *Thought and Object.* Oxford: Clarendon Press.

McKenna, M., and R. Robinson. 1980. *An Introduction to the Cloze Procedure: An Annotated Bibliography.* Newark, N.J.: International Reading Association.

McKevitt, P. (ed.). 1996. *Integration of Natural Language and Vision Processing,* vol. 3, *Computational Models and Systems.* Dordrecht, Holland: Kluwer. Forthcoming.

Meini, C., and A. Paternoster. 1996. "Understanding Language through Vision." In McKevitt 1996.

Miceli, G., L. Giustolisi, and A. Caramazza. 1991. "The Interaction of Lexical and Non-lexical Processing Mechanisms: Evidence from Anomia." *Cortex* 27:57–80.

Minsky, M. 1975. "A Framework for Representing Knowledge." In P. Winston (ed.), *The Psychology of Computer Vision,* 211–277. New York: McGraw Hill.

Montague, R. 1974a. "English as a Formal Language." In Montague 1974b. First published in 1970.

Montague, R. 1974b. *Formal Philosophy: Selected Papers of Richard Montague.* Edited by R. H. Thomason. New Haven: Yale University Press.

Montague, R. 1974c. "The Proper Treatment of Quantification in Ordinary English." In Montague 1974b. First published in 1973.

Moravcsik, J. 1981. "How Do Words Get Their Meanings?" *Journal of Philosophy* 78:5–24.

Neisser, U. (ed.). 1987a. *Concepts and Conceptual Developments: Ecological and Intellectual Factors in Categorization.* Cambridge: Cambridge University Press.

Neisser, U. 1987b. "From Direct Perception to Conceptual Structure." In Neisser 1987a, 11–23.

Osherson, D. N., and E. E. Smith. 1981. "On the Adequacy of Prototype Theory as a Theory of Concepts." *Cognition* 9:35–58.

Palazzi, F., and G. Folena. 1992. *Dizionario della lingua italiana.* With the collaboration of C. Marello, D. Marconi, and M. Cortelazzo. Torino, Italy: Loescher.

Partee, B. 1981. "Montague Grammar, Mental Representations, and Reality." In S. Oehman and S. Kanger (eds.), *Philosophy and Grammar*, 59–78. Dordrecht, Holland: Reidel.

Pears, D. 1979. "The Relation between Wittgenstein's Picture Theory of Propositions and Russell's Theory of Judgment." In C. G. Luckhardt (ed.), *Wittgenstein: Sources and Perspectives*, 190–212. Ithaca: Cornell University Press.

Peirce, C. S. 1934–1948. *Collected Papers.* Cambridge: Harvard University Press.

Perry, J. 1977. "Frege on Demonstratives." *Philosophical Review* 86:474–497.

Perry, J. 1994. "Fodor and Lepore on Holism." *Philosophical Studies* 73:123–138.

Pustejovsky, J. 1991. "The Generative Lexicon." *Computational Linguistics* 17:409–441.

Putnam, H. 1975a. "The Analytic and the Synthetic." In *Philosophical Papers*, vol. 2, *Mind, Language, and Reality*, 33–69. Cambridge: Cambridge University Press. First published in 1962.

Putnam, H. 1975b. "Is Semantics Possible?" In *Philosophical Papers*, vol. 2, *Mind, Language, and Reality*, 139–152. Cambridge: Cambridge University Press. First published in 1970.

Putnam, H. 1975c. "The Meaning of 'Meaning'." In *Philosophical Papers*, vol. 2, *Mind, Language, and Reality*, 215–271. Cambridge: Cambridge University Press.

Putnam, H. 1979. "Reference and Understanding." In A. Margalit (ed.), *Meaning and Use*, 199–217. Dordrecht, Holland: Reidel.

Putnam, H. 1981. "Brains in a Vat." In *Reason, Truth, and History*, 1–21. Cambridge: Cambridge University Press.

Putnam, H. 1983a. "Models and Reality." In *Philosophical Papers*, vol. 3, *Realism and Reason*, 1–25. Cambridge: Cambridge University Press. First published in *Journal of Symbolic Logic* 45 (1980): 464–482.

Putnam, H. 1983b. "Reference and Truth." In *Philosophical Papers*, vol. 3, *Realism and Reason*, 69–86. Cambridge: Cambridge University Press.

Putnam, H. 1983c. "'Two Dogmas' Revisited." In *Philosophical Papers*, vol. 3, *Realism and Reason*, 87–97. Cambridge: Cambridge University Press. First published in 1976.

Putnam, H. 1992. *Renewing Philosophy*. Cambridge: Harvard University Press.

Quillian, M. R. 1968. "Semantic Memory." In M. Minsky (ed.), *Semantic Information Processing*. Cambridge: MIT Press.

Quine, W. V. O. 1952. "Notes on Existence and Necessity." In Linsky 1952, 75–91. First published in *Journal of Philosophy*, 1943.

Quine, W. V. O. 1953. "Two Dogmas of Empiricism." In W. V. O. Quine, *From a Logical Point of View*. Cambridge: Harvard University Press. First published in *Philosophical Review*, 1951.

Quine, W. V. O. 1969. *Ontological Relativity and Other Essays*. New York: Columbia University Press.

Quine, W. V. O. 1970. *Philosophy of Logic*. Englewood, N.J.: Prentice-Hall.

Quine, W. V. O. 1973. *The Roots of Reference*. La Salle, Ill.: Open Court.

Quine, W. V. O. 1986. Replies. In Hahn and Schilpp 1986.

Quine, W. V. O. 1991. "Two Dogmas in Retrospect." *Canadian Journal of Philosophy* 21:265–274.

Récanati, F. 1993. *Direct Reference*. Oxford: Blackwell.

Reiter, R., and G. Criscuolo. 1980. "Some Representational Issues in Default Reasoning." Technical report 80-7, Dept. of Computer Science, University of British Columbia.

Rescher, N. 1994. *Philosophical Standardism*. Pittsburgh: University of Pittsburgh Press.

Rey, G. 1983. "Concepts and Stereotypes." *Cognition* 15:237–262.

Riddoch, M. J., and G. W. Humphreys. 1987a. "Visual Object Processing in Optic Aphasia: A Case of Semantic Access Agnosia." *Cognitive Neuropsychology* 4: 131–185.

Riddoch, M. J., and G. W. Humphreys. 1987b. "A Case of Integrative Visual Agnosia." *Brain* 110:1431–1462.

Rich, E. 1983. *Artificial Intelligence*. New York: McGraw-Hill.

Rorty, R. 1979. *Philosophy and the Mirror of Nature*. Princeton: Princeton University Press.

Rosch, E. 1973. "On the Internal Structure of Perceptual and Semantic Categories." In E. E. Moore (ed.), *Cognitive Development and the Acquisition of Language*. New York: Academic Press.

Rosch, E. 1975a. "Cognitive Representation of Semantic Categories." *Journal of Experimental Psychology: General* 104:192–233.

Rosch, E. 1975b. "Universals and Cultural Specifics in Human Categorization." In R. Brislin, S. Bochner, and W. Lonner (eds.), *Cross-Cultural Perspectives on Learning*, 177–205. New York: Sage/Halsted.

Rosch, E. 1978. "Principles of Categorization." In E. Rosch and B. B. Lloyd (eds.), *Cognition and Categorization*. Hillsdale: Erlbaum.

Rosch, E. 1987. "Wittgenstein and Categorization Research in Cognitive Psychology." In M. Chapman and R. A. Dixon (eds.), *Meaning and the Growth of Understanding*. Berlin: Springer.

Rosch, E., C. B. Mervis, W. D. Gray, D. M. Johnson, and P. Boyes-Braem. 1976. "Basic Objects in Natural Categories." *Cognitive Psychology* 8:382–439.

Rosenfeld, A. 1988. "Computer Vision." In *Advances in Computers*, 27:265–308. New York: Academic Press.

Russell, B. 1950. *An Inquiry into Meaning and Truth*. London: Allen and Unwin.

Sartori, G., M. Coltheart, M. Miozzo, and R. Job. 1994. "Category Specificity and Informational Specificity in Neuropsychological Impairment of Semantic Memory." In C. Umiltà and M. Moscovitch (eds.), *Conscious and Nonconscious Information Processing*, Attention and Performance, no. 15, 537–544. Cambridge: MIT Press.

Schubert, L. K. 1976. "Extending the Expressive Power of Semantic Networks." *Artificial Intelligence* 7:163–198.

Searle, J. 1980. "Minds, Brains, and Programs." *Behavioural and Brain Sciences* 3:417–457.

Searle, J. 1982. "The Chinese Room Revisited." *Behavioural and Brain Sciences* 5:345–348.

Shallice, T. 1988. *From Neuropsychology to Mental Structure*. Cambridge: Cambridge University Press.

Shapiro, S. C. 1971. "A Net Structure for Semantic Information Storage, Deduction, and Retrieval." *Proceedings of the International Joint Conference on Artificial Intelligence* (London) 2:512–523.

Smith, B. C. 1991. "The Owl and the Electric Encyclopedia." *Artificial Intelligence* 47:251–288.

Stalnaker, R. 1993. "Twin Earth Revisited." *Aristotelian Society Proceedings* 93:297–311.

Strawson, P. F. 1952. *Introduction to Logical Theory*. London: Methuen.

Taylor, W. C. 1953. "'Cloze' Procedure: A New Tool for Measuring Readability." *Journalism Quarterly* 30:416–438.

Thomason, R. H. 1974. Introduction to Montague 1974b.

Thomason, R. H. 1991. "Knowledge Representation and Knowledge of Words." In J. Pustejovsky and S. Bergler (eds.), *Lexical Semantics and Knowledge Representation*, 1–8. Berkeley, Calif.: Association for Computational Linguistics.

Tye, M. 1991. *The Imagery Debate*. Cambridge: MIT Press.

Warrington, E. K. 1975. "The Selective Impairment of Semantic Memory." *Quarterly Journal of Experimental Psychology* 27:635–657.

Warrington, E. K. 1985. "Agnosia: The Impairment of Object Recognition." In J. A. M. Frederiks (ed.), *Clinical Neuropsychology*, Handbook of Clinical Neurology, rev. ser. no. 1 (= no. 45), 333–349. Amsterdam: Elsevier Science Publishers.

Warrington, E. K., and R. McCarthy. 1983. "Category Specific Access Dysphasia." *Brain* 106:859–878.

Warrington, E. K., and T. Shallice. 1984. "Category Specific Semantic Impairments." *Brain* 107:829–853.

Wettstein, H. 1986. "Has Semantics Rested on a Mistake?" *Journal of Philosophy* 83:185–209.

White, J. S. 1991. "Lexical and World Knowledge: Theoretical and Applied Viewpoints." In J. Pustejovsky and S. Bergler (eds.), *Lexical Semantics and Knowledge Representation*, 139–149. Berkeley, Calif.: Association for Computational Linguistics.

Wilks, Y. 1982. "Some Thoughts on Procedural Semantics." In W. G. Lehnert and M. H. Ringle (eds.), *Strategies for Natural Language Processing*. Hillsdale: Erlbaum.

Winston, P. H., and B. K. P. Horn. 1984. *LISP*. 2nd edition. Reading: Addison-Wesley.

Wittgenstein, L. 1922. *Tractatus Logico-philosophicus*. London: Routledge and Kegan Paul.

Wittgenstein, L. 1953. *Philosophische Untersuchungen*. Oxford: Blackwell.

Wittgenstein, L. 1958. *The Blue and Brown Books*. Edited by R. Rhees. Oxford: Blackwell. 2nd edition, 1969.

Wittgenstein, L. 1974. *Über Gewißheit*. Oxford: Blackwell.

Woods, W. A., and J. C. Schmolze. 1992. "The KL-ONE Family." *Computers and Mathematics with Applications* 23:133–177.

Index